POSTCARD HISTORY SERIES

# *Winfield*

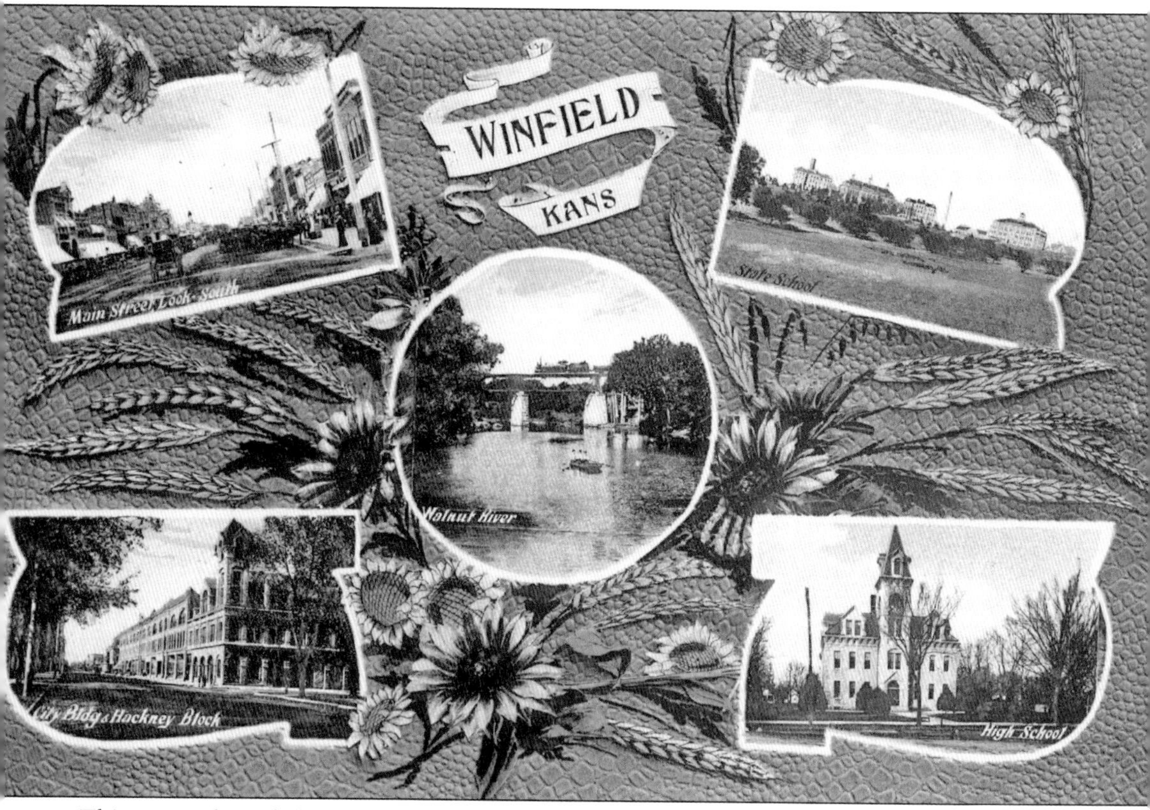


This postcard, mailed in 1909, boasts of Winfield's assets at that time: a prosperous Main Street, a state school for the mentally handicapped, a redbrick block of buildings housing the city office and fire department, a central high school, and, at the center of it all, the Walnut River. (Courtesy of Loyette Polhans Olson's collection.)

**ON THE FRONT COVER**: The intersection of Ninth Avenue and Main Street remains Winfield's hallmark and center of commerce to this day. Flanked by two limestone banks built in 1886 but easily recognized today, this corner was and is the gateway to Winfield's many attractions. (Courtesy of Loyette Polhans Olson's collection.)

**ON THE BACK COVER:** In 1541, Coronado and his men crossed the Walnut River near Winfield, Kansas, and camped on its banks. By the turn of the century, appreciation grew for the river's recreational aspects. Since 1971, its valley has housed an internationally known music festival that keeps Winfield in the spotlight each September. (Courtesy of Loyette Polhans Olson's collection.)

POSTCARD HISTORY SERIES

# *Winfield*

*Beverley Olson Buller*

ARCADIA PUBLISHING

ISBN 978-1-4671-1308-3

Published by Arcadia Publishing
Charleston, South Carolina

Printed in the United States of America

Library of Congress Control Number: 2014941312

For all general information contact Arcadia Publishing at:
Telephone 843-853-2070
Fax 843-853-0044
E-mail sales@arcadiapublishing.com
For customer service and orders:
Toll-Free 1-888-313-2665

Visit us on the Internet at www.arcadiapublishing.com

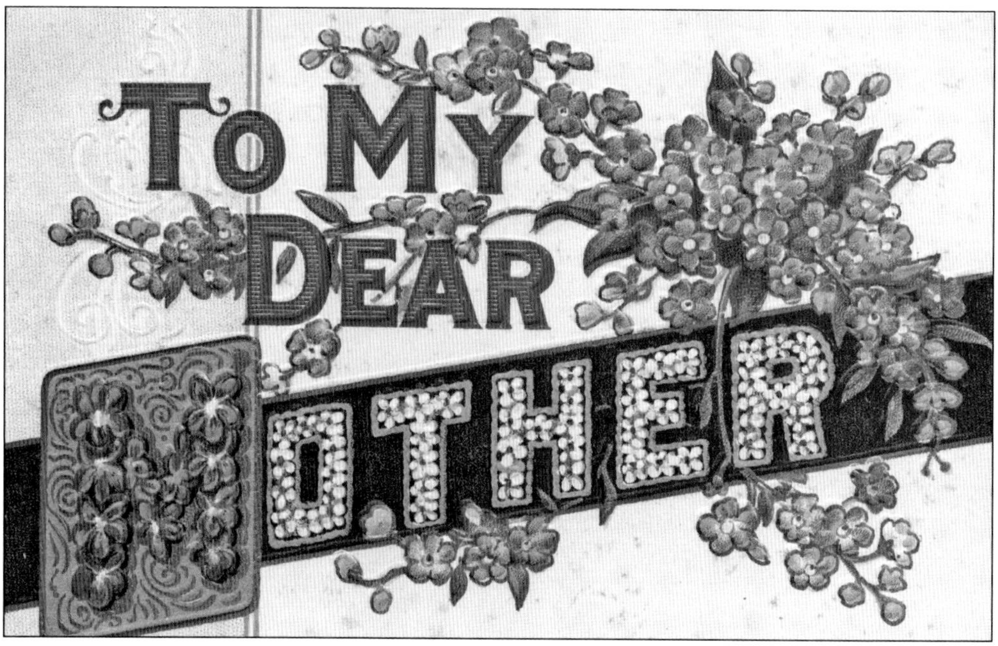


*This book is dedicated to my mother, Loyette Polhans Olson (1932–2014), and to my father, Dr. Robert Olson (1925–1994), who started her antique postcard collection. (Courtesy of Loyette Polhans Olson's collection.)*

# Contents

# Acknowledgments

When the thought of this book presented itself, I turned immediately to the Cowley County Historical Society. Members of the board and some volunteers met with me early on to discuss the book, and the staff at the museum, especially director Shawn Stover, was most helpful. The hours I spent in the Frankie Cullison Research Collection brought forth gems of primary source material and, as research should, guided me to other sources. The Celebrate Winfield History Committee, both past and present, deserves commendation for bringing together local history buffs since 2000 with the annual presentation of papers on Winfield's past. Roland Mueller wrote papers on the Chautauqua assembly in 2001, the Lutheran Children's Home and the Winfield-Arkansas City interurban in 2013, and the 1916 reservoir break in 2014, while Jerry Wallace shared his findings on Jack Welfelt in 2008, the beginnings of Southwestern College in 2009, E.C. Manning in 2010, and P.H. Albright in 2014. The work of these two men, and their willingness to reply to my questions, enriched my work, and I thank them. Longtime historically minded Winfield residents and dear friends Beverly Bergdall Johnson, Kay Roberts Light, and Marilyn Powers McNeish made themselves available for clarification and discussion of various Winfield landmarks. Cindy Goertz, Larry Hatteberg, Kathy Swain, and Nancy Tredway helped with specific information needs. William Botorff and Mary Ann Wortman provided a wealth of information through Botorff's website (now available through the museum's website under "Resources"). Thanks to my sister Mary Olson Beach and her husband, Chris, for their help and for providing a home away from home when I was in town. The support of my husband, Paul, as well as his patience and assistance in selecting which postcards to use and their placement, made all the difference.

I hope this book will create interest in the "Winfield That Was" and will ignite discussion of historic preservation as the images remind us of what has been lost. Please consult this book's bibliography as well as the Cowley County Historical Society Museum Library and the Winfield Public Library to learn more. All postcards are from the collection of Loyette Polhans Olson.

# Introduction

Penny postcards presented a simple and interesting way to communicate with friends, customers, and family into the 20th century. They speak of what a community found important as well as how it wanted to present itself to the wider world at the time. For this reason, illustrating the history of a city with postcards is by no means exhaustive; its view is quite literally based on the views chosen worthy of being placed on a postcard. That being said, each postcard offers the opportunity to dig deep into Winfield's past to discover the stories it contains.

The history of Winfield, Kansas, goes back to 1869, when Clifford M. Wood visited the area and felt it would be ideal for a town site. His wife, Melinda Jones Wood, even gave the town a name—Lagonda—because it reminded her of her hometown in Ohio located near Lagonda Creek. Within a month, however, Wood discarded the idea until he met Edward Cassander Manning, who was in the area looking for a place to establish a general store and a cattle ranch. Cowley County, created in 1864 by the Kansas State Legislature and named for Civil War casualty Matthew Doll Cowley, belonged to the Osage Indians by treaty rights, part of the Osage Diminished Reserve, which ran through eight Kansas counties. When Wood claimed land on the west side of what is now Winfield and built a structure, Indians burned it down. Manning, with T.H. Baker, a business partner he had met in Manhattan, Kansas, claimed over 40 acres of land in the area and paid Chief Chetopa $6 for rent. In June 1869, he placed a foundation on his claim and before the year was out built a 14-foot-by-16-foot log cabin at the north end of what is now Manning Street in Winfield.

At the beginning of 1870, Manning put together a town company of 12 other men, with Clifford M. Wood as vice president. He gave 40 acres of his claim to the town company; the other men agreed to pay half of the cost of building a log store and sell parts of their own claims later to create a 160-acre town site. A member of the town company, W.W. Andrews, suggested the name Winfield for the new town when the well-known Baptist minister Winfield Scott offered to provide a church if the town received his name. In November 1870, Scott came to the town that now bore his name and began the proceedings to establish a Baptist church. Manning acted fast in February 1870 to ensure Winfield was named the county seat when he heard that Cresswell (now Arkansas City) had been suggested. Manning, meanwhile, planned the town and aligned Main Street with the North Star. The original town site went north from Ninth Avenue to Fifth Avenue and a half mile west to Mansfield Street. The first building erected on the new Main Street was the log cabin store, built in April 1870 at the northwest corner of Ninth Avenue and Main Street. Some forethought went into its construction, as it had two stories, which allowed space on the second floor for county offices and other public uses, while the first floor housed the Manning & Baker store and rented space for other merchants. Manning allowed free public use of the second floor for two years, after which he claimed the whole building for his purposes. In April 1870, Manning built a residence near Eighth and Manning Streets and brought his family from Manhattan to Winfield. The next month, Manning set up a post office in his log store, distributing the mail being brought from the Douglass, Kansas, post office until the mail coach established regular delivery to Winfield in June 1870. When Winfield celebrated its first Fourth of July that year, a flag sewn by local women hung from the top of the log store, and after a day of games, picnicking, and patriotic music citizens danced at a ball on the second floor of the store. Further reason for celebration came in July 1870, when Pres. Ulysses S. Grant authorized the purchase of Indian land, including that on which Winfield had been built. Expecting a flood of settlers, Manning persuaded J.P. Short to open Winfield's first hotel at the northeast corner of Ninth Avenue and Main Street in October 1870.

The official survey of Cowley County began in January 1871. Upon its completion, the Winfield Town Association formed with E.C. Manning, J.C. Fuller, D.A. Millington, W.A. Mansfield, and A.W. Tousey as its members. The town site consisted of the east half of Manning's claim and the west half of Fuller's. Millington used his surveying skills to lay out the town's streets, alleys, blocks, and lots. Once the Winfield town site, with 72 lots and 80 buildings, entered the land registry for Cowley County, it could truly begin to grow. Never a boomtown, Winfield experienced slow and deliberate growth thanks to the foundation provided by E.C. Manning and his business partners.

By 1872, Winfield's 700 citizens shopped its many stores on Main Street, could attend one of five churches, get their photograph taken, join a lodge, and began to plan for the first public school building, jail, and courthouse. On February 22, 1873, it became a third-class city with W.H.H. Maris elected the first mayor. At this point, 65 percent of the original 72 lot-holders no longer lived in Winfield, but others certainly came to take their place. In 1878, E.C. Manning constructed a large building on the site of the old log store, now moved down the street to 821 Main Street. By 1879, with the population grown to over 2,000 denizens, it became a city of the second class. The Santa Fe Railroad came to Winfield that same year, and its population grew more in that year than ever before.

By 10 years into the new century, Winfield began to receive notice as an attractive, thriving, interesting city. Its trolley system, annual Chautauqua assemblies in its beautiful Island Park, two colleges, hospital, state school, churches, and homes caught the eye of a reporter for *Kansas* magazine in 1909. In its April edition, he hailed it as "Beautiful Winfield, the little Athens of the Sunflower State," commenting on its position within the embrace of the Walnut River and surrounding hills. The *Christian Science Monitor* offered similar words in July 1913. Following a study by the welfare department of the University of Kansas in 1914–1915, Winfield received first prize among the 15 second-class cities considered for the honor. The McKeever Prize recognized the city as the most ideal in which to raise children for cities of its size.

It was during these heady years that penny postcards made their debut, and Winfield provided a ready source for their images as well as citizens proud to mail them to friends, customers, and family near and far. Let the images on the coming pages provide a glimpse into the 20th-century history of the city once called "the little Athens of the Sunflower State."

*One*

# On Main Street

*Main Street, Winfield, Kansas.*

City planner E.C. Manning envisioned a wide-open main thoroughfare for the people of Winfield, so its main street was platted at 120 feet wide. This 1909 view taken from Eighth Avenue looking south shows there was room for customers in their wagons or on horseback as well as a track for mule-drawn trolleys running through the center of the street.

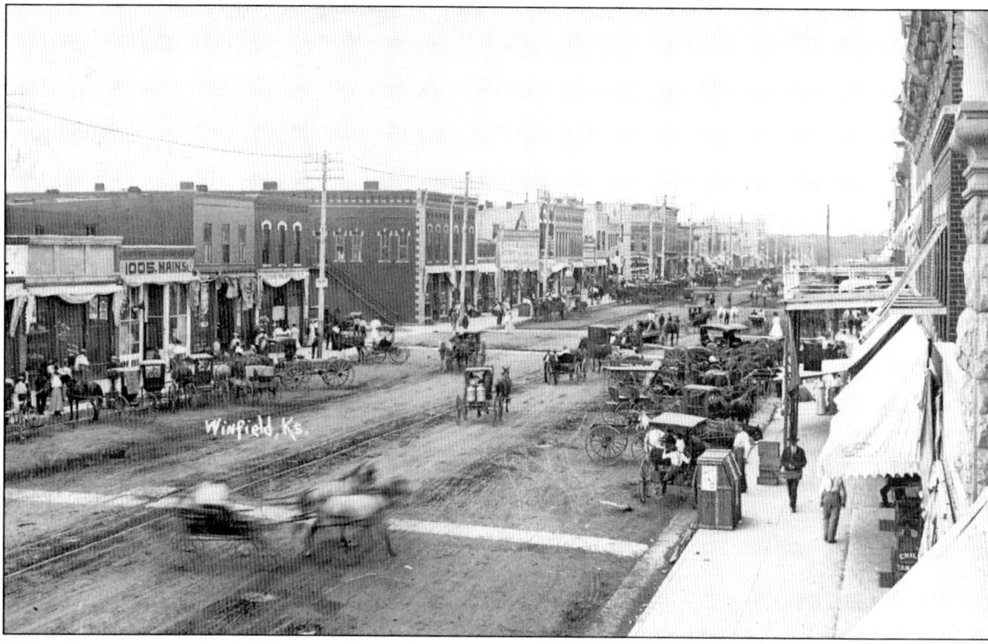


This view, postmarked 1908, catches a busy day in downtown Winfield from the middle of the 1000 block looking north. Note the milk cans in the back of the delivery wagon in the center of the image and the number of well-dressed ladies enjoying the walk between Tenth and Eleventh Avenues. By 1877, flagstones replaced many of the wooden sidewalks on Main Street, and the street was macadamized in 1888.

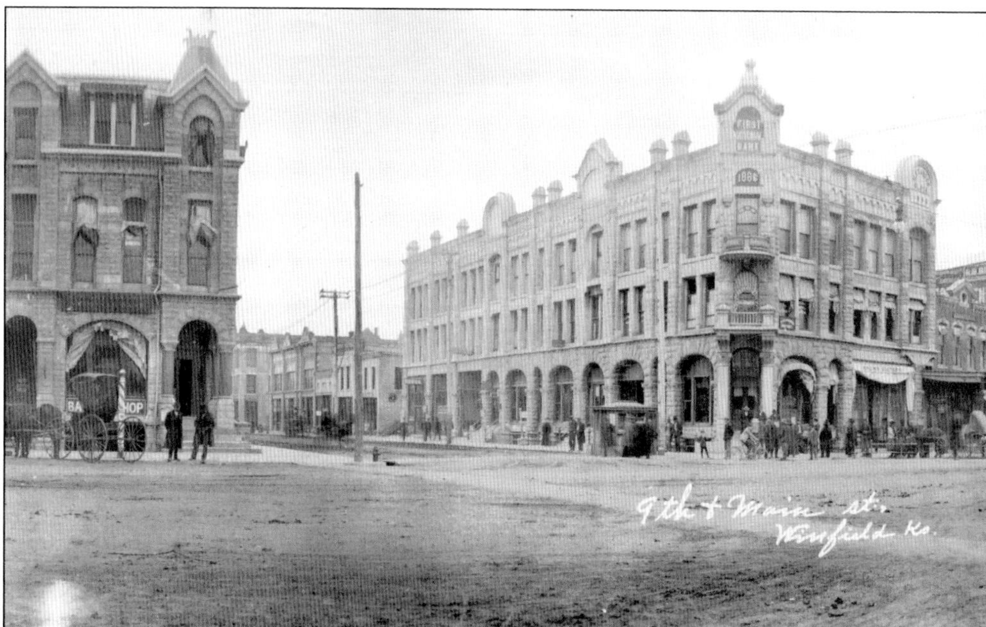


A slower day in Winfield appears in this view also postmarked 1908. The lack of crowds shows two of Winfield's major banks, both built in 1886, to good advantage. The street railway ticket booth on the southeast side of Ninth Avenue by the First National Bank is clearly visible as is the barber pole in front of the Cowley County National Bank on the northeast corner.

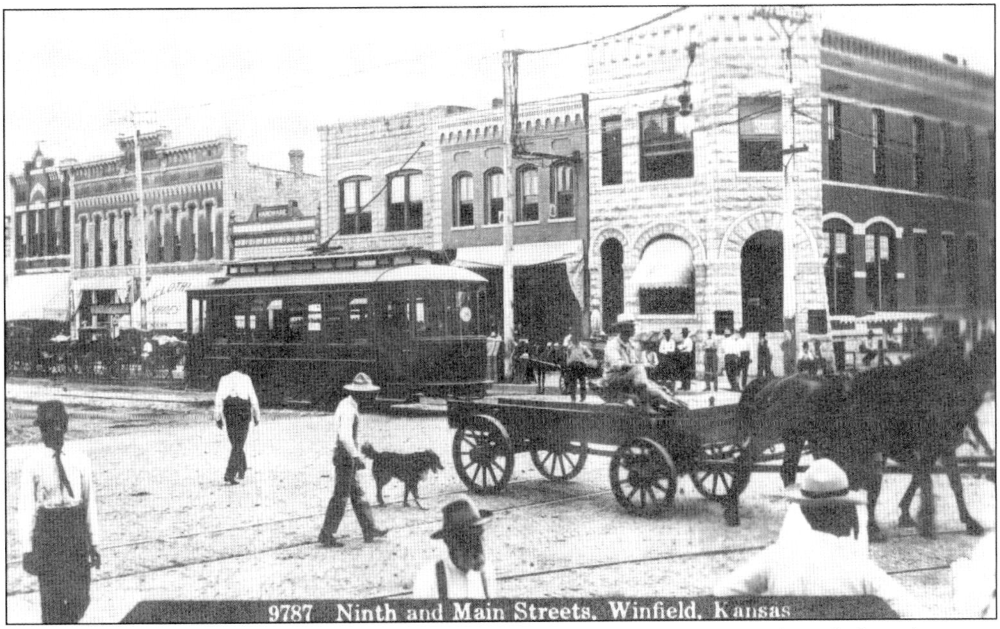


A 1910 card shows the row of buildings anchored by the Winfield National Bank directly across from the First National Bank block, as well as an electric interurban car with its web of wires. Note the lightbulb hanging in the center of the intersection above the dray wagon. Obviously, there were no leash laws in early Winfield, but dog licenses were issued as early as 1878.

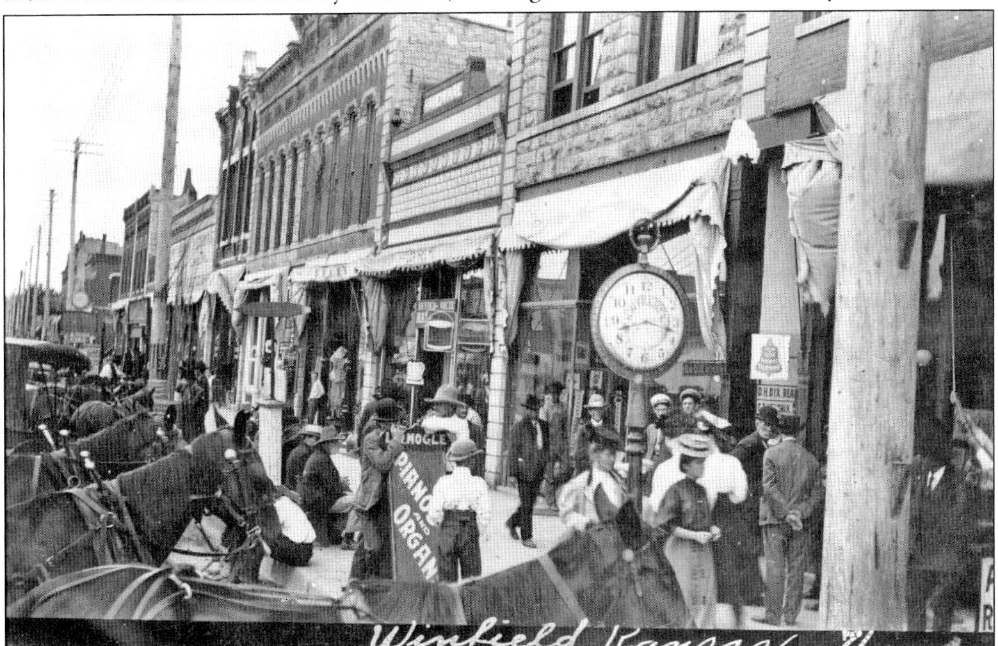


A close-up view of the west side of the 900 block of Main Street just south of the Winfield National Bank reveals a sign for the Missouri and Kansas Telephone office at 905 ½ Main Street, the Snyder-Nolte Hardware Store at 907 Main Street, and L.R. Mogle's Jewelry and Music Store. Also on that block were R. Hudson and Co. Jewelry, J.S. Mann clothiers, Dautschmann's meat market, Kyer's Furniture, and Mitschler's meat market.

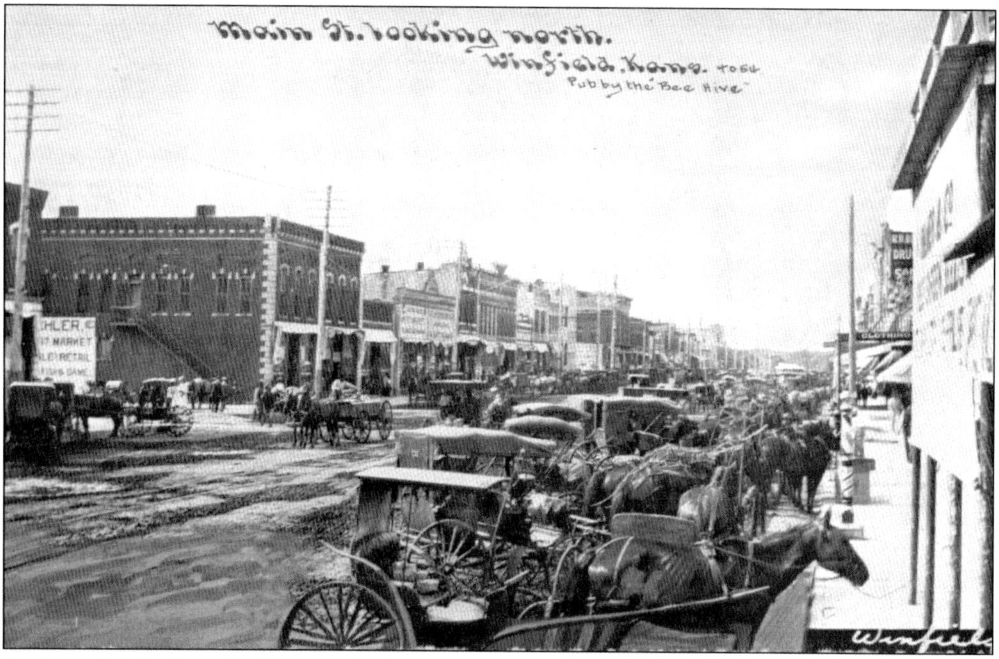


A view of Main Street looking north from just south of Tenth Avenue shows a large advertisement for Mitschler's meat market on its redbrick building on the corner of Tenth Avenue and Main Street, constructed on the site of the Spotswood grocery, one of Winfield's earliest stores. Meat markets also dealt in pelts and hides and offered cold storage in 1910 when this card was mailed.

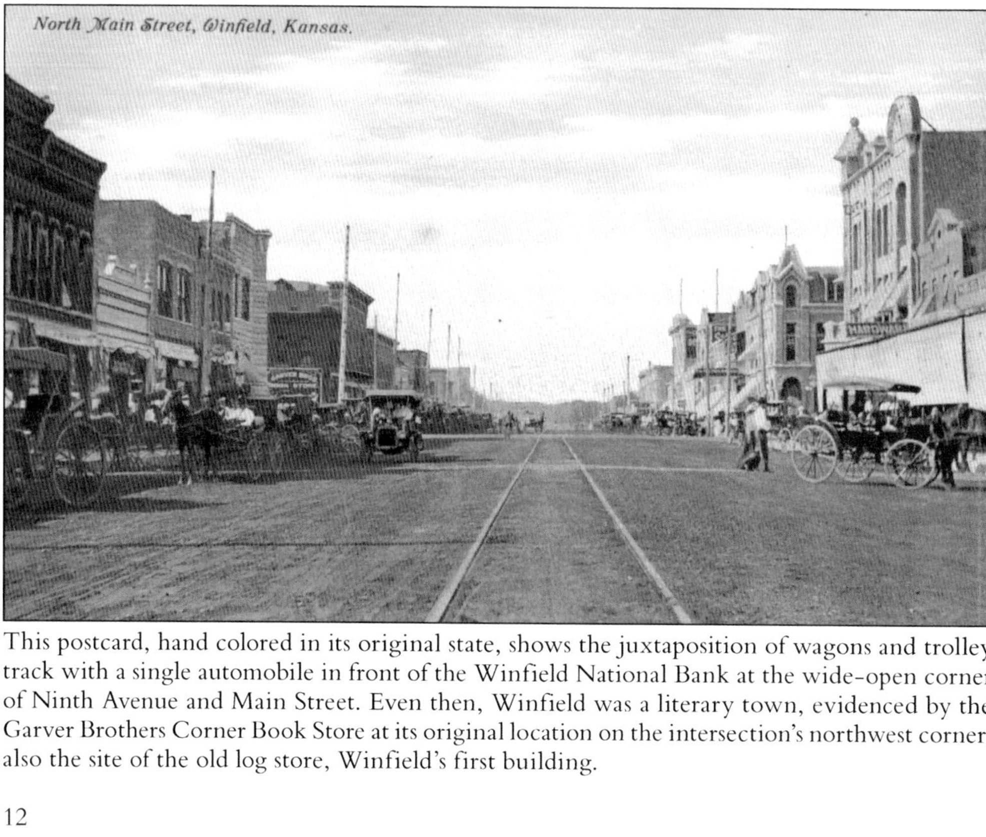


This postcard, hand colored in its original state, shows the juxtaposition of wagons and trolley track with a single automobile in front of the Winfield National Bank at the wide-open corner of Ninth Avenue and Main Street. Even then, Winfield was a literary town, evidenced by the Garver Brothers Corner Book Store at its original location on the intersection's northwest corner, also the site of the old log store, Winfield's first building.

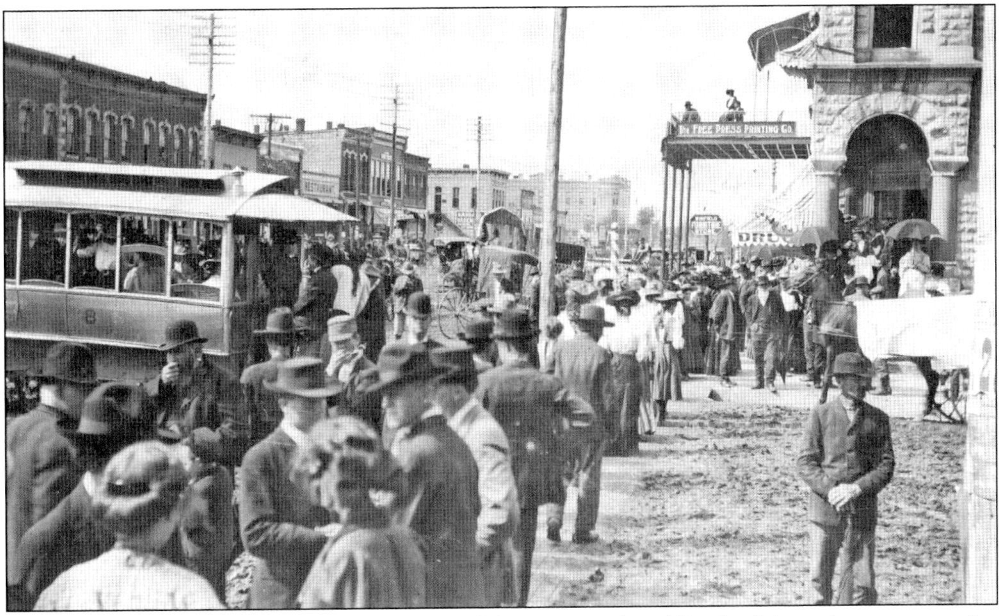



In a photograph likely taken from the steps of the First National Bank, this card captures mule-drawn trolley car No. 8 loading passengers, as well as well-dressed citizens navigating the wooden sidewalks across Ninth Avenue and taking in the view from the balcony provided by the awning of the Columbian Parlors north of the Cowley County National Bank. Women with parasols stand on the steps of the Cowley Bank.

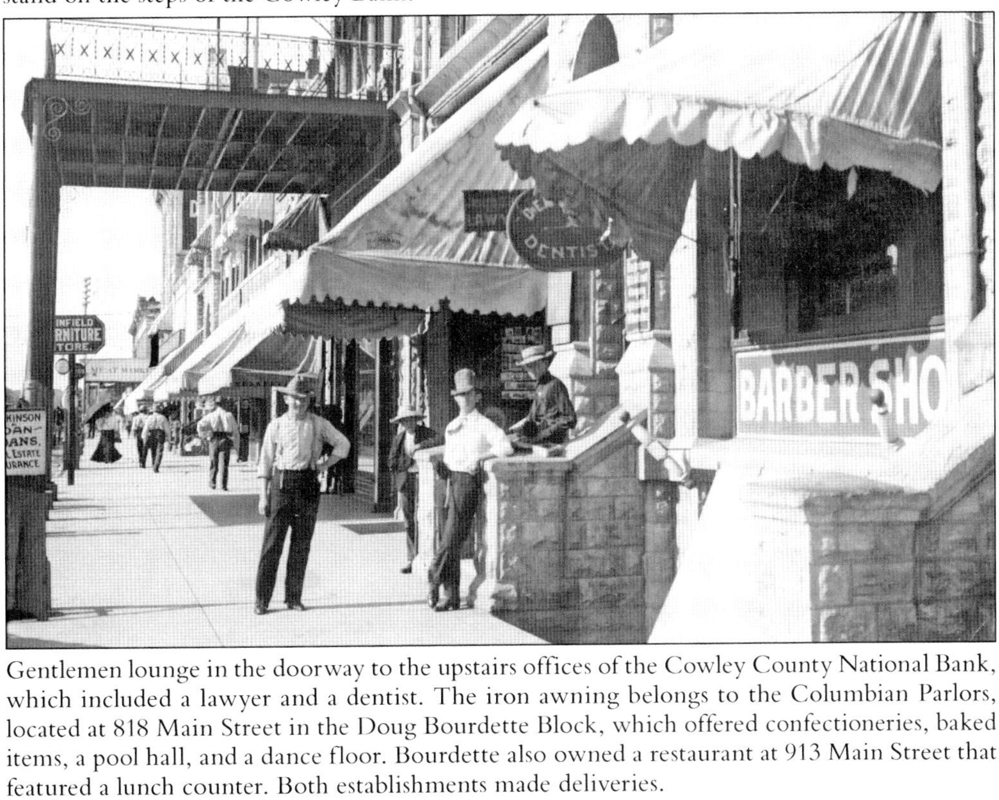



Gentlemen lounge in the doorway to the upstairs offices of the Cowley County National Bank, which included a lawyer and a dentist. The iron awning belongs to the Columbian Parlors, located at 818 Main Street in the Doug Bourdette Block, which offered confectioneries, baked items, a pool hall, and a dance floor. Bourdette also owned a restaurant at 913 Main Street that featured a lunch counter. Both establishments made deliveries.

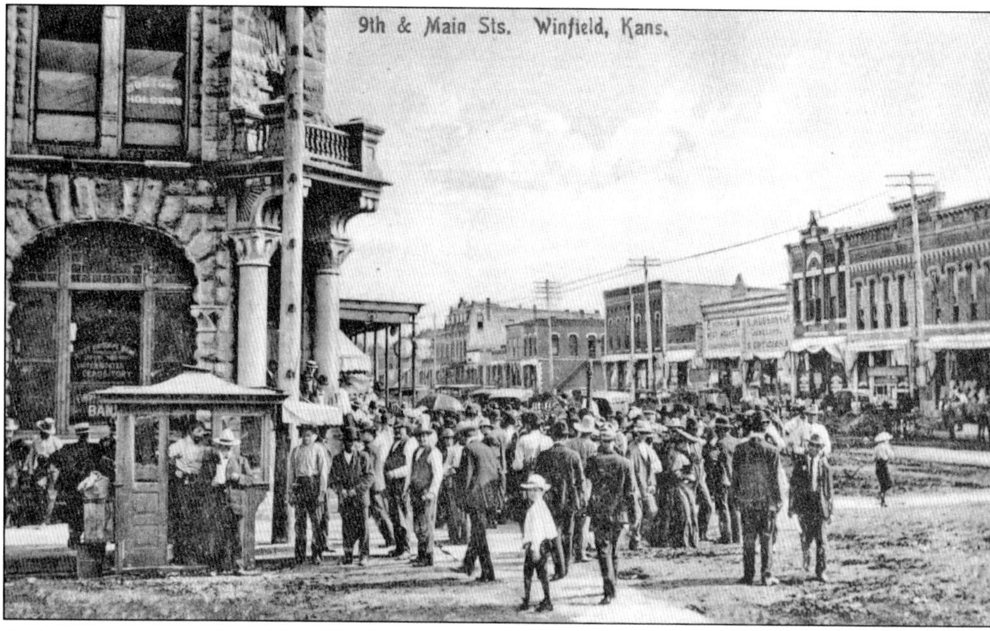


This postcard, postmarked 1909, provides a view of the west side of Main Street across from the First National Bank building, with R. Hudson Jewelers and Dautschmann's meat market in the center of the block. It also evidences the detail on the limestone bank, such as the Romanesque window and the Corinthian columns marking the front door, and provides a clear view of the street railway ticket booth and its operator.

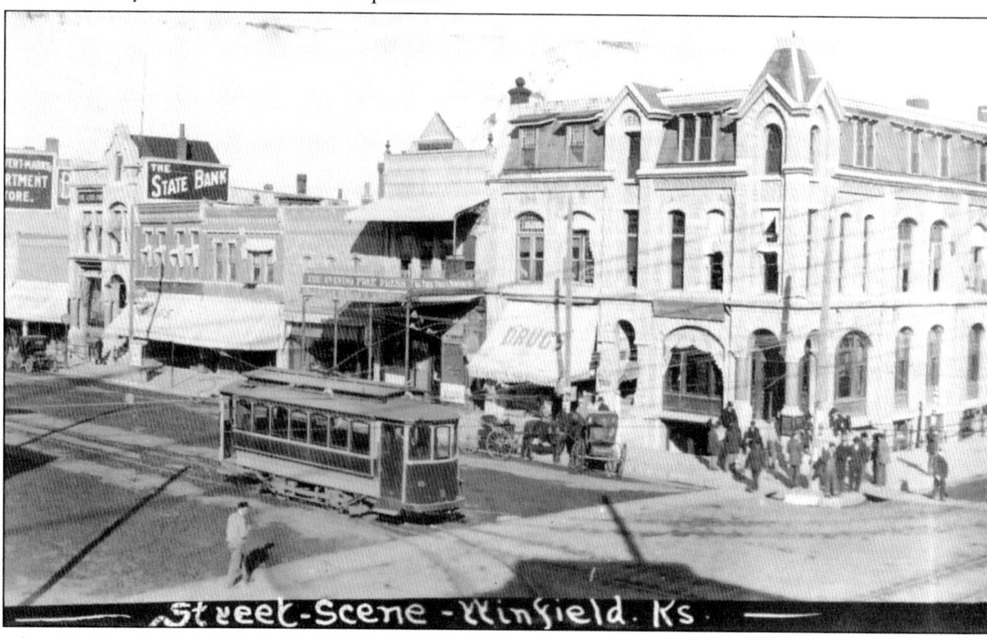


This charming scene puts the Cowley County National Bank and other buildings north of it along with one of Winfield's electric interurban cars on fine display. This postcard sent in 1914 clearly shows the State Bank's original location as well as the front of the Columbian Parlors. The Free Press Printing Company, at 818 ½ Main Street, provided a newspaper six days a week as well as job printing.

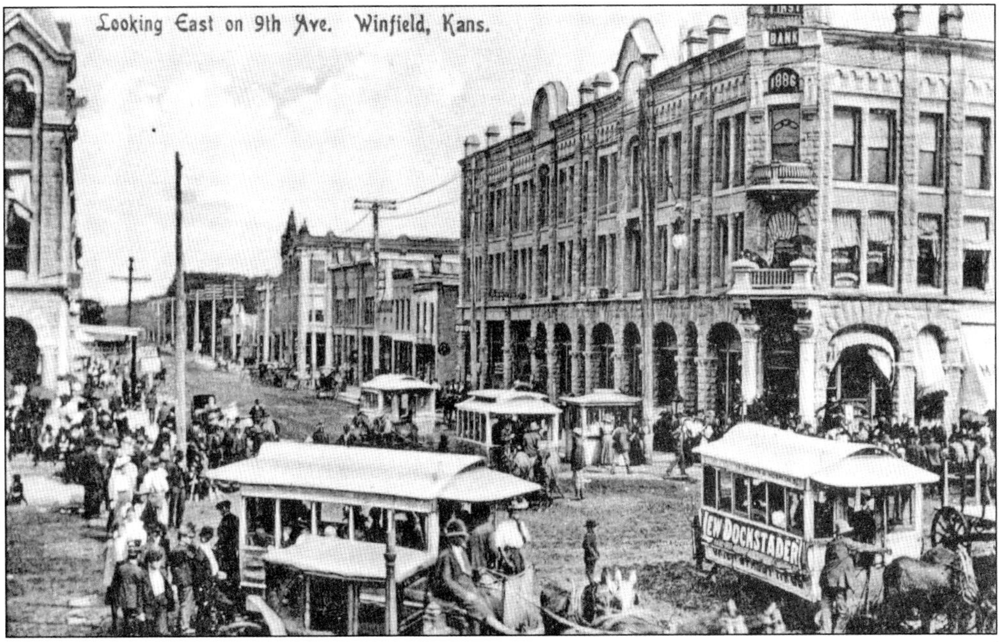


This view of the side of Main Street looking east on Ninth Avenue shows a city thriving and looking ahead. Crowds on foot, in wagons and buggies, in mule-drawn trolley cars, and seated individuals provide evidence the intersection of Ninth Avenue and Main Street was the place to see and be seen. Note the electrical lines; Winfield first received electricity in June 1905.

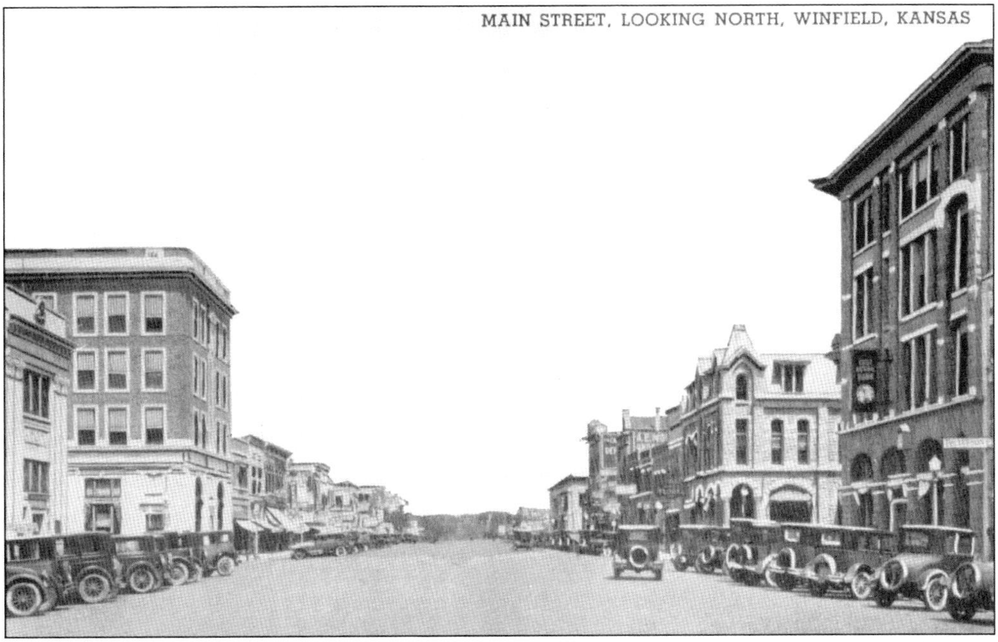


Winfield appears much cleaner in this card sent in 1929. Main Street maintains its wide-open feel but angle-parked cars have replaced the wagons now lining its sides, and no evidence of interurban tracks remain in its center. A proud, remodeled, four-story State Bank appears at the intersection's northwest corner, the First National Bank sports a new clock, and light poles dot the sidewalks.

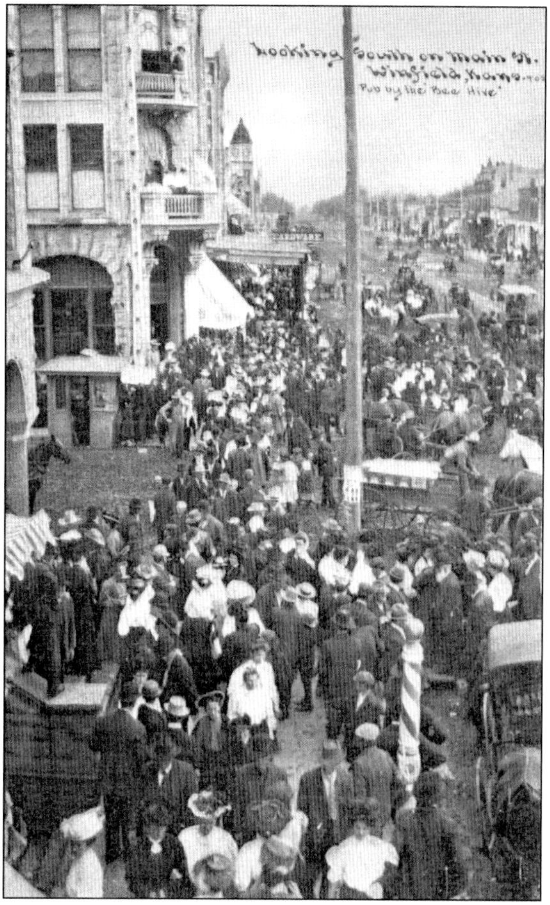


Farmers in overalls, women in hats, and deliverymen in wagons join the throng at the corner of Ninth Avenue and Main Street looking south from the Cowley County National Bank. Others watch the action from the balconies on the First National Bank and the S.C. Black hardware store awning south of it. The clock tower of Dauber's Dry Goods at Tenth Avenue and Main Street is visible in the distance.

Muddy streets, a mule-drawn trolley car, and horse-drawn vehicles fill this view of Winfield's Main Street looking south from Eighth Avenue. This postcard, sent in 1912 to folks living in Chicago, would have been nostalgic as the mule cars stopped running years earlier. The card also provides a different aspect of the bank corner of Ninth Avenue and Main Street and a clearer view of Dauber's Dry Goods Company a block south.

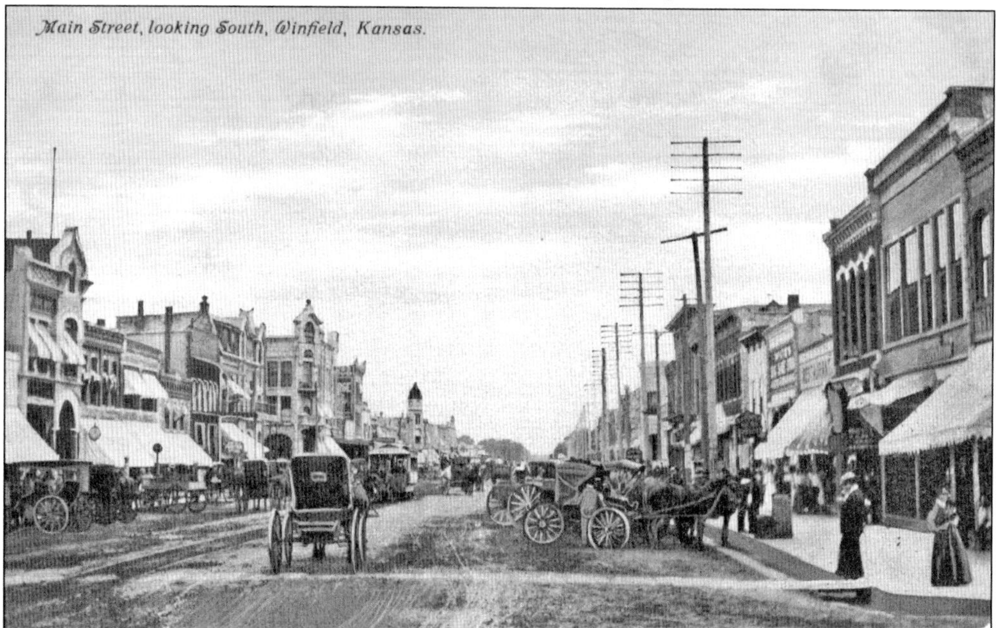

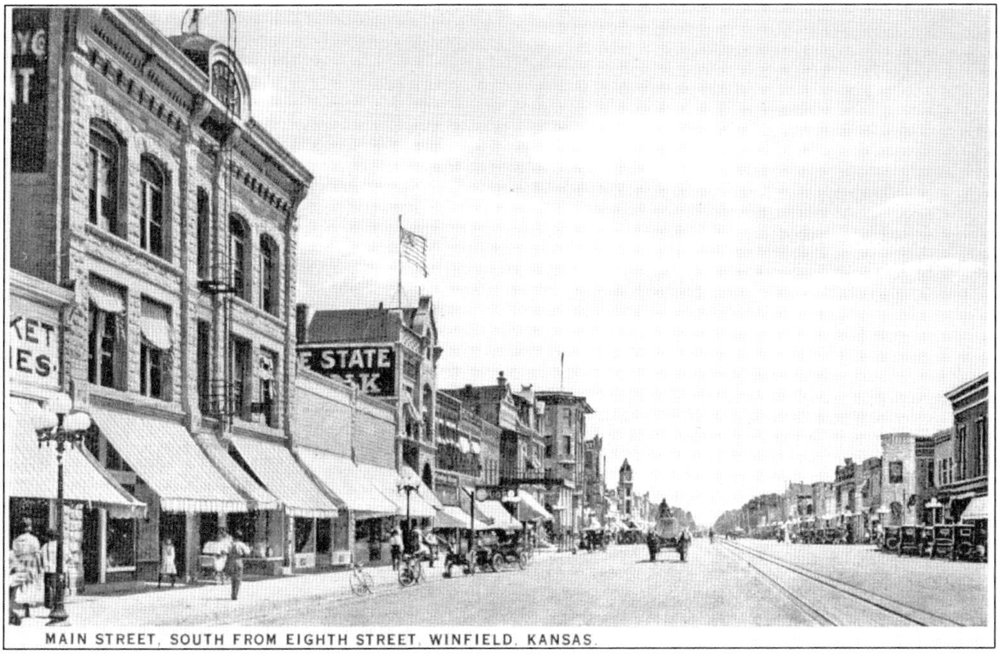


A later view of Winfield's Main Street south of Eighth Avenue shows the addition of five-globe electric lamp posts. The first location of the State Bank is clearly visible on the east side of the street, as is the Baden Block inscription on the limestone building north of it that housed the Brady Brothers Department Store at the time. Note the bicycles and baby pram in the photograph.

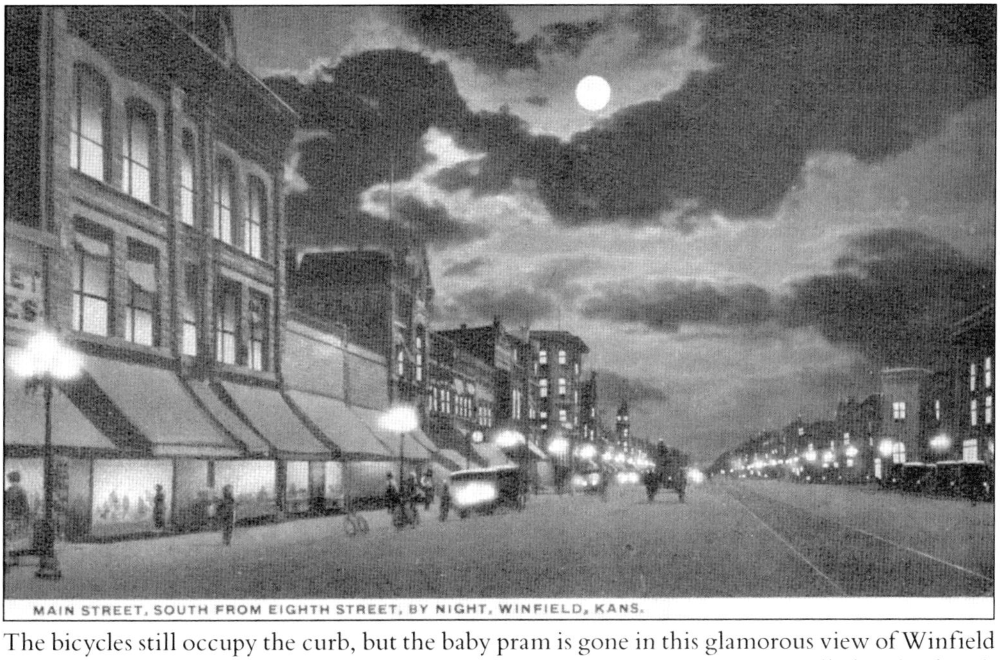


The bicycles still occupy the curb, but the baby pram is gone in this glamorous view of Winfield at night, using the same postcard from Eighth Avenue looking south. Originally hand colored, this postcard, with every window lit, celebrates the addition of electric streetlights along Main Street. Winfield's electrical plant supplied lights for businesses, streetlights, and wealthy customers first, but they quickly spread throughout the city.

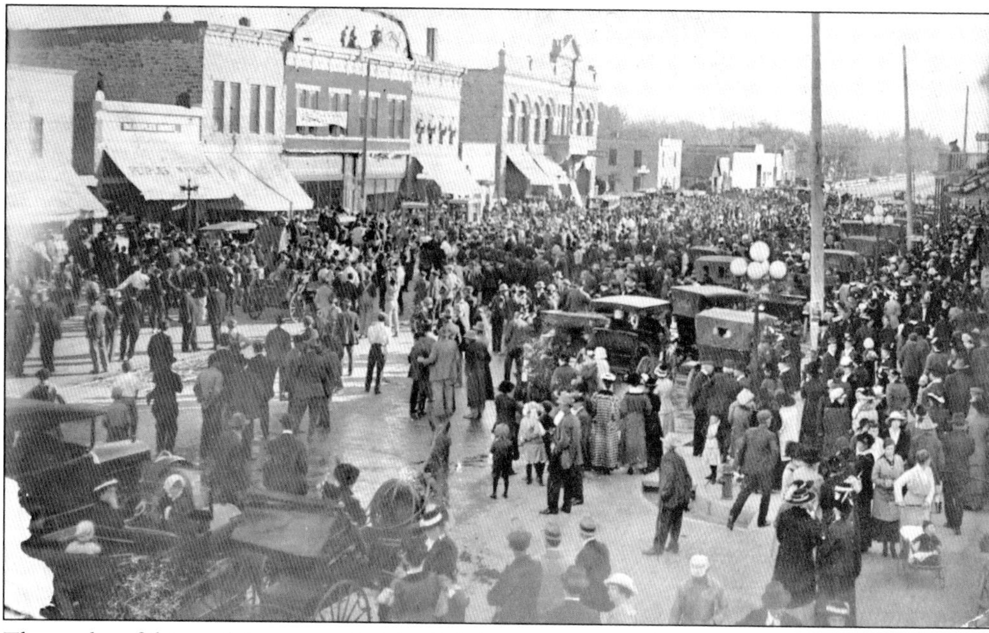

The sender of this card drew an arch, highlighting some unusual creatures and their handlers atop the A.E. Morris Furniture Store at 1010–1012 Main Street. A crowd has gathered for a turkey drop on Saturday, November 20, 1915. Every five minutes, for an hour, starting at 2:30 p.m., a turkey dropped into the crowd, free for whoever caught it without use of a club or gun.

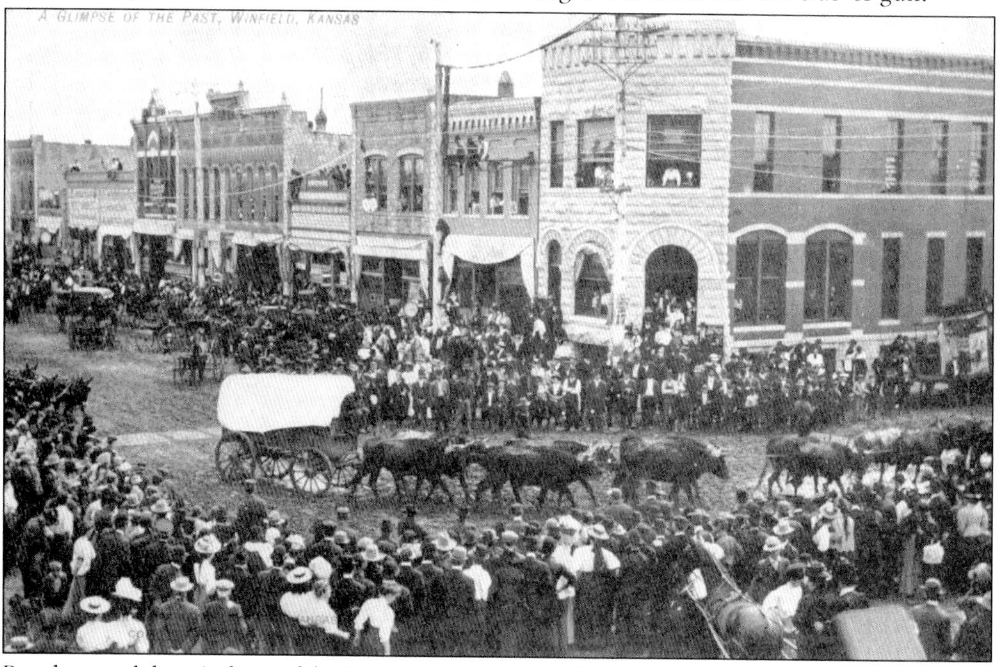


People crowd the windows of the Winfield National Bank, line the streets, and perch precariously on buildings at the southwest corner of Ninth Avenue and Main Street to witness a true glimpse from Winfield's past. As they turn the corner, the cattle run past the site of the city's first building, E.C. Manning's log all-purpose store and meeting place. Appreciation of history is not new in Winfield.

Winfield loves a parade. In the old days, parades celebrated Grand Army of the Republic encampments, sports championships, and circuses, among other things. Thanks to the breadth of Main Street, Ringling Brothers' elephants and their keepers navigate the turn east onto Ninth Avenue in full view of people taking advantage of virtually every balcony, awning, and upper-story window of surrounding buildings. Just as in modern times, traffic stopped for parades on Main Street.

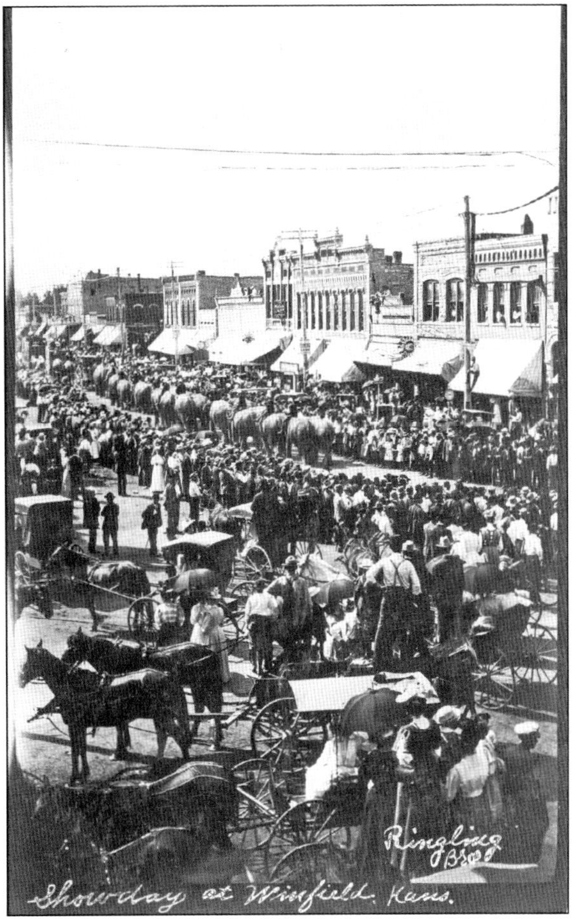


Ringling Brothers swung through Kansas at least twice a year. In 1897, they came to Winfield for an October 2 show after being in Guthrie, Oklahoma, the day before. While the novelty of elephants parading down Main Street made people climb poles for a better view, there would have been musicians and caged animals to see as well. Early circuses set up on the Lowell School grounds, hence the turn east.

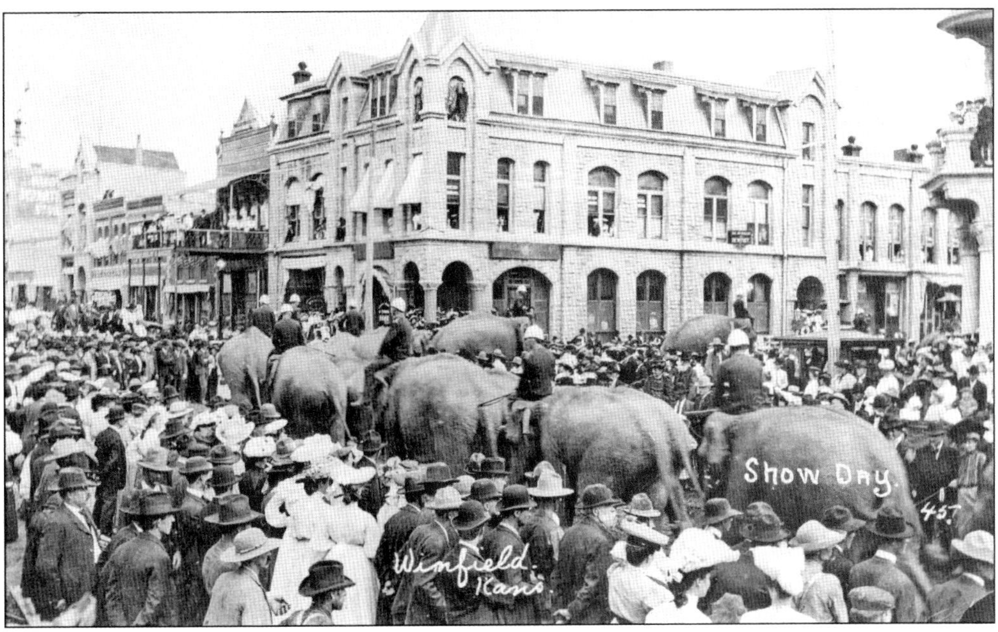

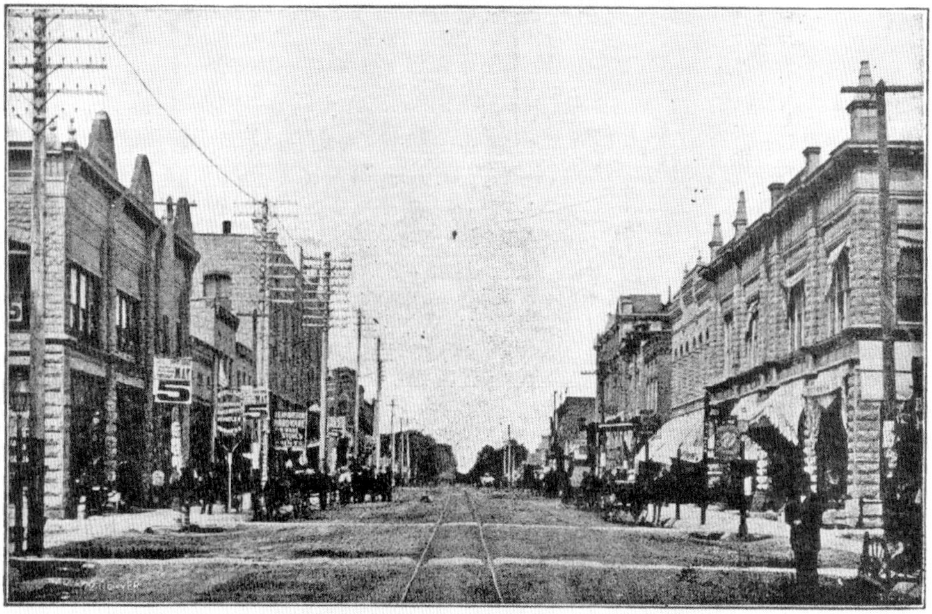


Ninth Avenue West, Winfield, Kansas

This postcard shows the corner of Ninth Avenue and Main Street viewed from Millington Street, a block east of Main Street looking west. First National Bank would be on the south and Cowley County National Bank on the north. Note the sidewalks crossing the street at both corners and the fliers for events and fairs posted. Signs for McGregor's Hardware in its original location can be seen on the south side of the street.

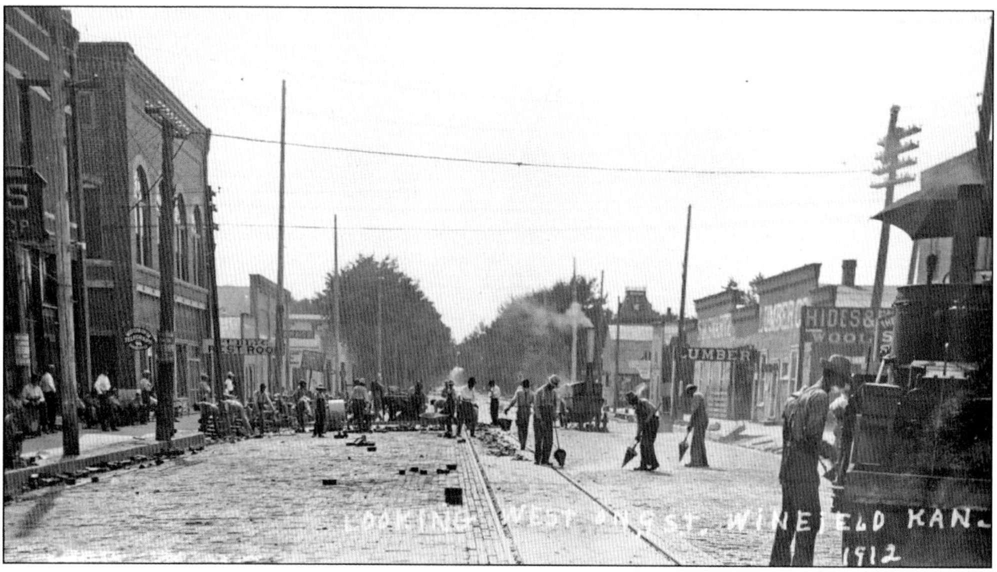


Winfield's streets were macadamized in the 1890s, putting an end to the muddy mess. In 1912, they began to be bricked. Here, men work around the tracks of the interurban railway on Ninth Avenue just west of Main Street. Only local men did the work, completing a block of paving every two and a half days. Winfield celebrated when Main Street north of Ninth Avenue was ready for the 1914 Chautauqua.

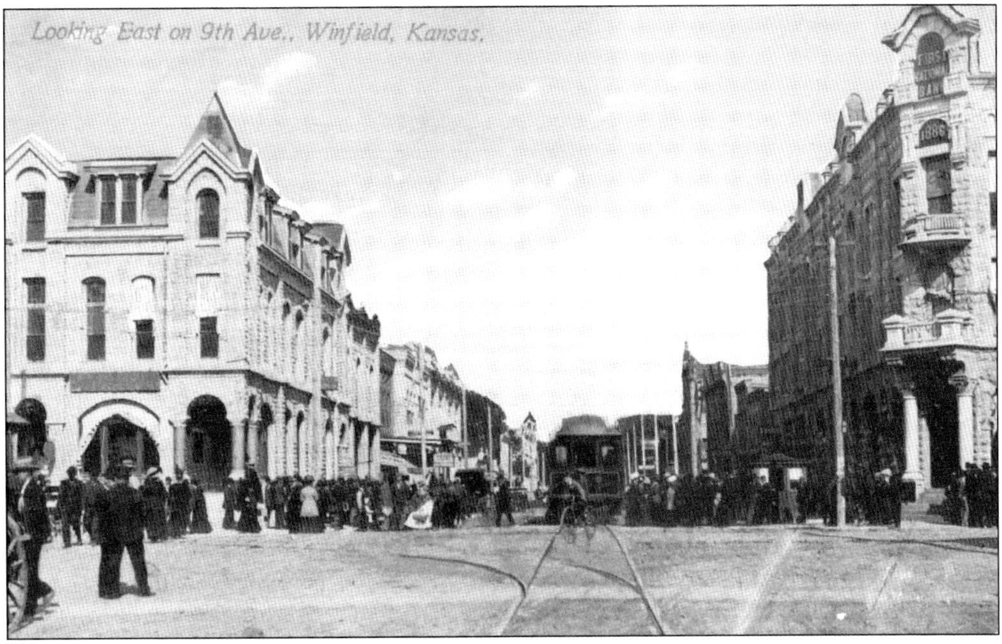


In front of the Cowley County National Bank, toward the north in this image, a bronze star with an *S* on it can still be found imbedded in the pavement. It marks the spot where Constable H.H. Siverd fell in the line of duty on October 25, 1893. The star, made from the badges of 26 members of fraternal organizations to which Siverd belonged, was installed on May 21, 1894.

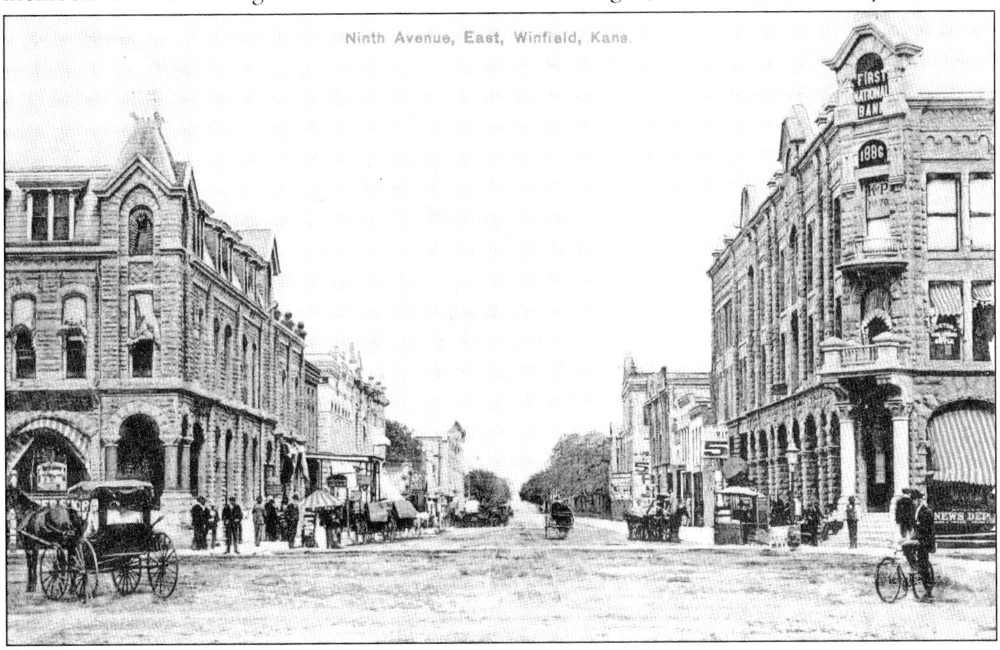


The corner of Ninth Avenue and Main Street was also the site of what came to be known as a massacre. At this intersection on the evening of August 13, 1903, a mentally unstable man fired eight shots while a crowd gathered for the weekly concert of Caman's Band, killing nine people and wounding 25. He then fled west to the alley behind the Corner Book Store, where he shot himself.

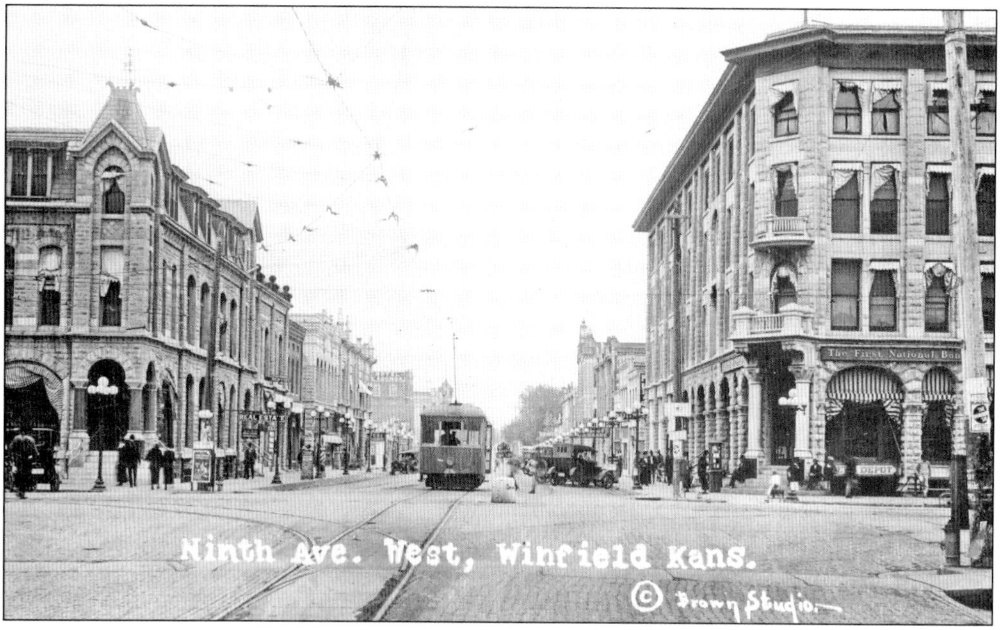


This view, looking east on Ninth Avenue from Main Street, reflects the 1918 addition of a fourth floor to the First National Bank and the absence of the street railway ticket booth. Other additions are brick streets, five-globe streetlights, and Hotel Lagonda, northeast of this intersection. Main Street was still a place to spend leisure time, as evidenced by the child and her wagon in front of First National Bank.

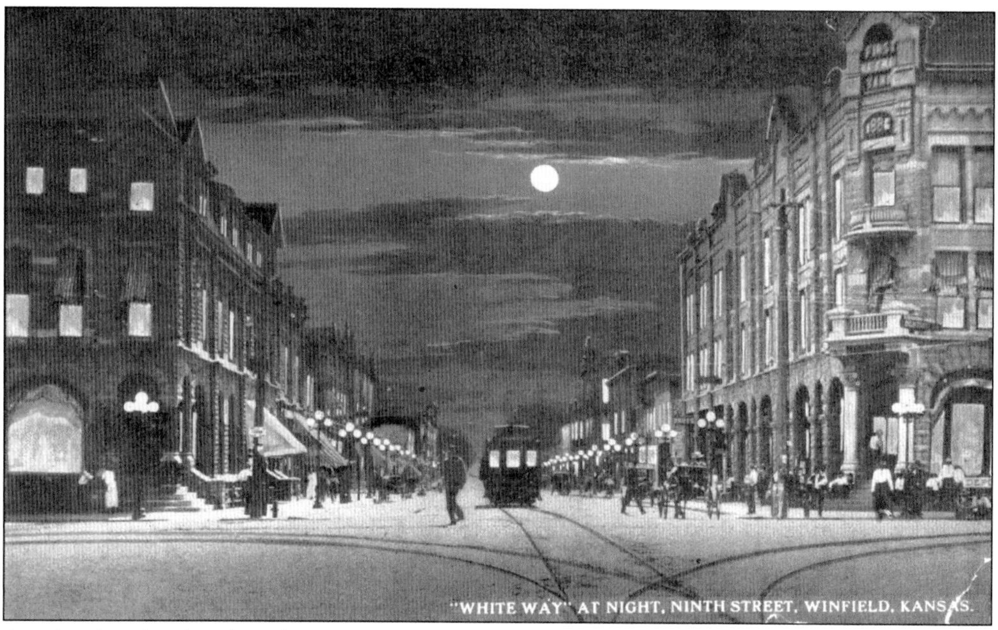


Another hand-colored nighttime Main Street scene looking east on Ninth Avenue shows the intersecting interurban tracks as well as the steps leading up to the Cowley County National Bank, which are generally covered with people in other views. These steps disappeared in 1930 when the first floor was lowered to street level. September 5, 1914, marked the "white way," when electric lighting lit up Main Street from Fifth to Eleventh Avenues.

# *Two*

# Winfield at Work

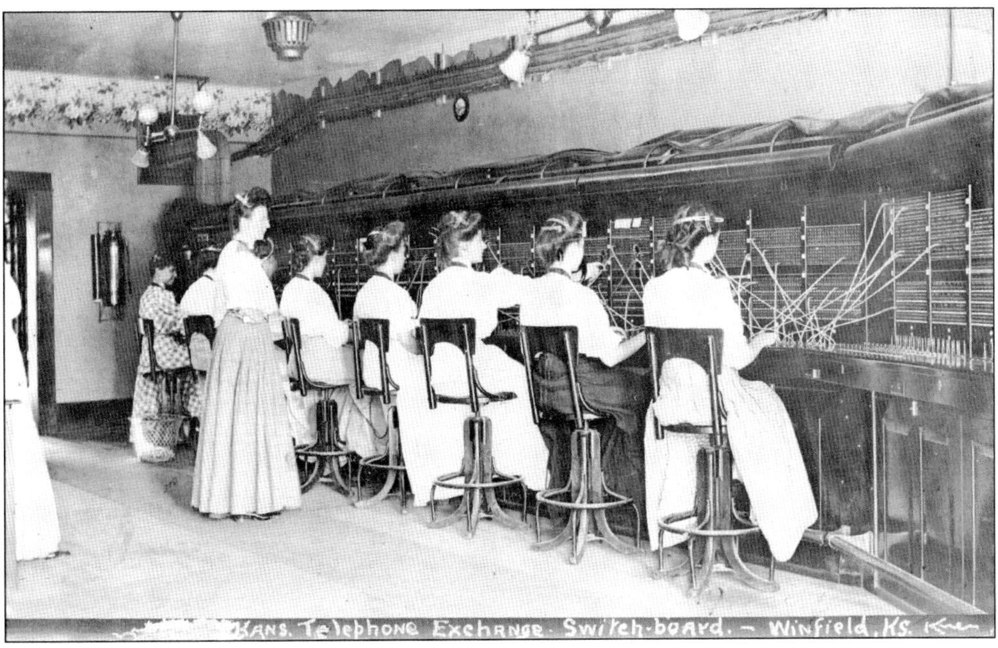


Women found work in a variety of settings in early Winfield, which established its first telephone exchange in 1881. The Winfield Telephone Exchange opened in 1901 and eventually became part of the Missouri & Kansas Telephone Company. By 1910, Winfield had 1,760 telephones, using hand-cranked machines until 1926. With Winfield's new telephone office at 720 Millington Street, the city moved to the dial system in 1960.

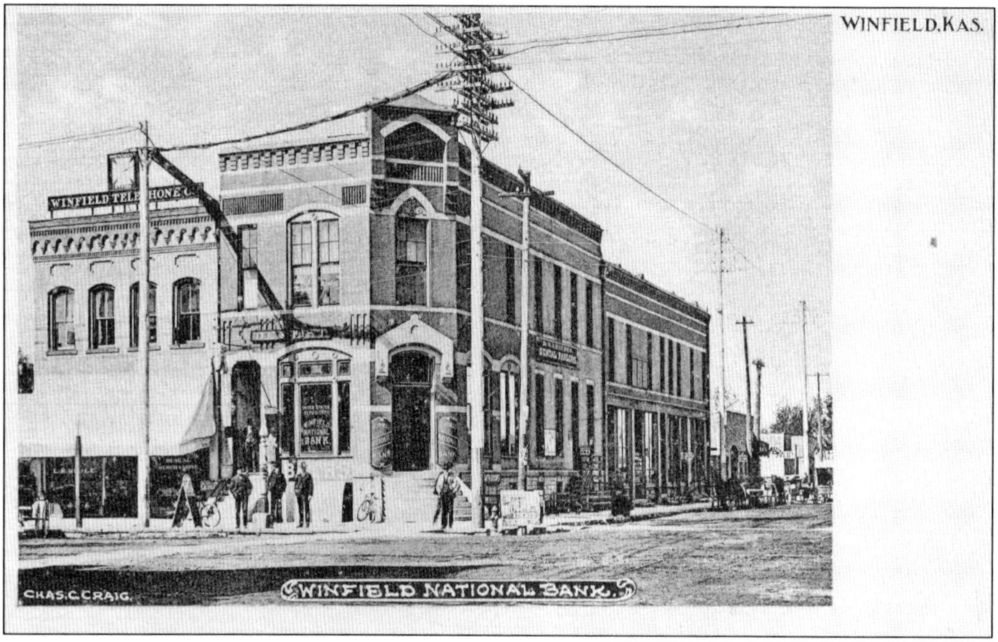


J.C. Fuller established Winfield's first bank in 1871 on the southwest corner of Ninth Avenue and Main Street. It was also the first in Cowley County and the first bank south of Emporia, Kansas. In 1879, Col. J.C. McMullen incorporated it as the Winfield Bank. H.B. Schuler bought it in 1885, making it Winfield National Bank. In 1923, it received a new stone building but merged with First National Bank in 1945.

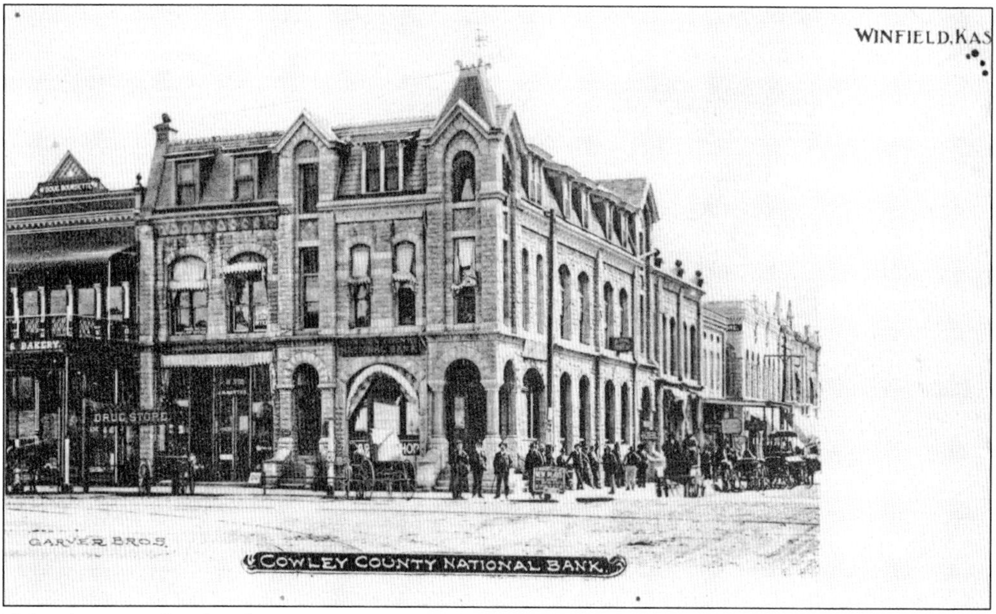


What became the Cowley County National Bank organized in 1883 as the Farmers Bank. In 1886, the ornate limestone building pictured here went up on the northeast corner of Ninth Avenue and Main Street. Farmers Bank reorganized as the Cowley County National Bank in 1891. This bank closed in 1922 when it merged with the First National Bank. The building remains in the National Register of Historic Places.

The State Bank, chartered in 1905, originally shared the east side of the 800 block of Main Street north of the Cowley County National Bank. Construction began in 1916 on the building pictured here at the northwest corner of Ninth Avenue and Main Street, property first owned by E.C. Manning and later sold to Henry Goldsmith for his Corner Book Store. The bookstore, named Garver Brothers by 1916, moved to 823 Main Street.

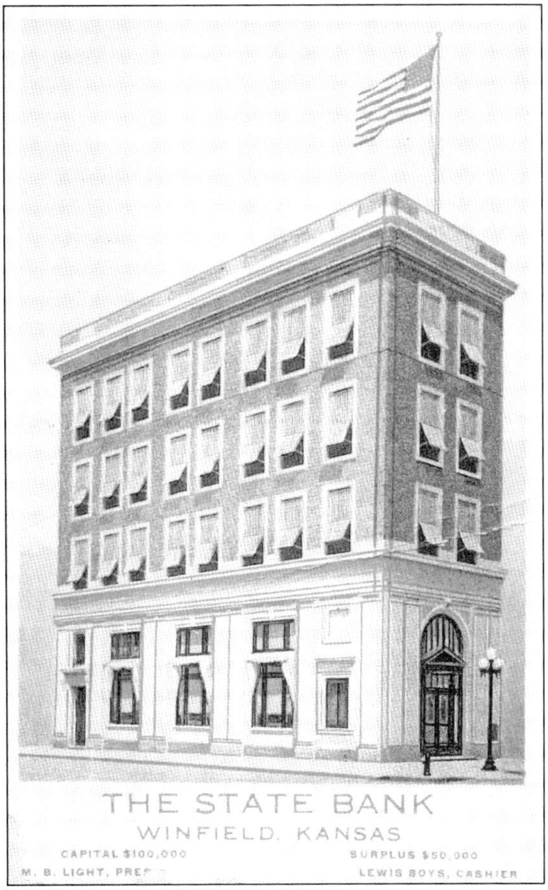


A series of these postcards, personalized for the bank sending them, went out monthly in 1909 to the customers of various banks around the state, including Winfield's State Bank. Only 25 feet wide when first built, the State Bank continued to grow, more than doubling its size in 1927 with expansion to the north and continuing in business to this day as Union State Bank.

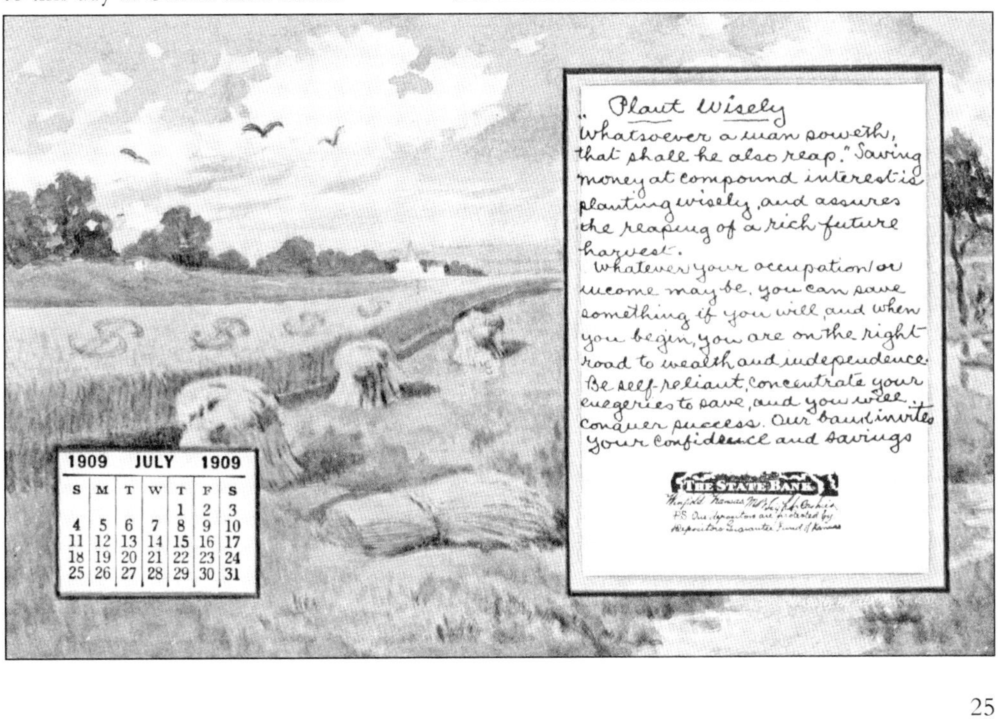

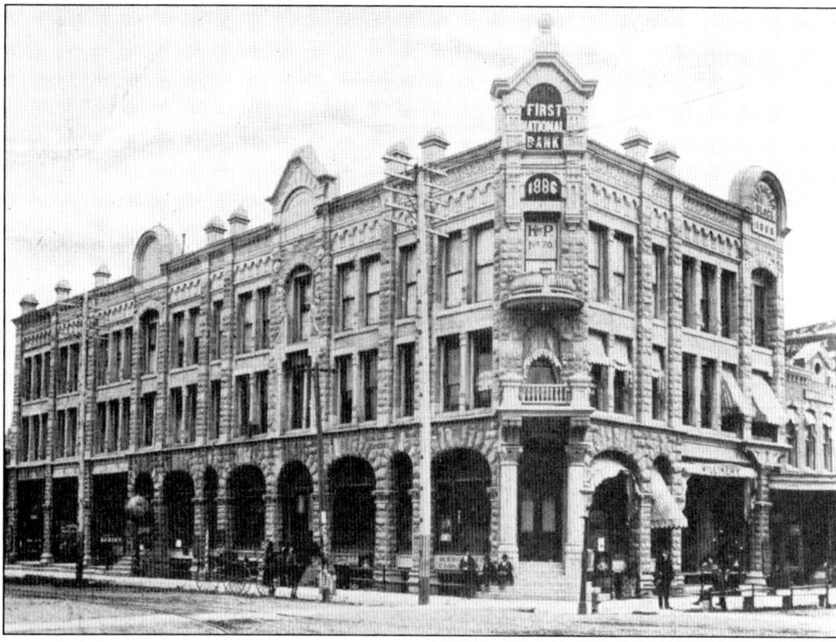


First National Bank, Winfield, Kans.

Winfield's second bank started in 1872 at 905 Main Street as Read's Bank, located in the first brick building in the county just south of the Winfield National Bank. In 1884, it became the First National Bank and a year later purchased the lot across the street at the southeast corner of Ninth Avenue and Main Street for its imposing three-story limestone building, which still stands today. It became the Corner Bank in 1999.

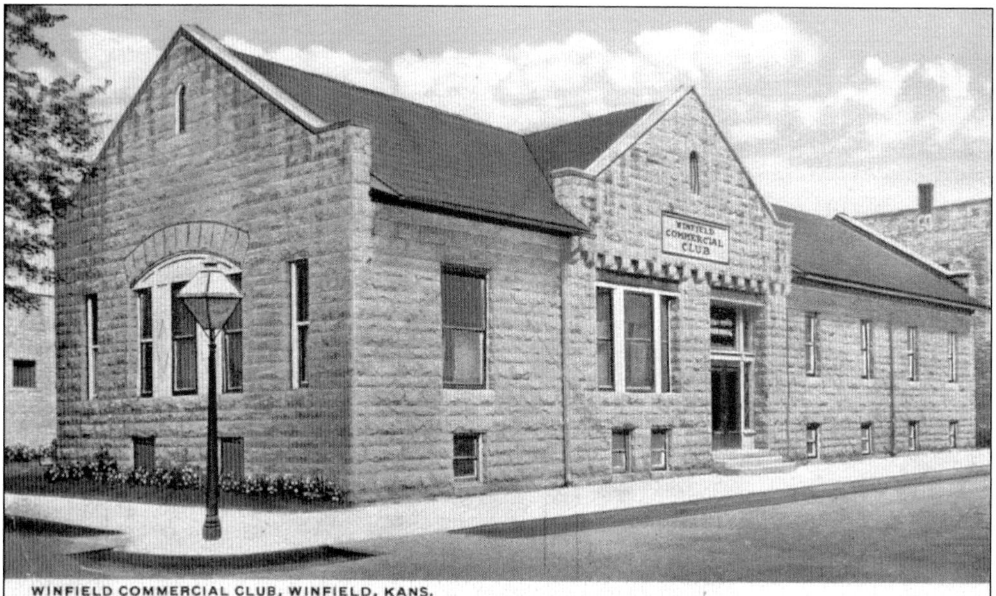


WINFIELD COMMERCIAL CLUB, WINFIELD, KANS.

In 1897, fourteen charter members formed the Winfield Commercial Club with the purpose of promoting Winfield and its businesses. By 1900, membership increased to 56. This postcard, postmarked 1920, shows the club's later location in the former YMCA building at Tenth Avenue and Millington Street around the time it became known as the chamber of commerce. A parking lot now occupies its location.

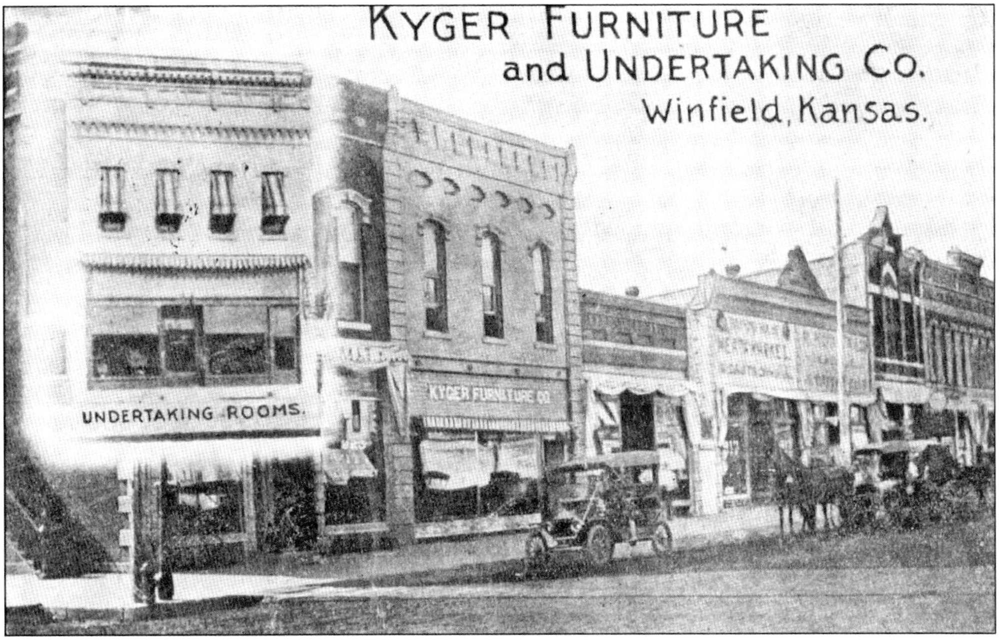


Kyger Furniture started life in 1883 on East Ninth Avenue before moving to what became its permanent location a few years later. In its early years, it provided furnishings for every aspect of life, including its end. This advertising card shows the store's undertaking business, located at 1014 Main Street, superimposed next to the furniture store, which ran from 1895 until 1919, when it was sold to Durim and Swisher Co.

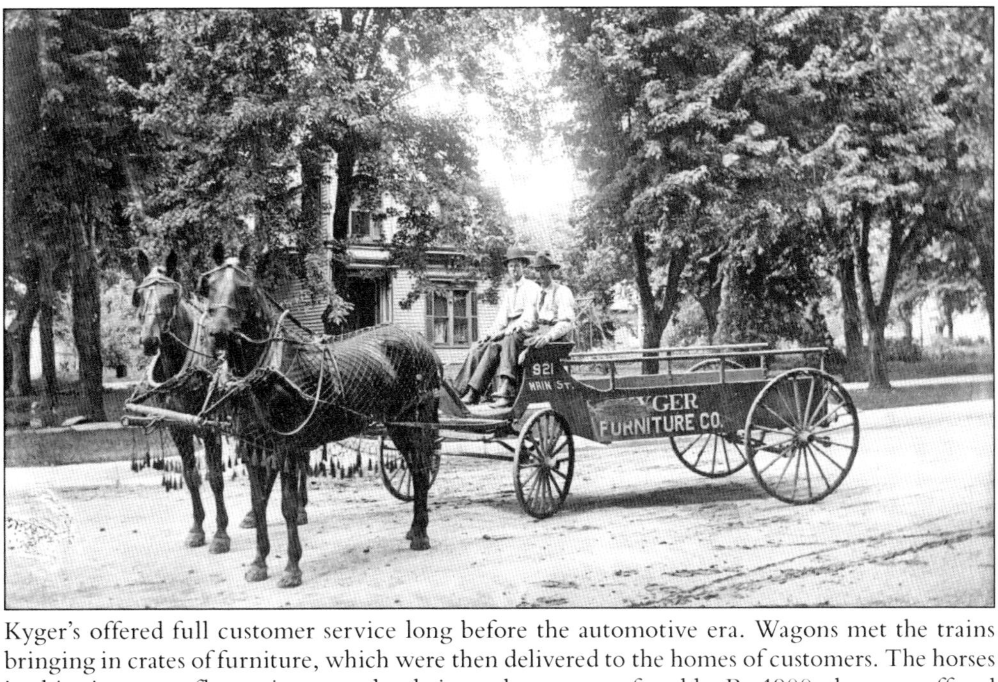


Kyger's offered full customer service long before the automotive era. Wagons met the trains bringing in crates of furniture, which were then delivered to the homes of customers. The horses in this view wear fly netting to make their work more comfortable. By 1900, the store offered 7,000 square feet of furniture display, southern Kansas's largest at the time. Kyger Furniture remains at 921 Main Street, and still family owned, today.

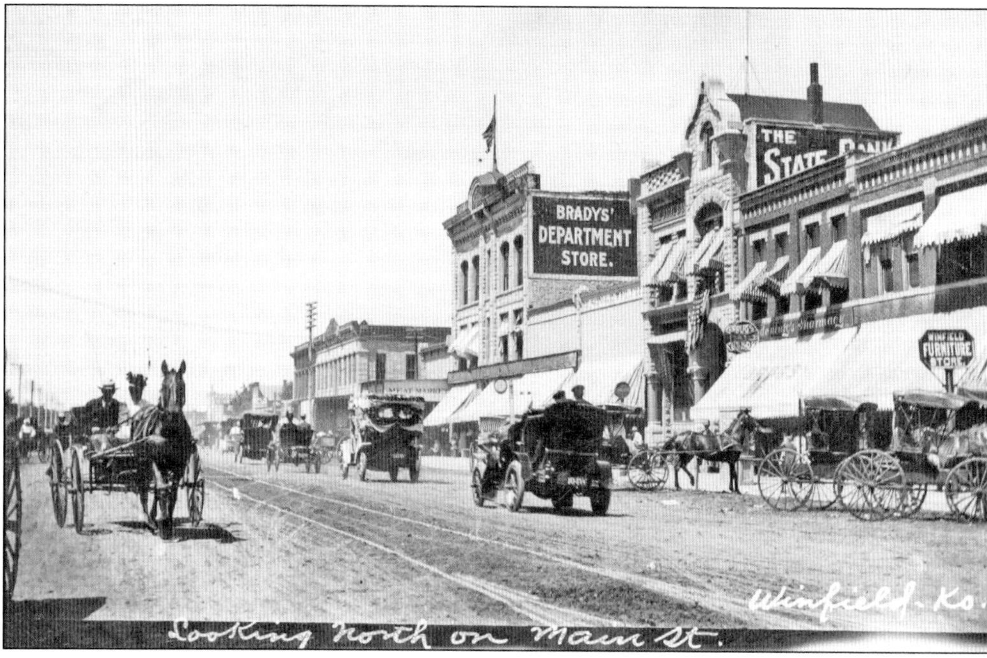


This view, looking north from Ninth Avenue on the east side of Main Street, shows the original location of the State Bank as well as the Brady Brothers and Company Department Store at Eighth Avenue and Main Street. Purchased from J.P. Baden in 1897, the store doubled in size by 1900 to include not only dry goods but also clothing, shoes, and groceries. The second floor housed a dressmaking department.

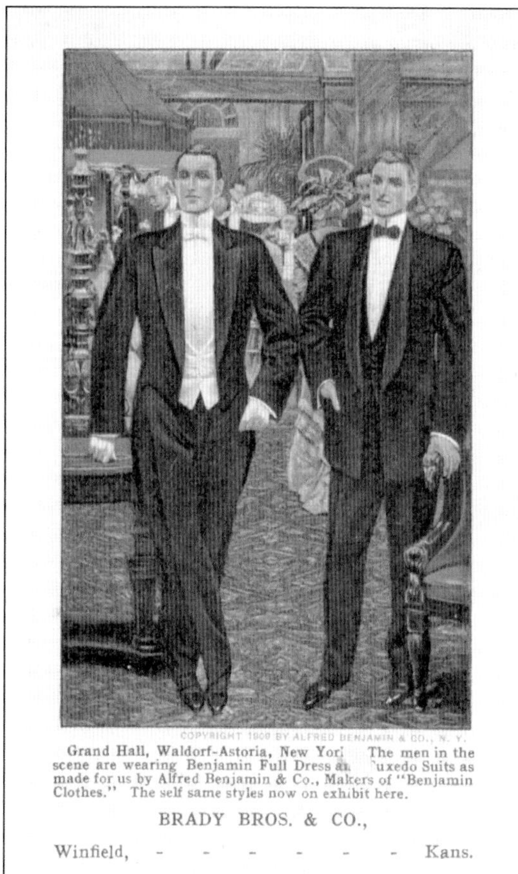


Brady Brothers stressed customer service, employing 27 people in 1900, twelve of them female. This 1909 advertising card provided by a ready-made clothing company could be sent to customers anywhere. The company sold the store to Calvert and Mabry Co. in 1916. Following a fire that destroyed the Baden Block in 1984, the three-story 800 Main Place mini-mall, also constructed of limestone, opened in 1987.

This card provides a view of the interior of W.H. Somermeier's drug store at 209 East Ninth Avenue. With much to attract young and old, it offered a wide variety of grooming items, such as shaving and manicure sets, perfume, toothbrushes, soaps, and mirrors. Two pharmacists, including Somermeier (on the right), filled prescriptions. A.K. Snyder purchased the business in 1909, and it retained the Snyder name into modern times.

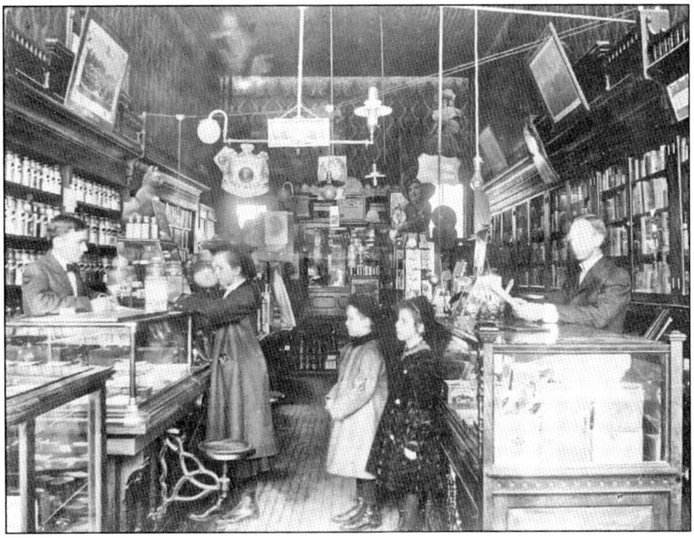

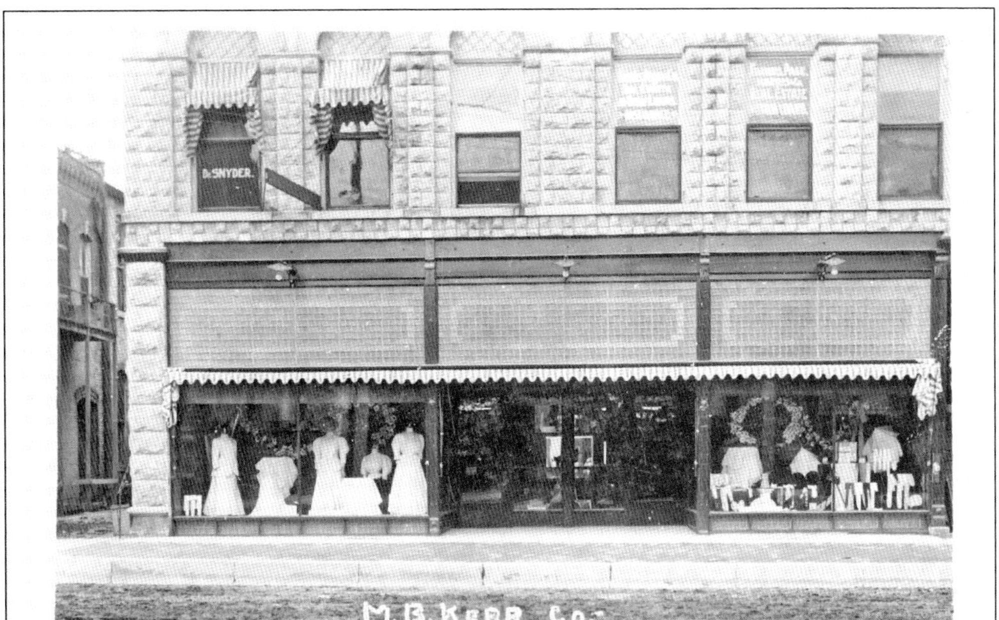


M.B. Kerr first opened a store for women in 1896 on the 900 block of Main Street. Within a few years, he moved it to 113 East Ninth Avenue and across the street to 112 East Ninth Avenue in 1903. At that time, Kerr's featured a millinery department and trained corset fitters. The store changed with the times and served Winfield women until it closed in 1994.

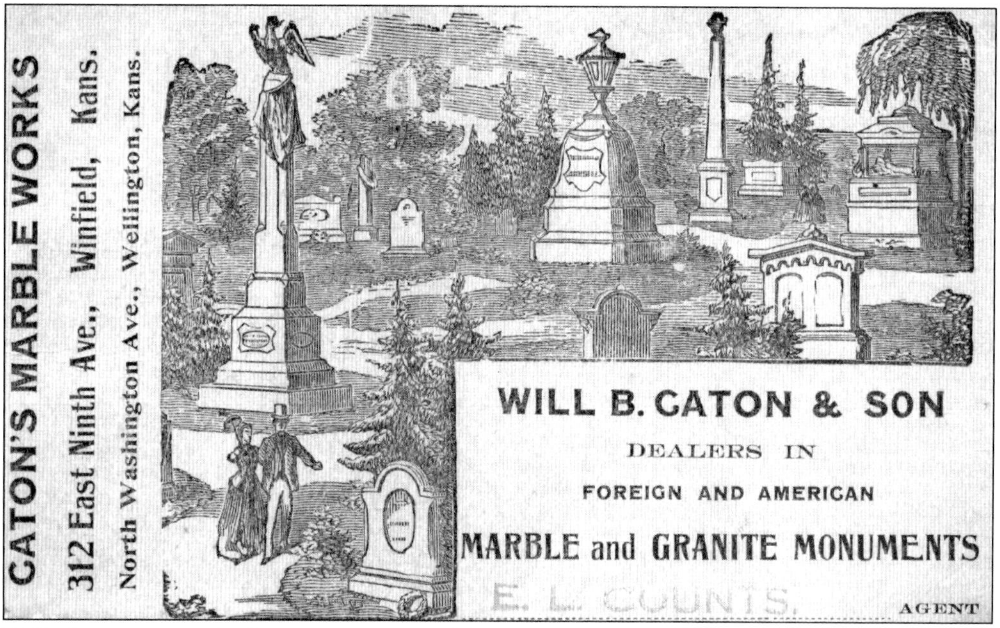


W.B. Caton apprenticed in a Missouri marble works following the Civil War and brought his skills to Winfield in 1879, the same year William H. Dawson opened the Winfield Marble Works. Caton's Marble Works shipped all over the state and into Oklahoma and Texas, employing salesmen, one of whose cards is shown here. Dawson's remains in business today at Main Street and Fourteenth Avenue.

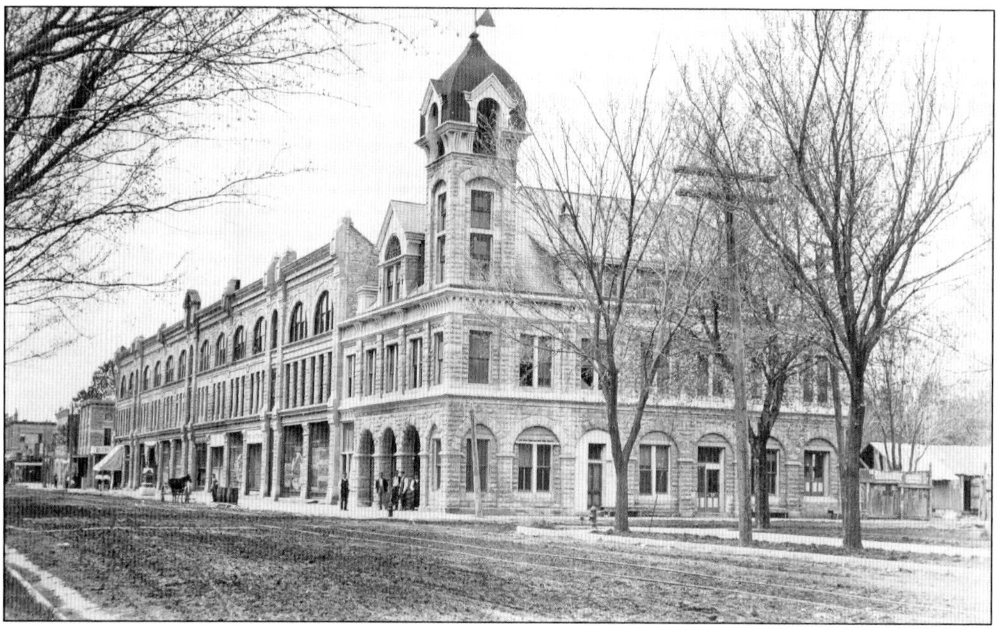

When the Hackney Block west of the city building at Ninth Avenue and Fuller Street suffered a fire about 1900, W.B. Caton took the opportunity to rebuild the west end of it as the home for his marble works, carving "1901 Caton Block" into the center of the roof pediment. In later years, the Central Commercial College and a Hudson-Essex service shop occupied the building, which was razed in 1975.

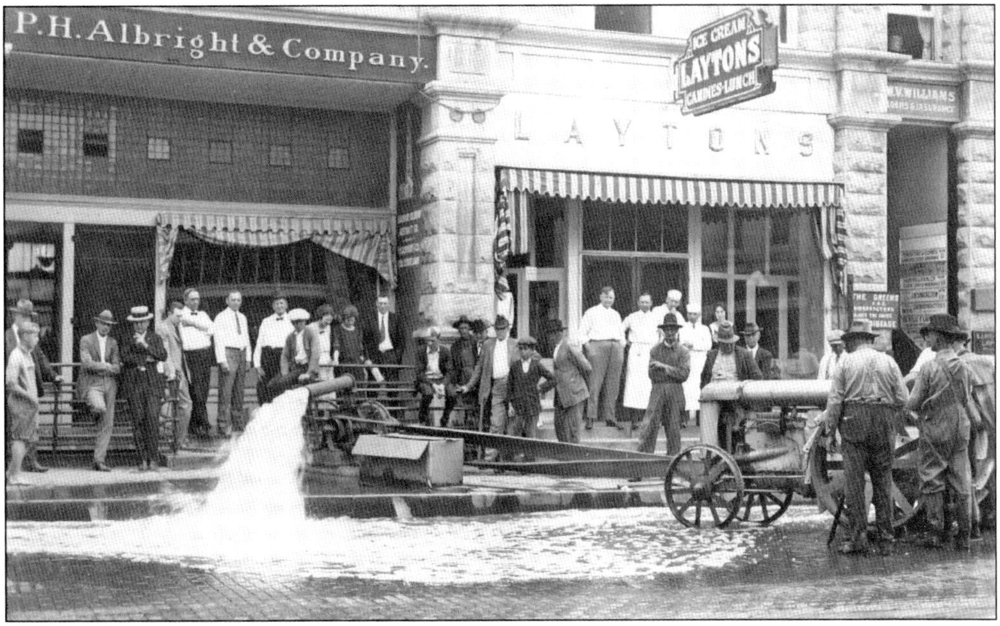


P.H. Albright opened a real estate loan agency and abstract firm in 1881 on the second floor of the post office at the northwest corner of Ninth Avenue and Main Street. By 1900, he and his partners had employed 20 people and moved. Layton's Confectionery did not last into the 21st century, but Albright's location on the 200 block of East Ninth Avenue served it well. It remains a family business today.

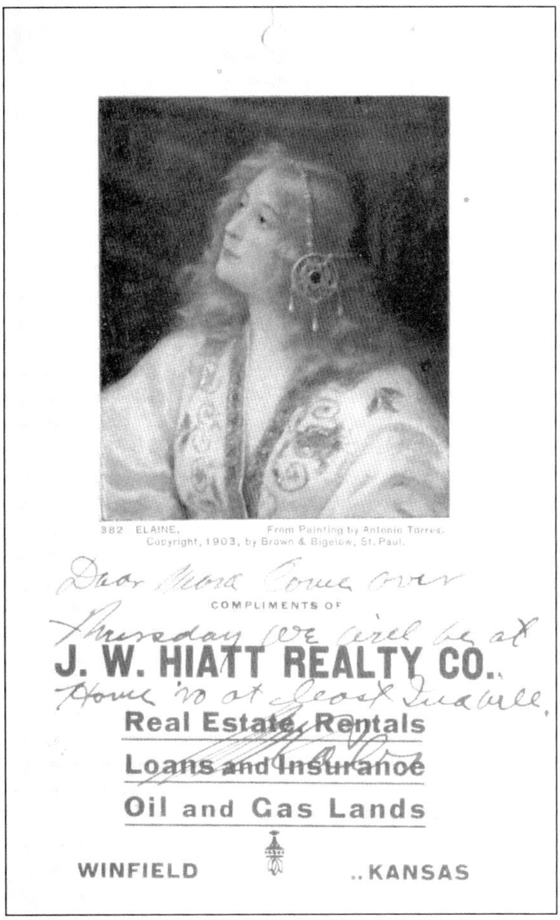


Jesse Hiatt came to Cowley County in 1871, creating a homestead and stock ranch. By 1901, he owned 8,000 acres of land. He purchased the brick home at 508 West Ninth Avenue from George Miller in 1902 and developed Hiatt's Park, west of Winfield. Until his death in 1919, Hiatt operated a realty company at 103 East Ninth Avenue. His great-granddaughter ran a restaurant in his former home from 1989 to 1996.

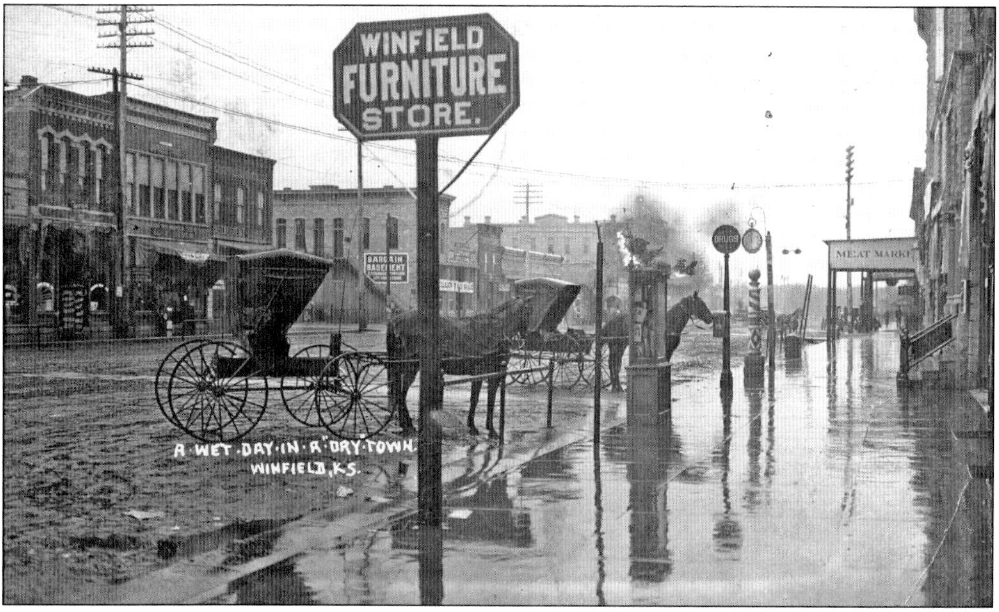


Liquor joints closed for good in 1891 by vote of residents, making Winfield a dry town and fodder for this 1911 postcard. This view shows the Winfield Furniture Store, organized in 1875 by J.W. Johnson, which moved to 816 Main Street in 1898. Also visible at the northwest corner of Eighth Avenue and Main Street is J.B. Lynn's Bargain Basement, which opened in 1902. Lynn's dry goods store itself dated to 1874.

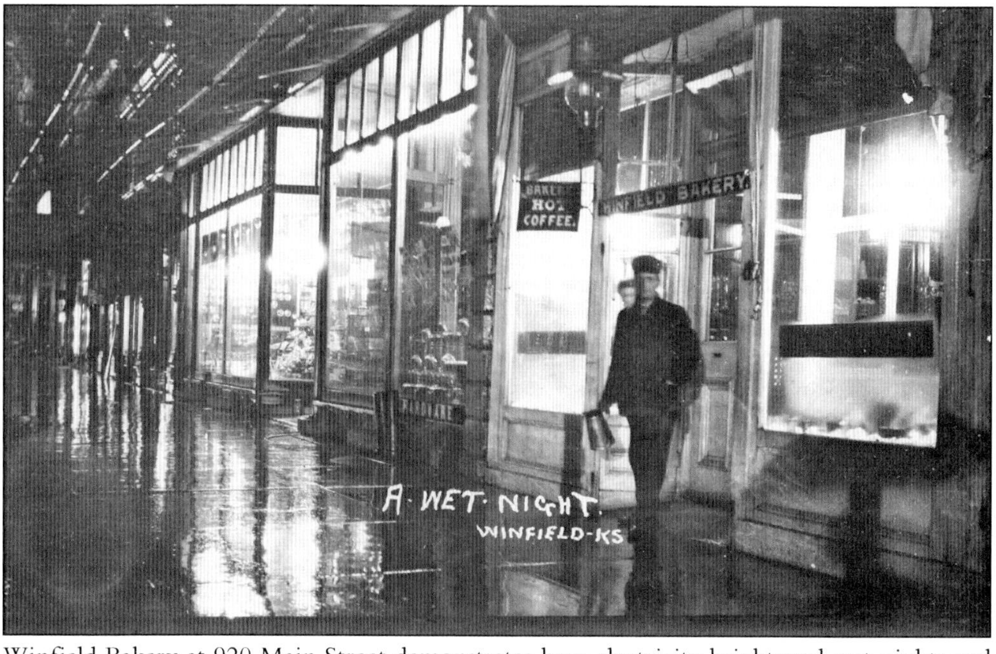


Winfield Bakery at 920 Main Street demonstrates how electricity brightened wet nights and shop windows as well. This bakery, started in the early 1900s by L.D. Holtke, was sold to his partners in 1917. William Ulrich bought the bakery in 1926, renaming it Peerless Bakery. His store manager, Merle Hatteberg, purchased it in 1941 and ran it at 609 Main Street until 1975, when it sold to Melvin Slagle.

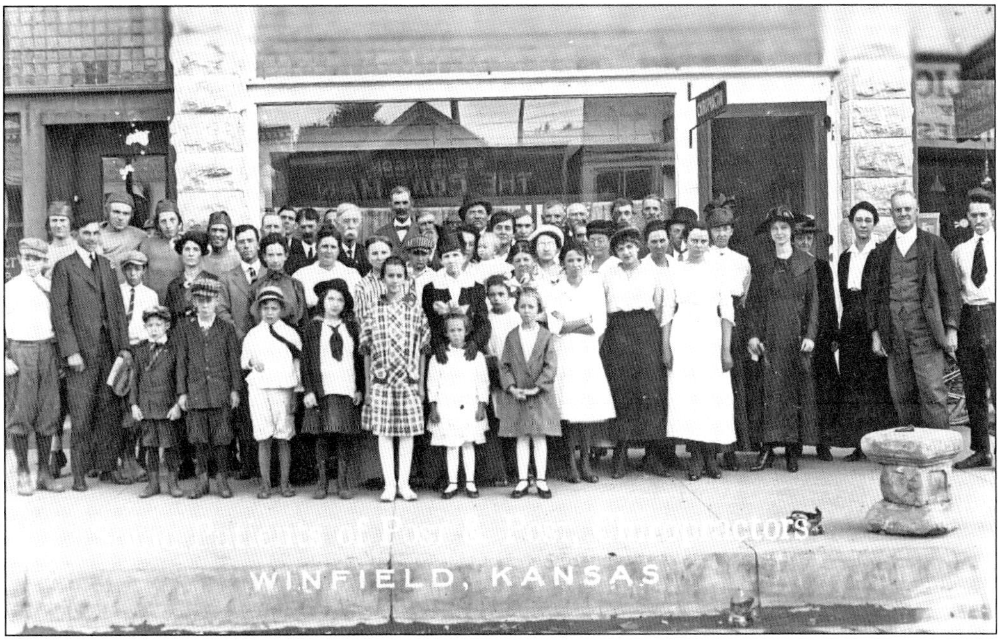


Patients of all ages turned out to help Post & Post Chiropractors advertise in front of their office at 211 East Ninth Avenue. Beginning in 1878, hitching posts were required in front of businesses. Note the fine limestone one here, as well as the set of discarded roller skates, likely from one of the children in the front row, and the football players in the back row.

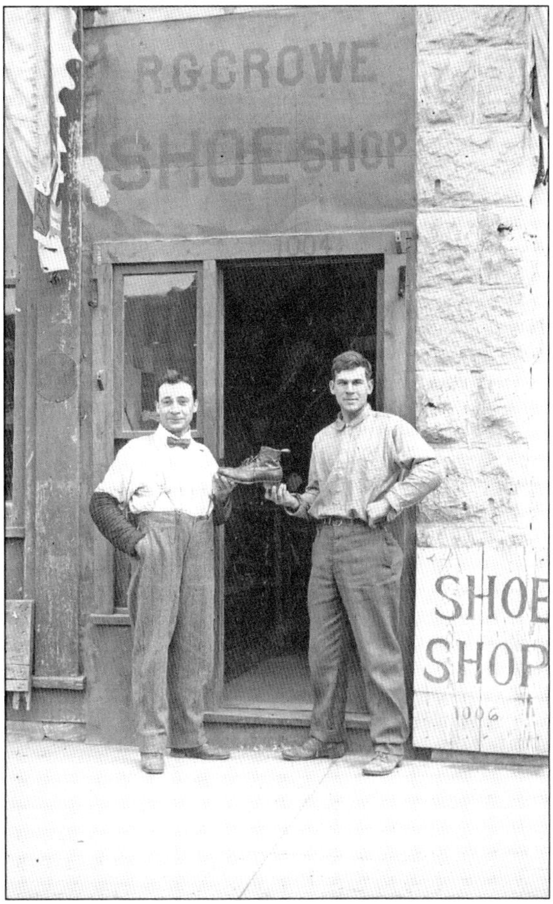


Businesses selling shoes were not in short supply in Winfield, Kansas. R.G. Crowe's Shoe Shop at 1004 ½ Main Street came and went, as department stores such as Brady Brothers carried shoes. Kerr's opened a shoe department in its store for women in 1924. The Orr-Crawford shoe store on the 900 block of Ninth Avenue opened in 1909 as the Winfield Booteria.

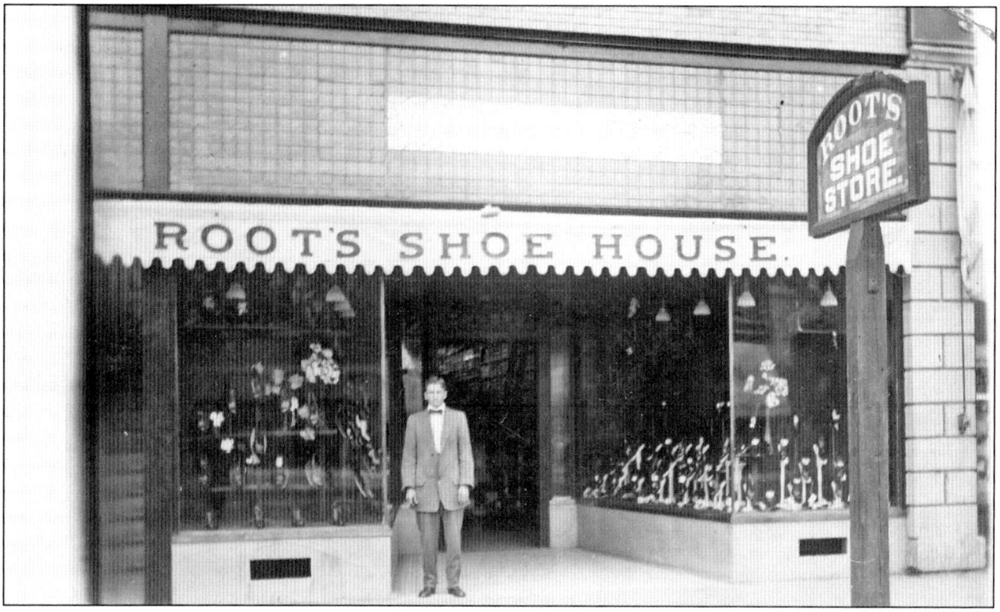


W.C. Root and S.H. Root began in the shoe business in 1881 and lasted into the 1930s. Later, S.H. moved to St. Louis, but he continued buying for his brother's store. By 1925, when this postcard was sent, the windows of the store at 817 Main Street brimmed with ready-to-wear shoes, and the company employed five salesmen and a bookkeeper. The name of the company appears in the tiles above the awning.

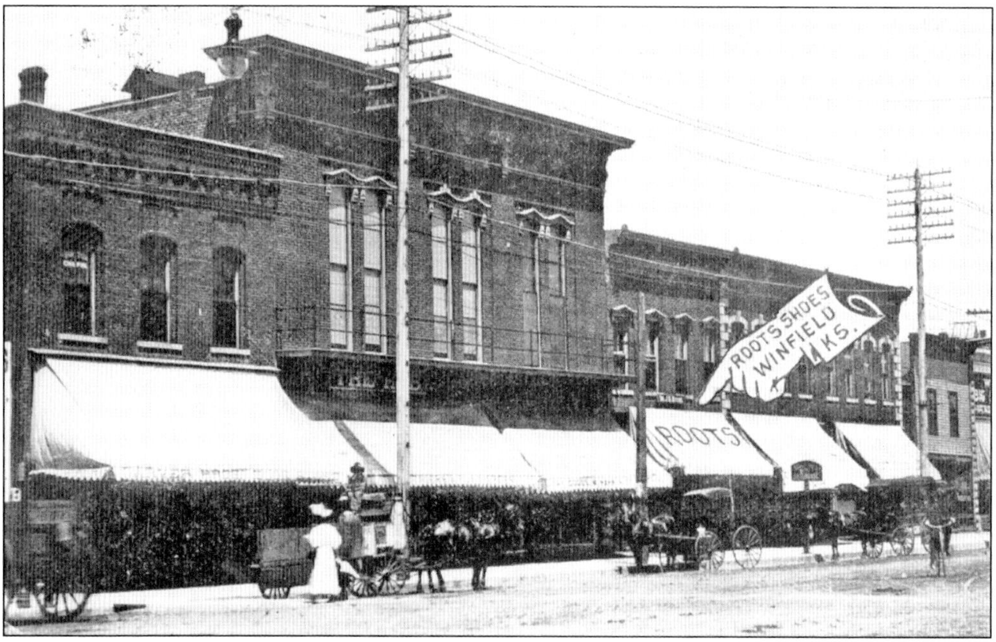


This advertising card signed on the back by W.C. Root himself also provides a view of Hahn's dry goods at 819 Main Street, the Hub at 821 Main Street (upper floor was the former location of Manning's Opera House), and Garver Brothers Book Store, then at 823 Main Street. The Hub outfitted men from head to toe, while Garver Brothers carried all manner of books, stationery, athletic goods, and Eastman Kodak products.

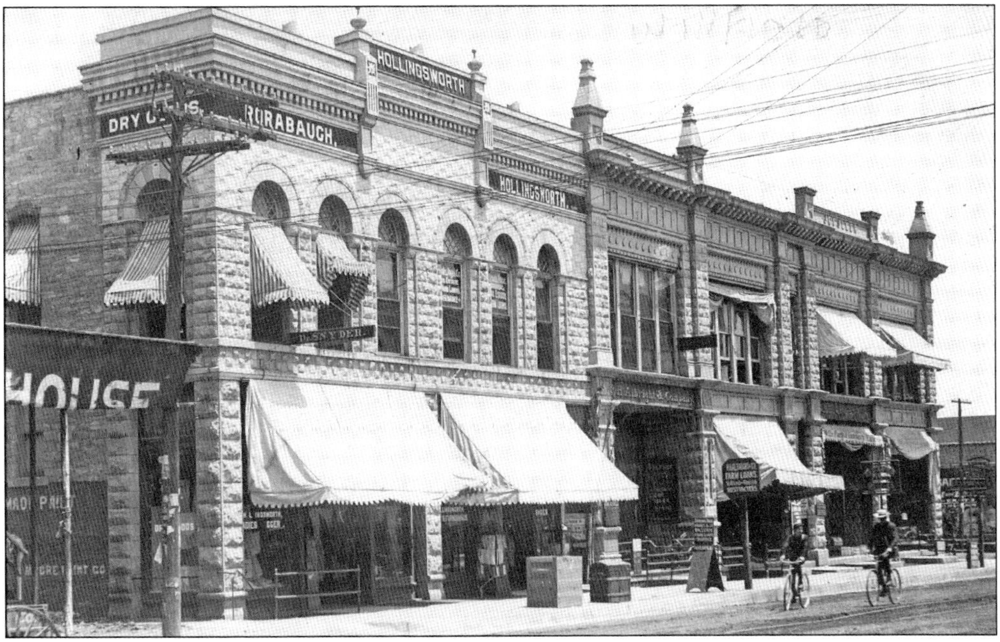


Postmarked 1910, this card displays the Hollingsworth and J.C. Fuller Buildings to good advantage. At that time, Rorabaugh Dry Goods occupied the west end of the block on East Ninth Avenue with the Wells Fargo Railway Express and S.J. Neer stationery and book store on the east end with P.H. Albright in the middle. E.H. Pierce purchased Neer's, moving it in 1935 to 810 Main Street, where Pierce's became a fixture.

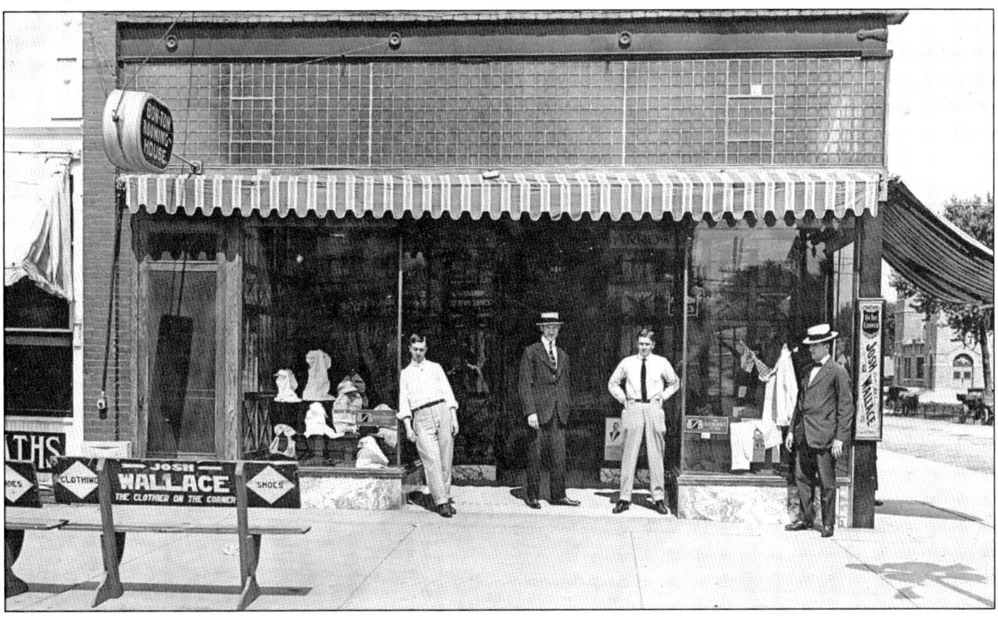


Josh Wallace, "the clothier on the corner," started his business at the northeast corner of Tenth Avenue and Main Street in 1905. Wallace's son took over the business in 1923, and in 1925 half of the business was sold to Fred Study. The building also housed the Bon Ton Boarding House upstairs. Note the First Methodist Church in the background at Tenth Avenue and Millington Street.

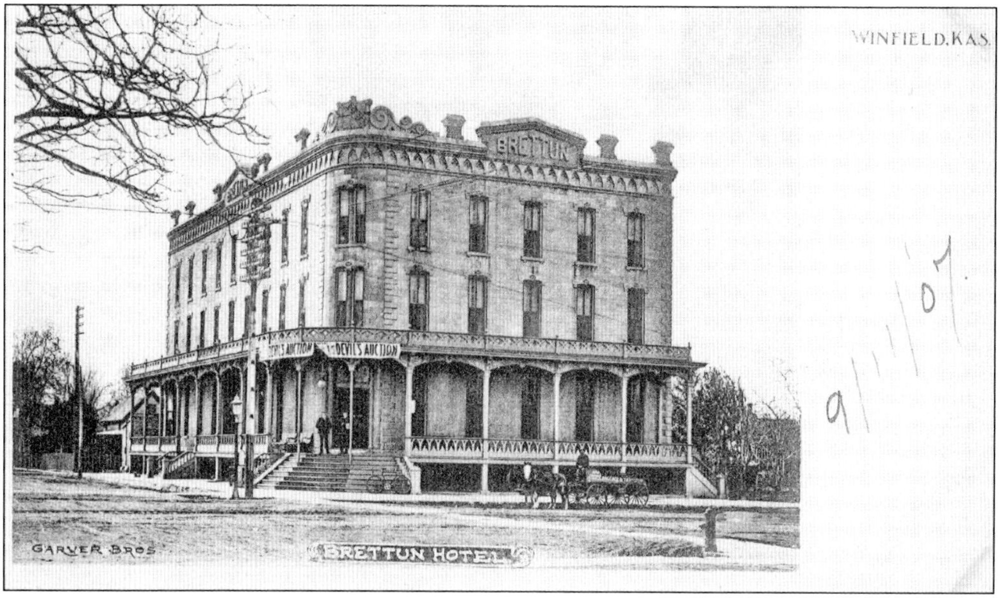


Winfield's first limestone hotel, the Brettun, was built in 1881 at the northwest corner of Seventh Avenue and Main Street. It had 50 guest rooms and 25 public rooms. In disrepair after the owner's death, it underwent remodeling in 1900 and again in the 1930s but was demolished in 1969. The building that housed the St. James Hotel, built in 1888 at 1009–1015 Main Street, survives today, minus its third floor.

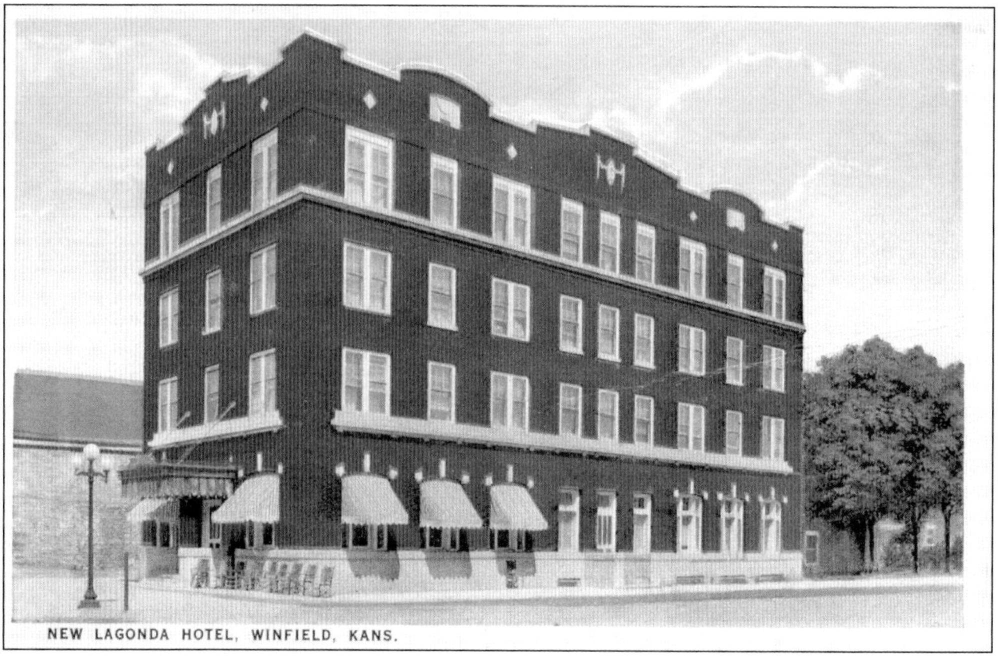


Even before the Brettun Hotel, the Lagonda existed as a frame building on the northwest corner of Eighth and Main Streets, one of many hotels in early Winfield. Called by various other names, it burned in 1879. On the site of the former frame Arlington Hotel at Ninth Avenue and Loomis Street, the four-story brick Lagonda Hotel went up in 1918 and still stands today as the Lagonda Apartments.

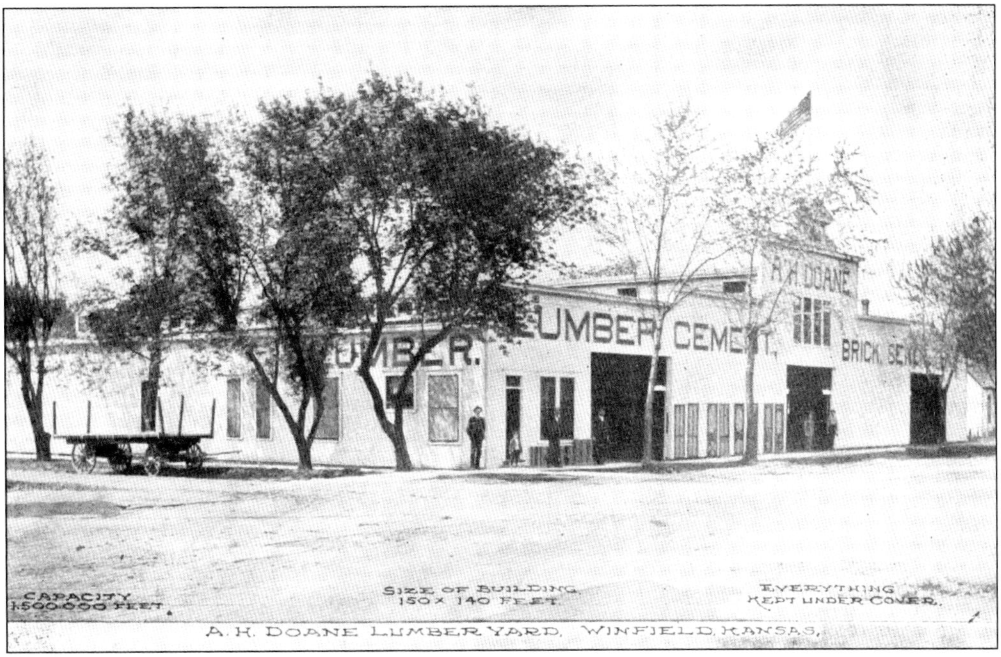


A lumberyard stood at 201 West Ninth Avenue well into the 20th century. In 1904, A.H. Doane established the business with a lumber shed at 502 East Sixth Avenue, advertising on this card "everything kept under cover." The business later became Swartz Lumber, then A.B. Everly Lumber in 1919, and, finally, in a modernized building, Deal Lumber.

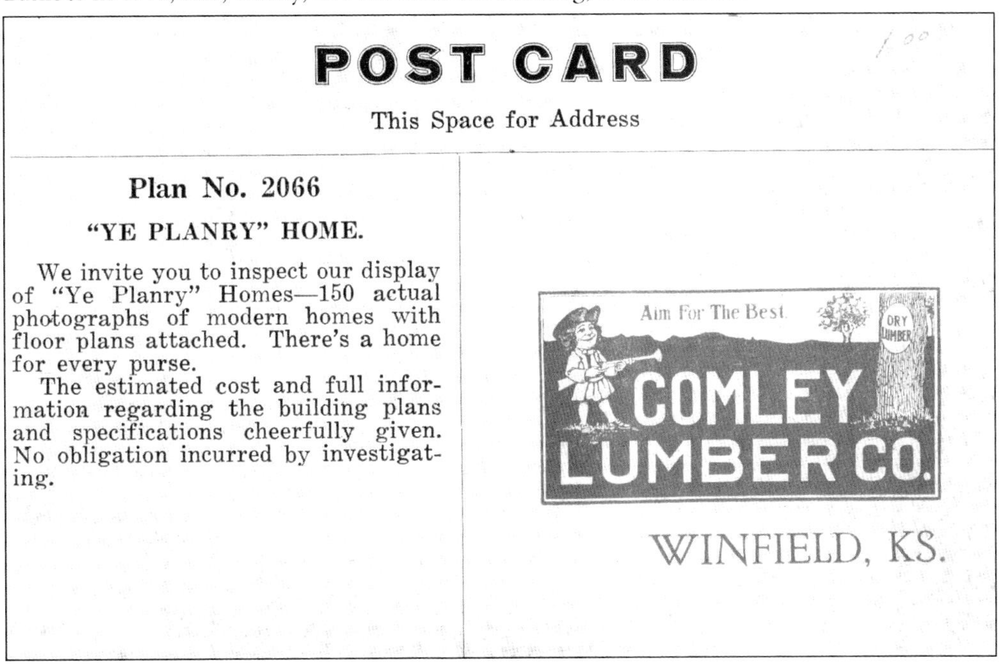


Another Winfield lumberyard grew in a different way. Comley Lumber Company began in 1879 as Pond and Comley. In 1909, Comley bought out Pond's interest in the store at 1201 Main Street, and the business eventually became a chain of 25 stores throughout the Midwest, centered in Wichita, Kansas.

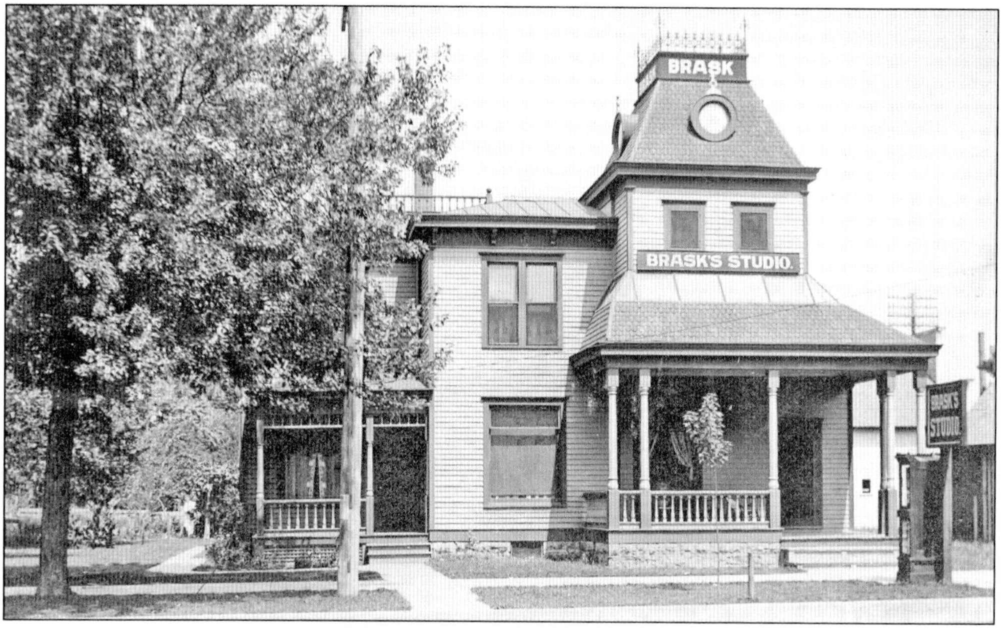


P.J. Brask based his business at 206 West Ninth Avenue from 1907 to 1921. Many postcards of Winfield bear his name, as well as that of George Dresser, an earlier photographer from whom Brask purchased the building. Brask sent this postcard in 1911 to inform an out-of-town customer to expect delivery of his photographs the next week. Winfield Floral moved its long-running business to the building in 1939.

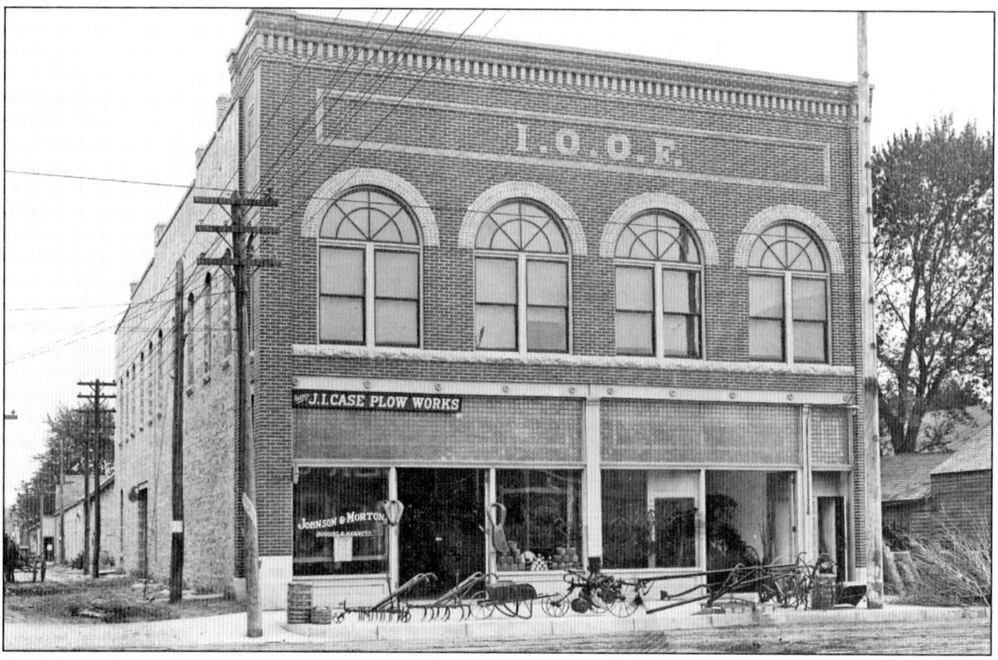


In 1911, when this card was sent, this building at 113 West Ninth Avenue served as a meeting place for the International Order of Odd Fellows and other fraternal organizations. Downstairs was Johnson & Morton's Buggies and Harness, which was also an agent for J.I. Case Plow Works. This building, with its "I.O.O.F." lettering, remains visible from Main Street today.

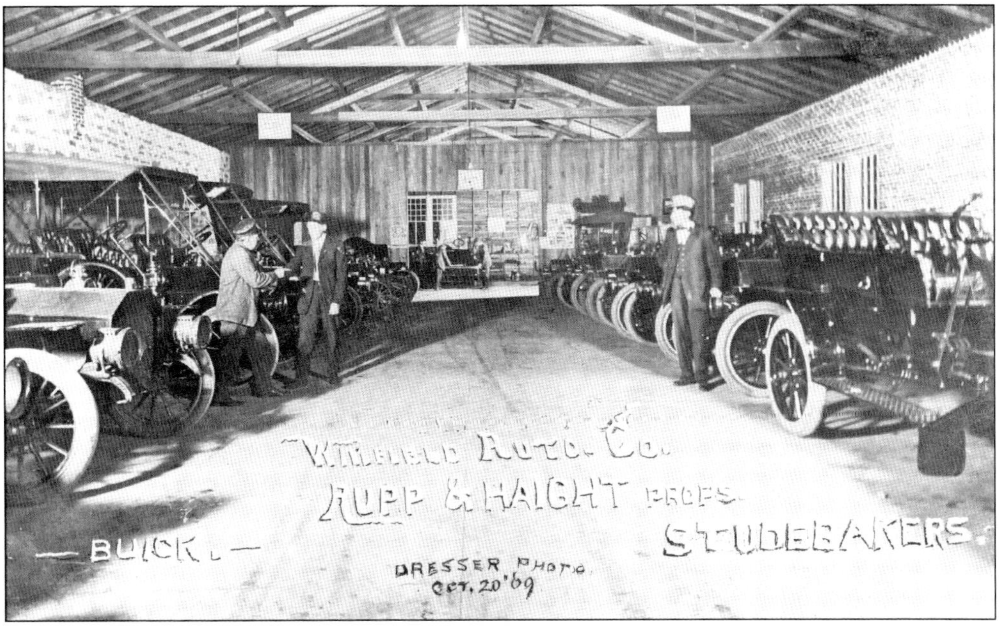


In 1909, Beason M. Rupp and Lloyd Haight sold Buicks and Studebakers from their Winfield Auto Company, located on West Ninth Avenue. Haight made a name for himself racing cars at the Winfield Fairgrounds. On October 16, 1909, he took first in the four-lap race for Winfield/Arkansas City vehicle owners driving, of course, a Buick. Haight married Rupp's daughter in 1911 and moved to California.

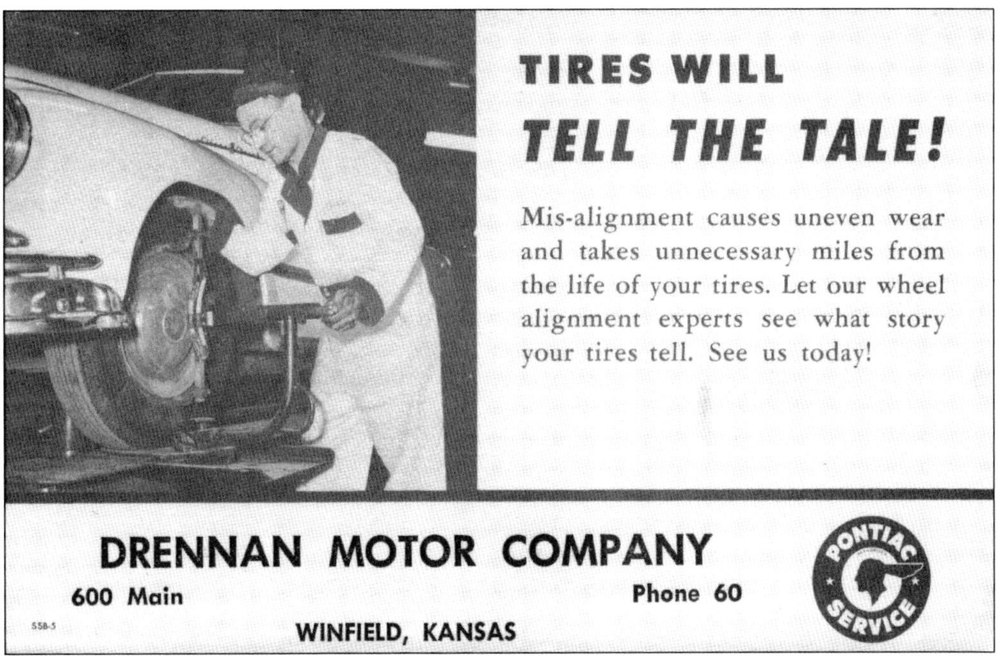


The Drennan Motor Company started life as Hill-Howard-Drennan at 214 East Ninth Avenue, but C.M. Drennan bought his partners out in 1917 and moved the business to 121–123 West Ninth Avenue, selling Saxon and Studebaker vehicles. By the time this card was sent, the business was at 600 South Main Street and sold Cadillacs, Pontiacs, and International Harvester trucks.

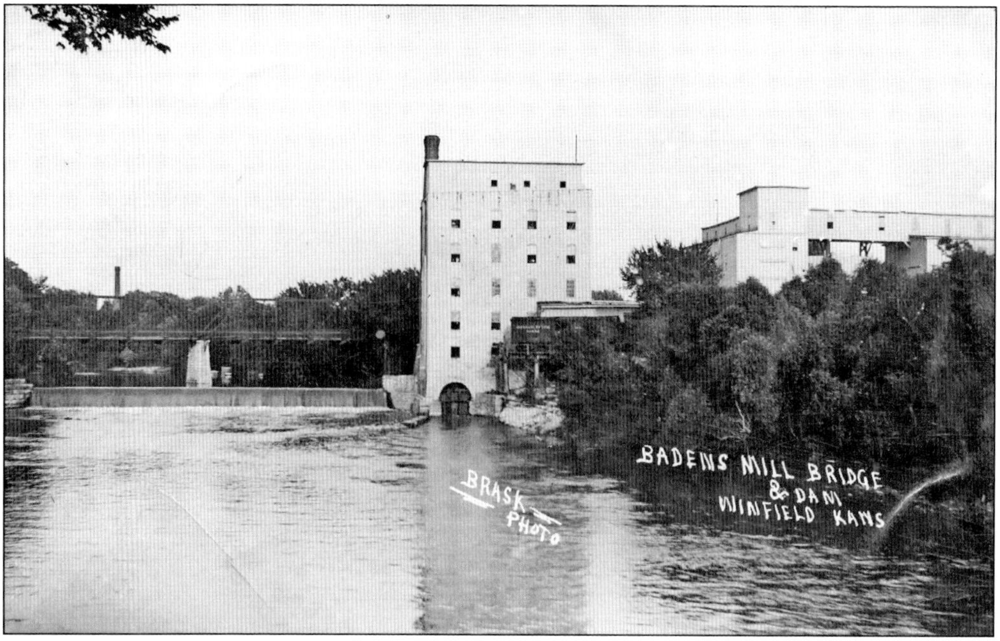


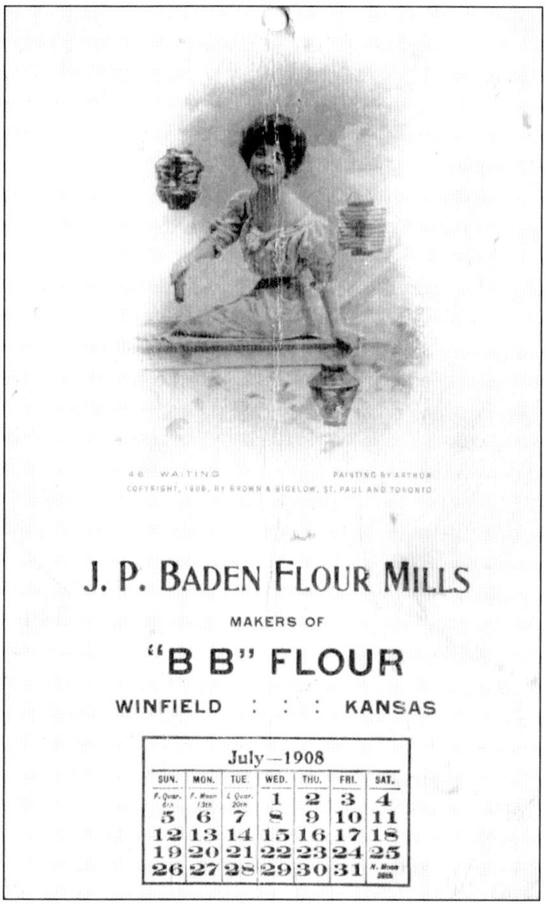


Two flour mills opened in Winfield in 1873. Bliss and Company established theirs north of Ninth Avenue on the Walnut River. Fire destroyed the original building, which was reconstructed in 1883. In 1889, J.P. Baden purchased and remodeled the mill. When Baden died in 1900, the mill employed 35 men. In later years, it became Winfield Consolidated Mills, which closed in 1966.

By the time this advertising card went out, Baden Mill continued in business due to Adelaide Elizabeth Baden and her sons maintaining the staff, which included three traveling salesmen, and her husband's business plan. The Santa Fe Railroad had a switch on the west side of the mill, while the Frisco loaded on the east. The Missouri-Pacific line could also reach the mill, and a scale track connected with all three railroads.

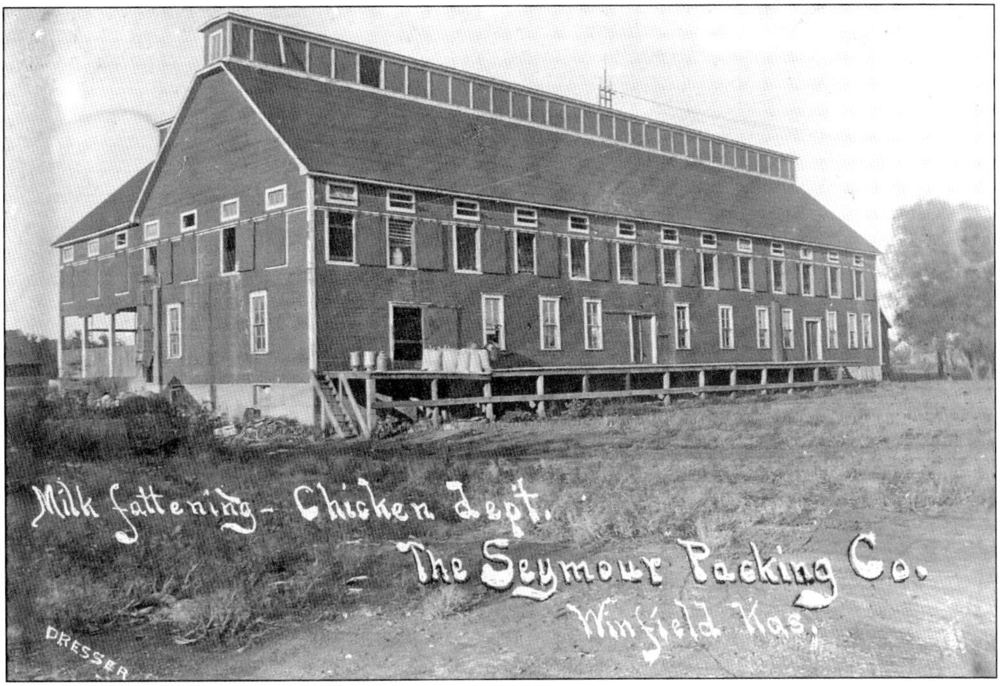


J.P. Baden also established a packinghouse, which he enlarged in 1895 with an ice plant and additional storage for dressed chickens, butter, and eggs. The plant had an egg-candling room and a creamery. Products from this packinghouse went all over the United States. In 1906, the plant became the Seymour Packing Company, headquartered in Topeka, Kansas, and another building was added in 1910.

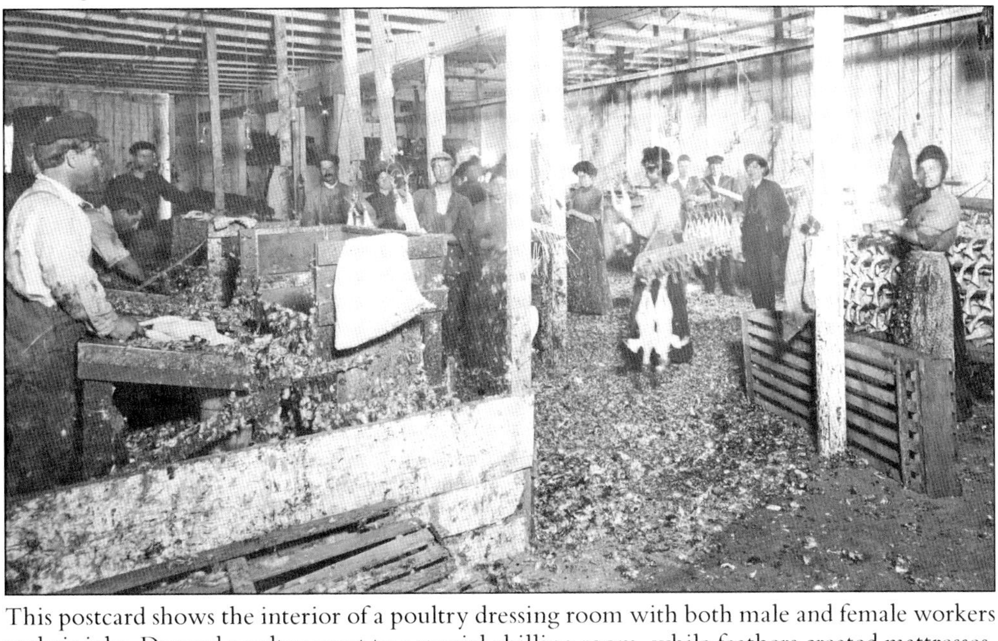

This postcard shows the interior of a poultry dressing room with both male and female workers at their jobs. Dressed poultry went to a special chilling room, while feathers created mattresses, pillows, and comforters. By 1900, all the buildings at Baden's plant were lit with electric lights from a duplex system in the plant's main engine room, and 60 to 100 people were employed there.

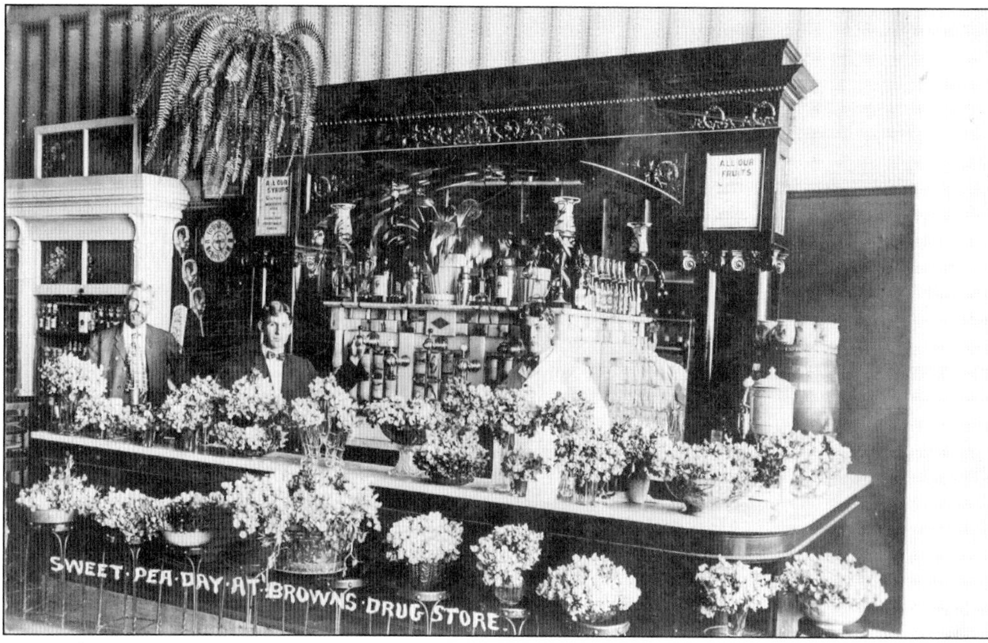


Located at 805 Main Street, Brown's Drug Store hung a sign in 1880 and was still around to advertise in the Southwestern College *Moundbuilder* in 1907, no doubt attracting the college crowd with its large soda fountain. This postcard, mailed July 3, celebrated an annual contest begun in 1902 for the best sweet peas grown from seeds given out by the store.

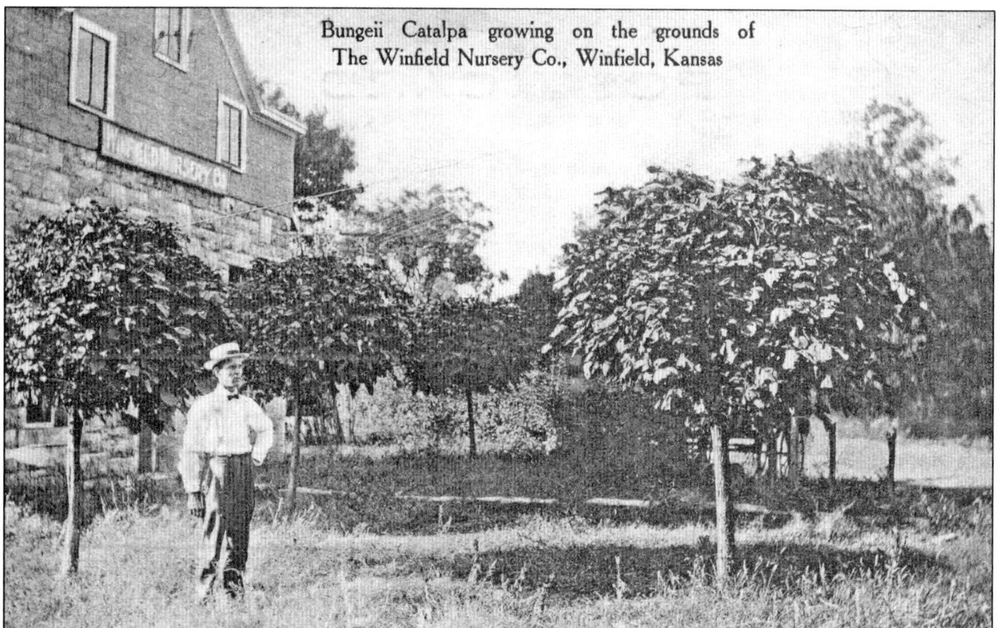


The Winfield Nursery Company began northwest of the city in 1874 but moved to one mile northwest of Island Park about 20 years later. By 1900, the nursery covered 65 acres with fruit trees as well as a grape arbor and berry bushes. Shrubs, roses, and other trees were also cultivated. A packing yard for the stock and an office were located west of Island Park.

*Three*

# WINFIELD'S CIVIC SIDE

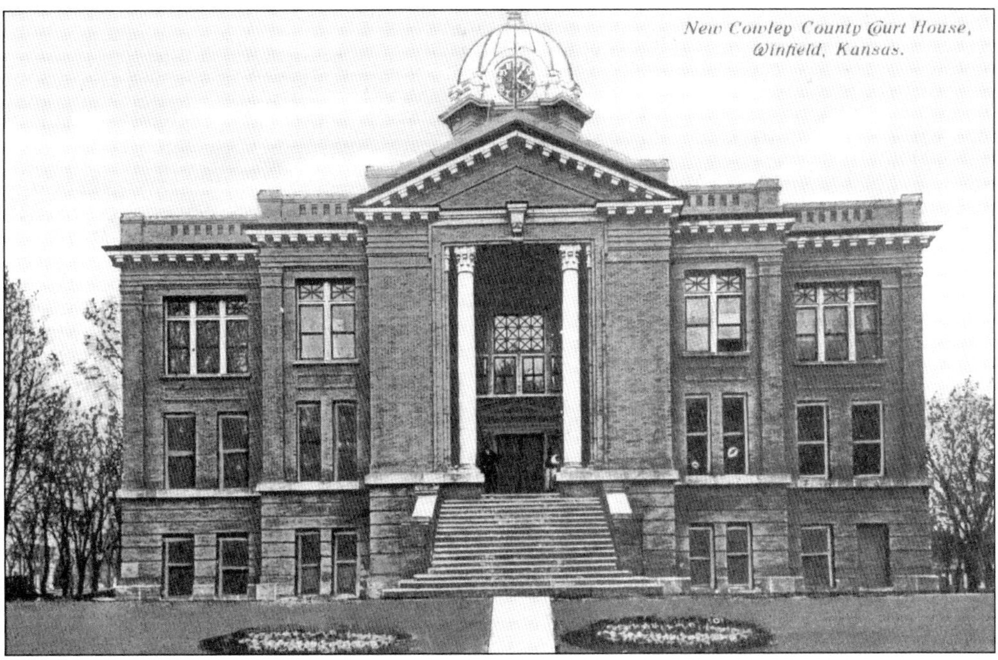


Were it not for quick action on the part of Col. E.C. Manning, the Cowley County Courthouse would be located in Arkansas City, Kansas. The bill organizing Cowley County in the 1870 state legislature named Cresswell (Arkansas City's name at the time) the county seat. Manning called for a census and garnered the needed votes in time to present them to Gov. S.J. Crawford, who proclaimed Winfield as the county seat.

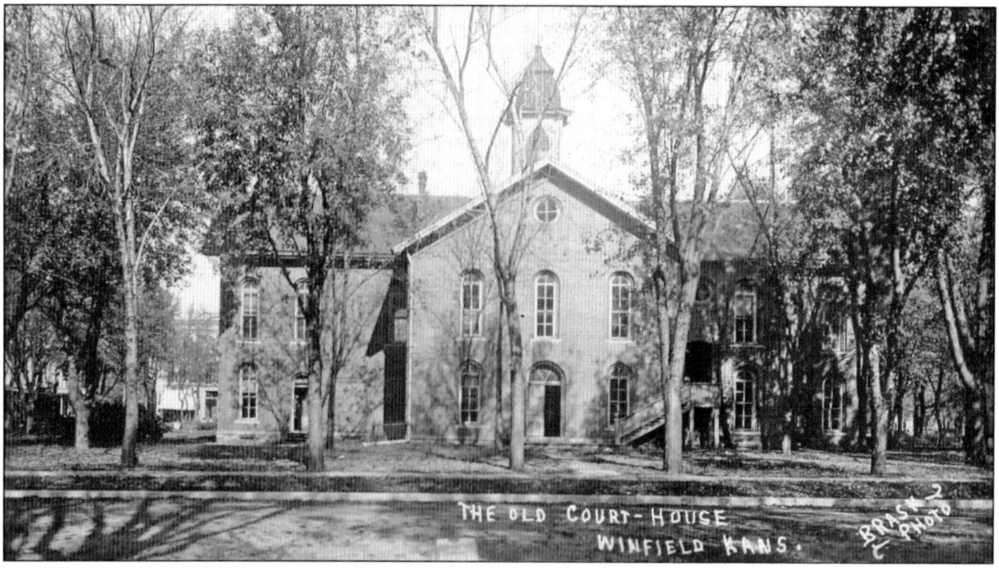


Cowley County's courthouses have always occupied the city block on Ninth Avenue between Loomis and Fuller Streets in Winfield. In 1873, the first courthouse, built on the south side of the block, faced Tenth Avenue. Eight years later, the east and west sides of the two-story building received one-story wings. Further remodeling later added second stories to these wings, allowing this courthouse to remain in service for 36 years.

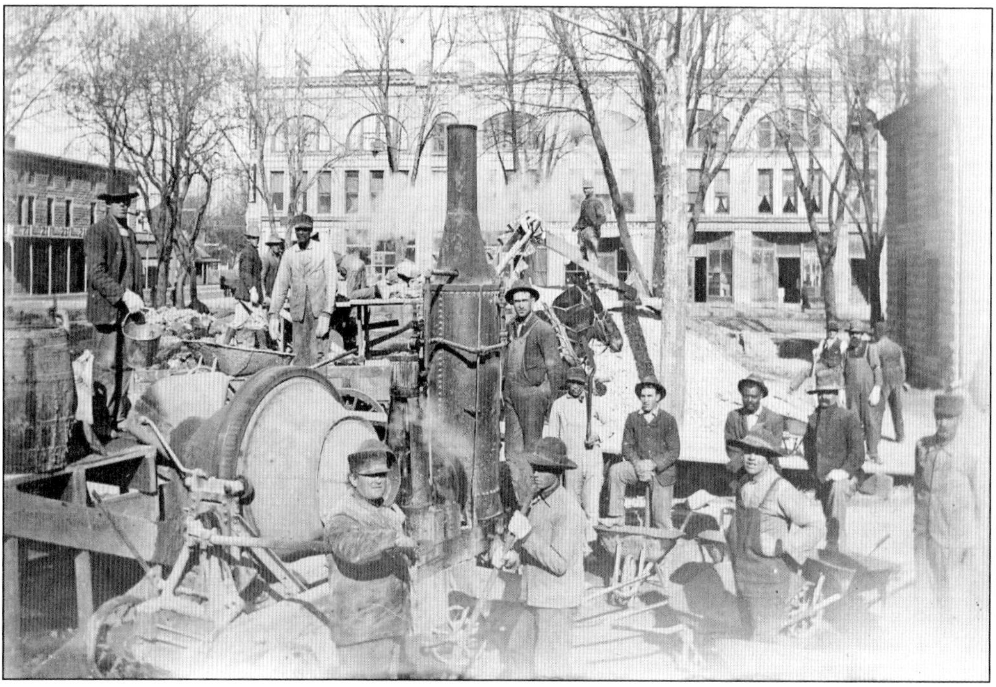

Construction work began in October 1908 on Cowley County's second courthouse, with its first still in operation. Its location placed it more in the center of the block but facing Ninth Avenue, requiring the removal of four large maple trees and some smaller ones to accommodate it. This view shows workmen in a staging area with the Hackney/Caton Block across the street on Ninth Avenue visible in the background.

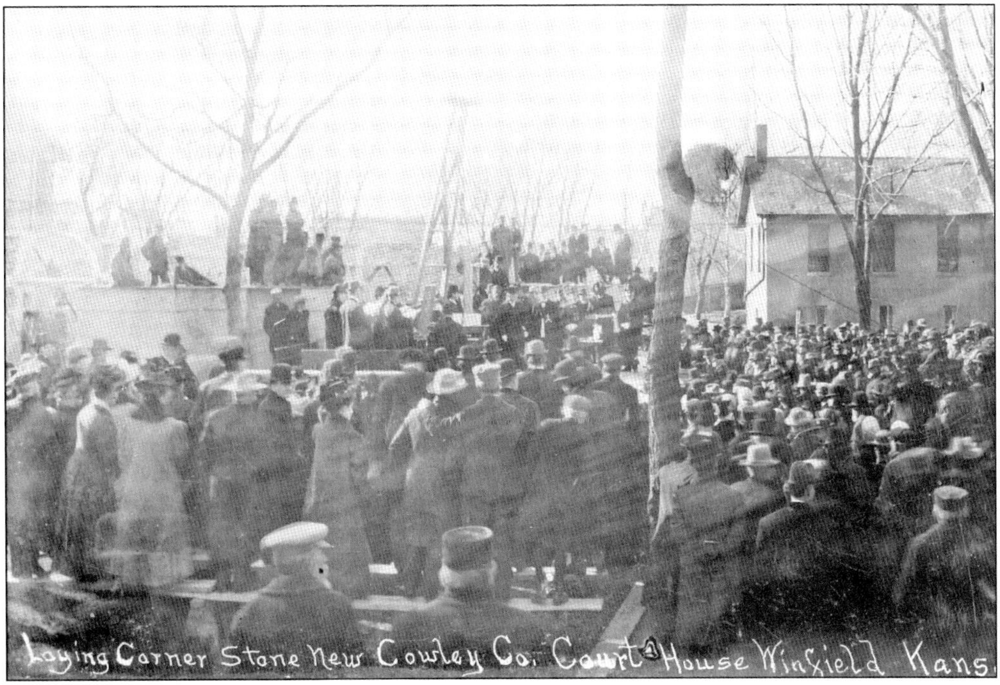


Because of encouragement for the public to attend, a crowd turned out for the laying of the cornerstone of the new courthouse at 2:00 p.m. on January 7, 1908. The Grand Lodge of Ancient, Free, and Accepted Masons led a ceremony, which included music provided by a Masonic quartet and placement of the cornerstone in the northeast corner of the building.

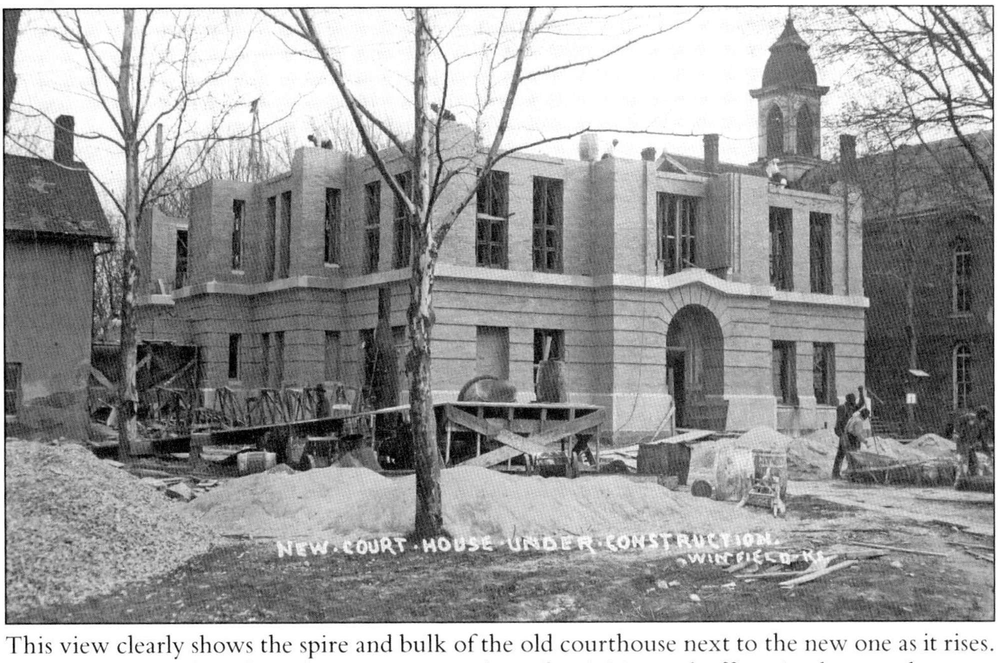


This view clearly shows the spire and bulk of the old courthouse next to the new one as it rises. Need for it arose based on the growing number of activities and offices in the courthouse as well as the need for more storage space for records. Once the move into the new courthouse was complete, the old one was demolished.

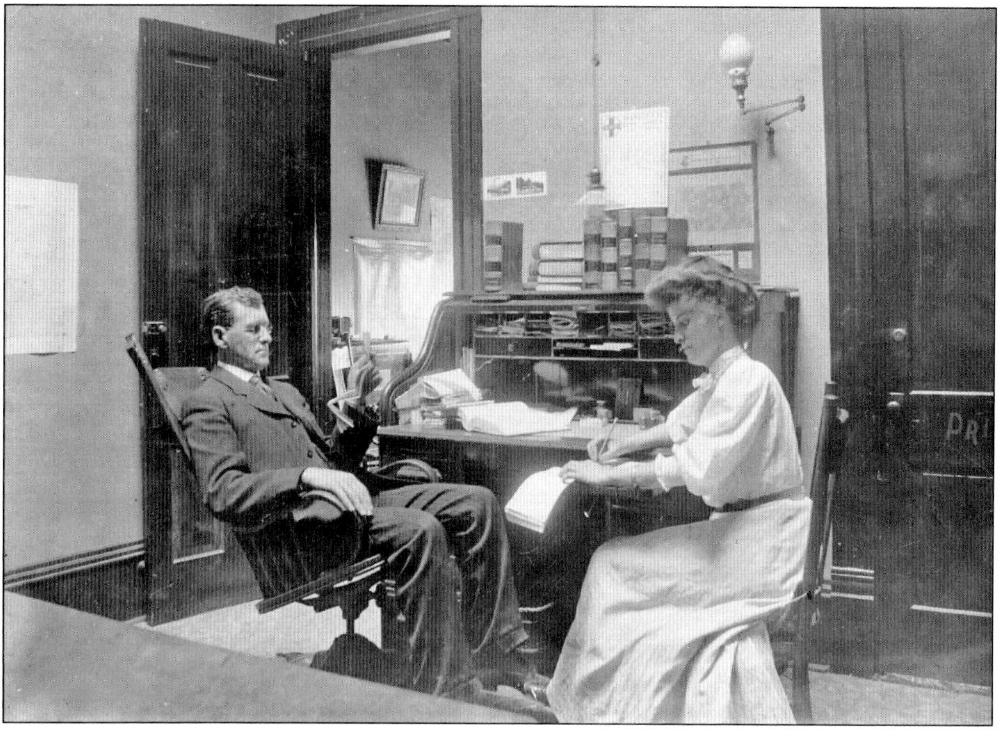

One of the people whose career spanned both courthouses was E.S. Torrance, pictured here in his law office upstairs on the Manning Block with Maude Gafney, legal assistant and notary public. Admitted to the bar in 1881, and elected county attorney in 1900, he served many years as the judge of the district court of Cowley County.

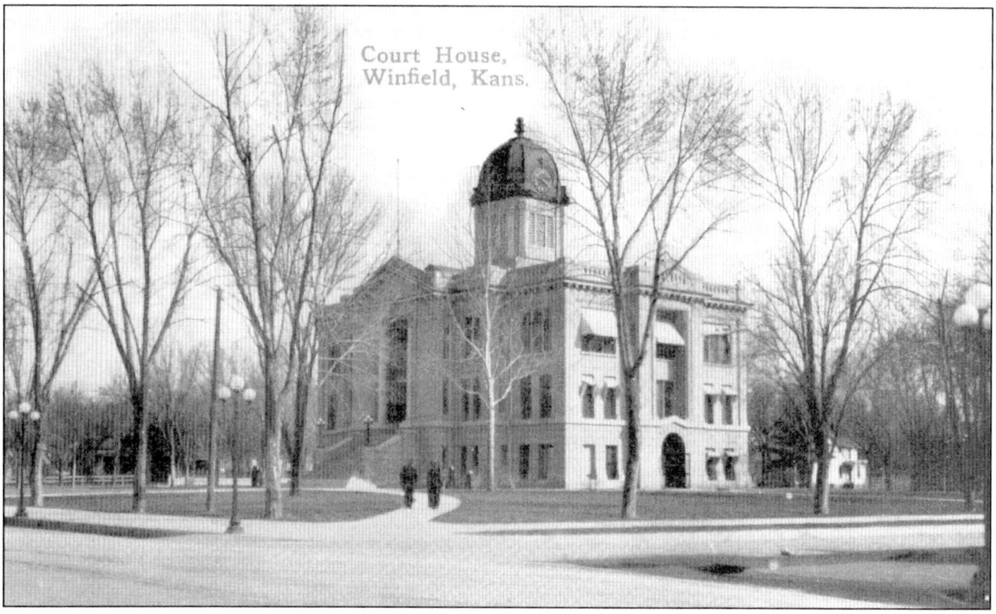


When completed in 1909, the courthouse sat proudly facing Ninth Avenue alone on the block with three stories of brick and stone, a clock tower, and ample grounds surrounding it. It served the county for over 50 years, giving way to the current courthouse built on the same site in 1963.

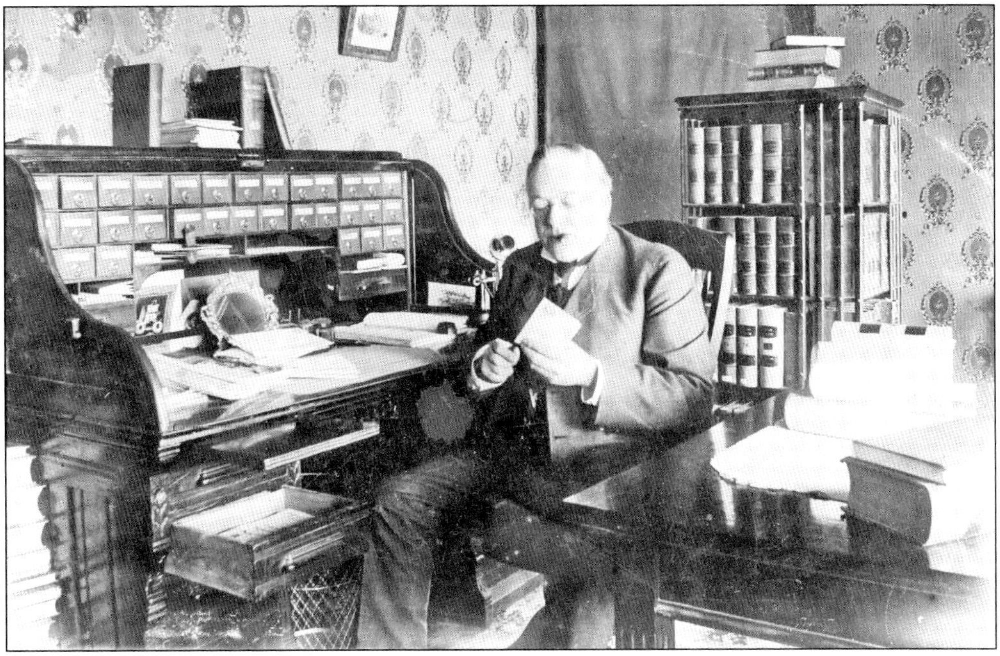

William Patrick Hackney served as a captain in the Civil War, was admitted to the bar in 1867 and set up practice in Winfield in 1870. In 1876, he represented Cowley County in the Kansas House of Representatives and from 1880 to 1881 in the state senate. As Winfield's mayor in 1887, he brought about the widening of the sidewalks on Main Street from 12 to 16 inches.

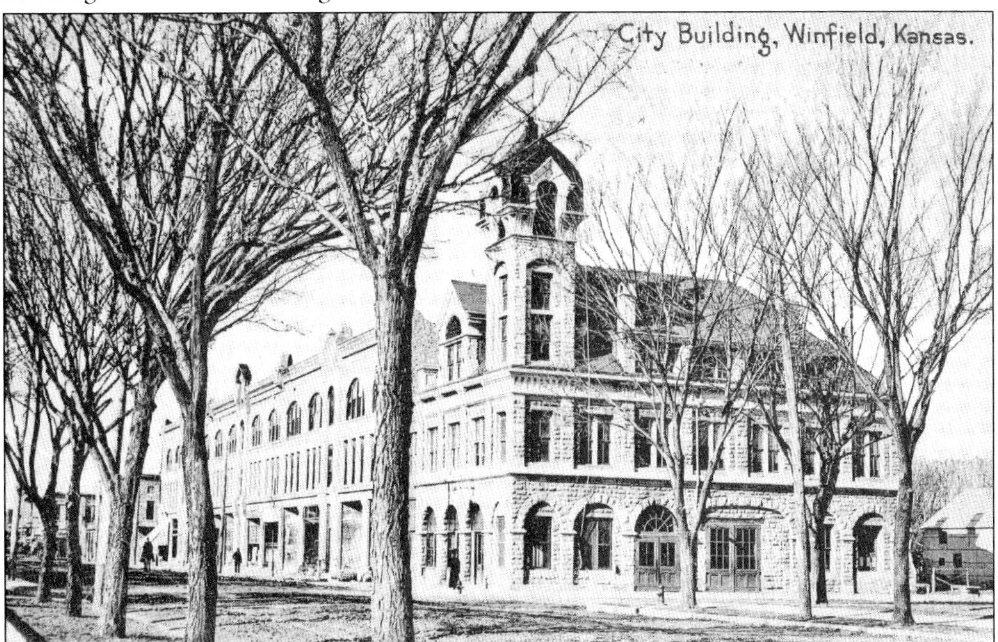


Before leaving Winfield in 1894 due to ill health, W.P. Hackney constructed nearly 10 buildings for the city. The Hackney Block, said to be one of the most beautiful buildings in the state, adjoined the city building on Ninth Avenue between Loomis and Fuller Streets. Hackney's own home at 417 East Tenth Avenue remains equally handsome.

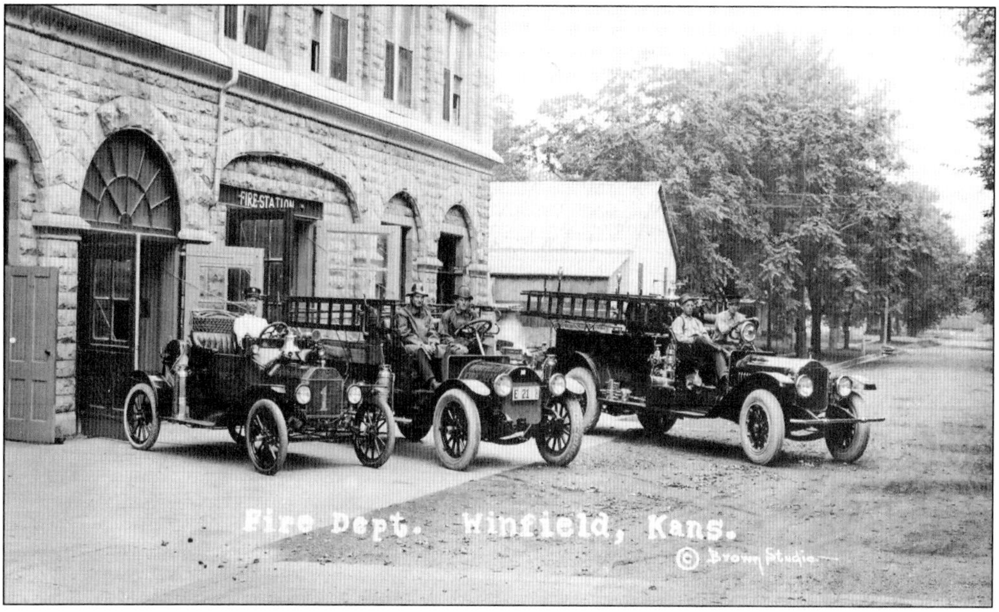


The Winfield Fire Department organized in 1883 and moved into the ground floor of the city building in 1886. Firefighters received pay of $1 per month and $1 per fire, but by 1904 they worked 24-hour paid shifts. In 1926, the city building moved to the corner of Ninth Avenue and Millington Street. The fire department remained in the old building with many upgrades in staffing, equipment, and the building over the years.

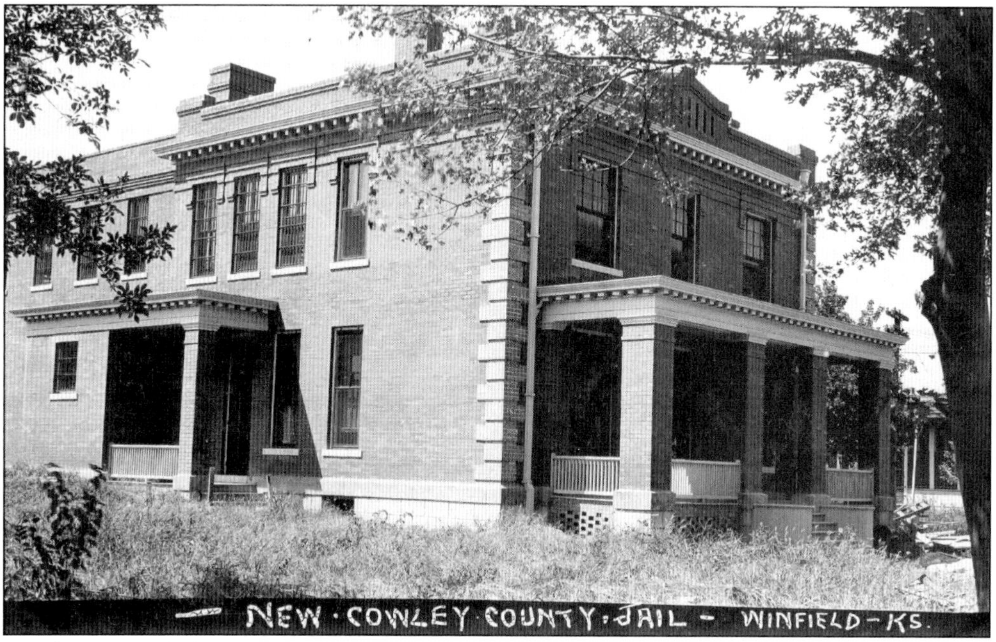


Cowley County's first jail was built in 1873 near the courthouse on land donated by the Winfield Town Association. In 1909, the county constructed a large brick jail on the northwest corner of Tenth Avenue and Loomis Street. Besides prisoners, it housed the sheriff and his family. This building stood in use until 1963, when the jail became part of the new courthouse complex across the street.

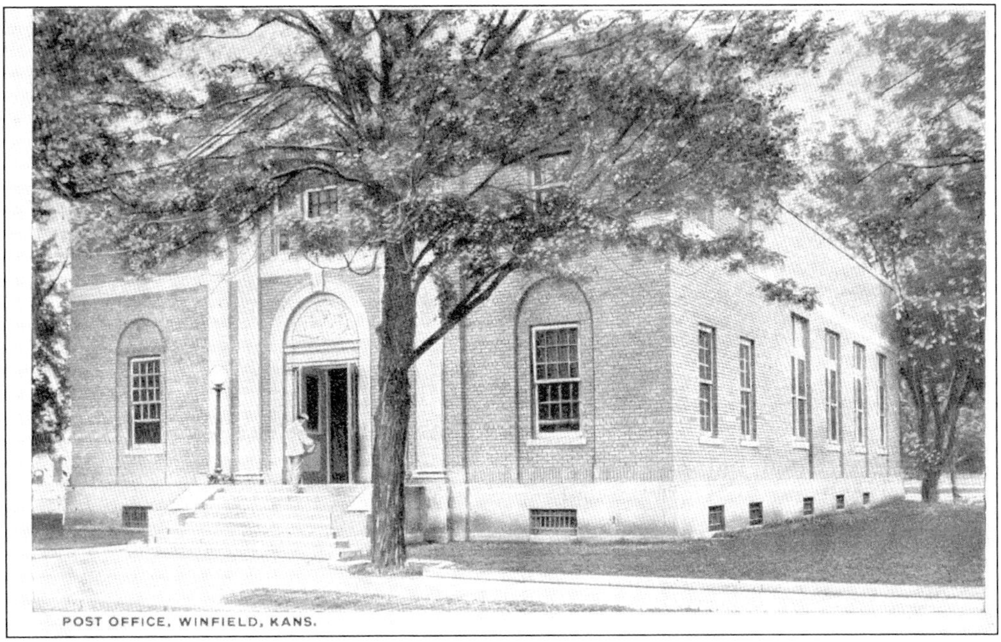


Postal service came early in Winfield's development as a city through the efforts of E.C. Manning, who operated an informal post office in his log store. An official post office was established in May 1870. The post office shown in this card went up at Tenth Avenue and Millington Street in 1916 and served until moving into its new building at Tenth Avenue and Loomis Street.

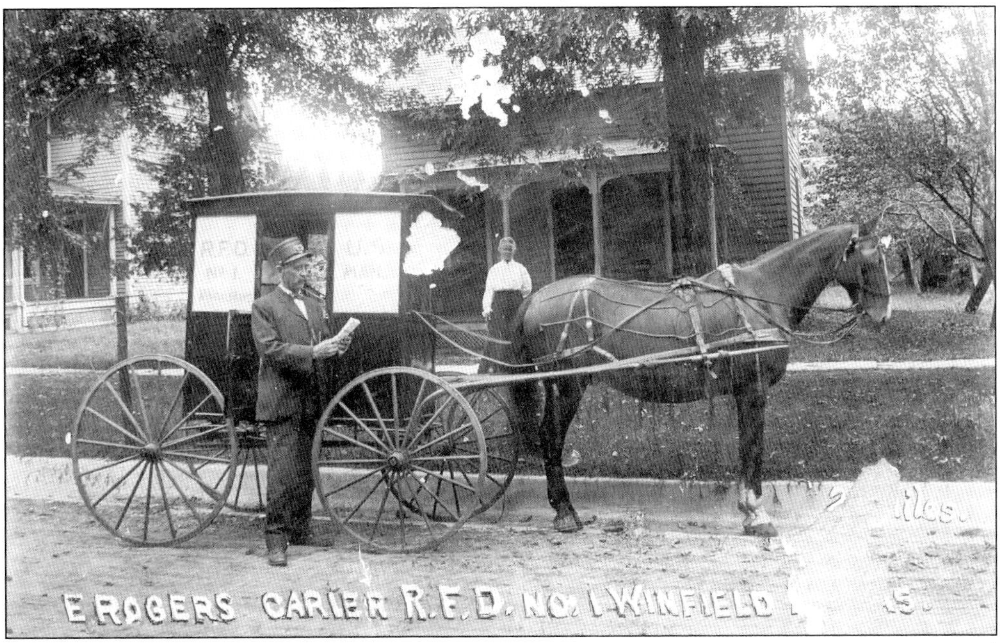


Winfield began receiving rural free delivery on September 2, 1901, according to the US Postal Service website, which also states that in 1902 weatherproof postboxes at the street and passable roads were required to receive mail. Carriers such as E. Rogers delivered mail Monday through Saturday, sold stamps and registered letters to patrons, and provided their own transportation. Many still used a horse and wagon into the 1920s.

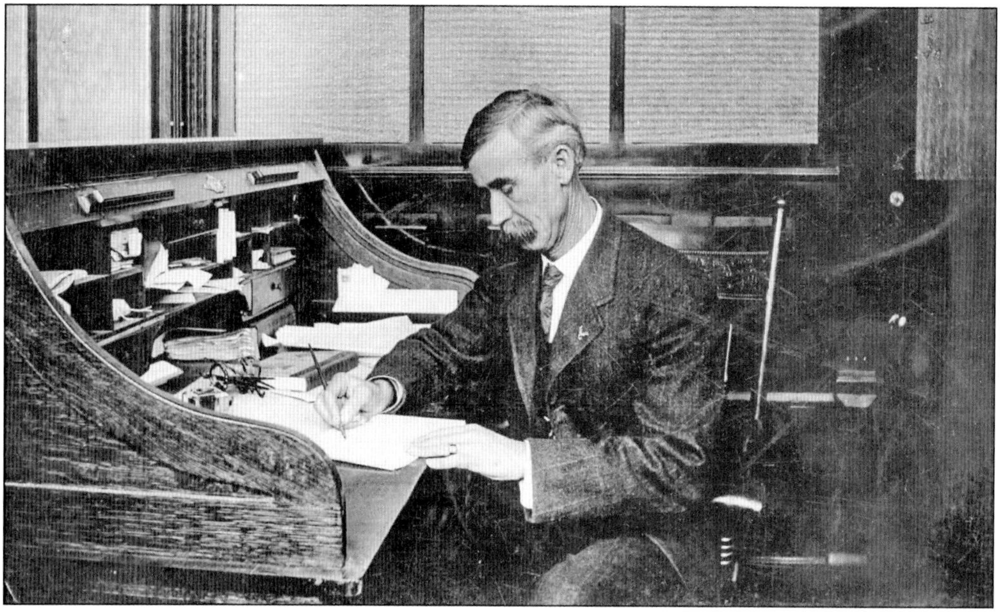

E.C. Manning served as Winfield's first postmaster from May to October 1870. Mail delivery to homes began in 1887. John W. Skinner, pictured here, held the job from June 1906 to October 1913. Like Manning, he brought a proven dedication to Winfield to the job, having already served two terms as Cowley County sheriff, started a livery business on East Ninth Avenue, and run a successful stock farm south of Burden, Kansas.

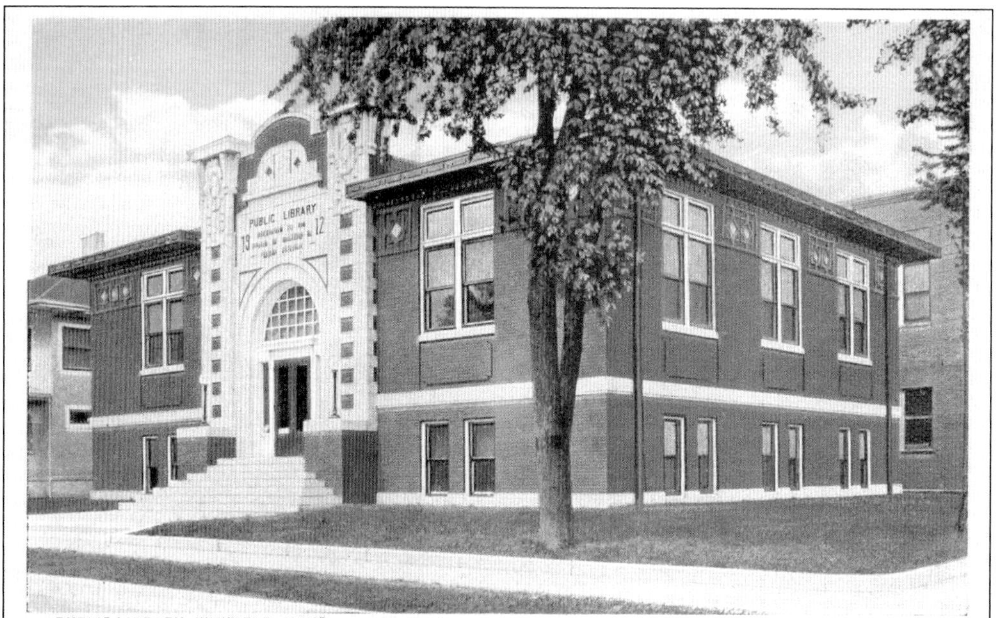


Private lending libraries existed in Winfield prior to the city receiving its first tax-supported public library through funding from Andrew Carnegie in 1912. Its grand opening on January 1, 1913, included a public reception. Popular vote allowed the library to move into the old St. John's library in 1990, where it celebrated its 100th anniversary in 2013. The 1912 building remains in the National Register of Historic Places.

*Four*

# Where Winfield Learned

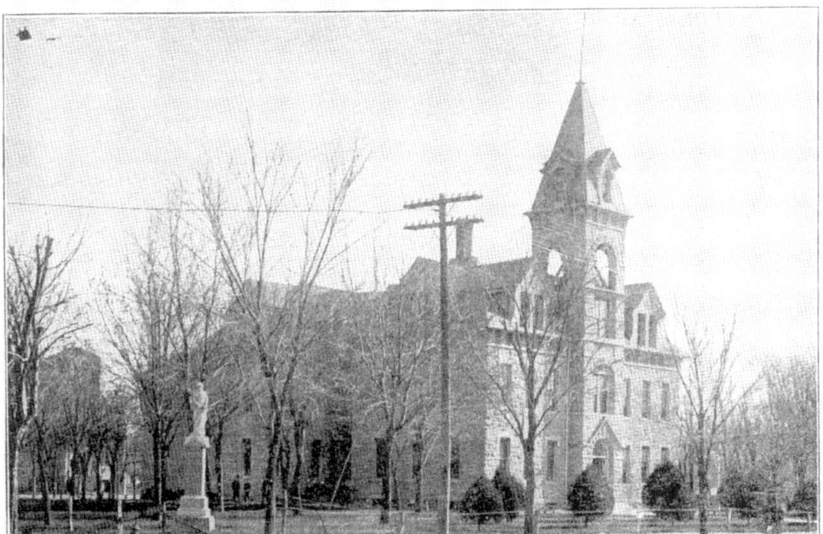

Central School Building, Winfield, Kansas

Winfield's first schoolroom was on the second floor of Manning's log store on Main Street. Central School was built in 1872 at Ninth Avenue and Fuller Street with bonds voted by Winfield's citizens. The 1891 statue, visible in this view at the corner of the yard, commemorates two high school students who drowned while ice-skating: Paul Bedillion, who fell through thin ice on Timber Creek, and Thomas Morgan, who tried to save him.

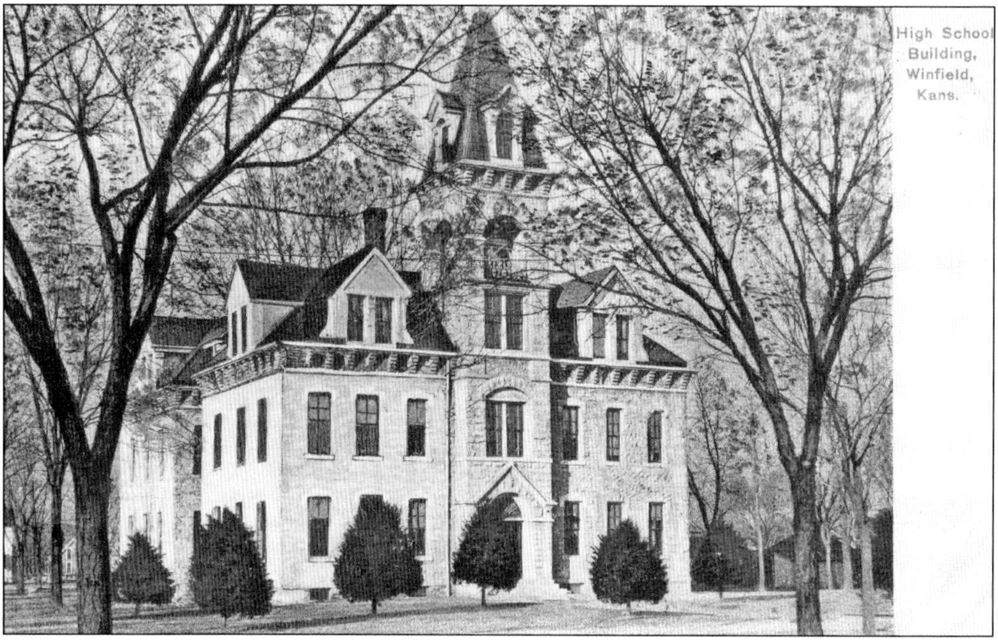


Before the turn of the century, with the completion of four elementary schools and an addition built in 1880 to ease overcrowding, Central School became the first Winfield High School. By this time, the grounds had been leveled and sidewalks installed. The great number of trees reflects the planting project celebrated on Arbor Day at Central School each year.

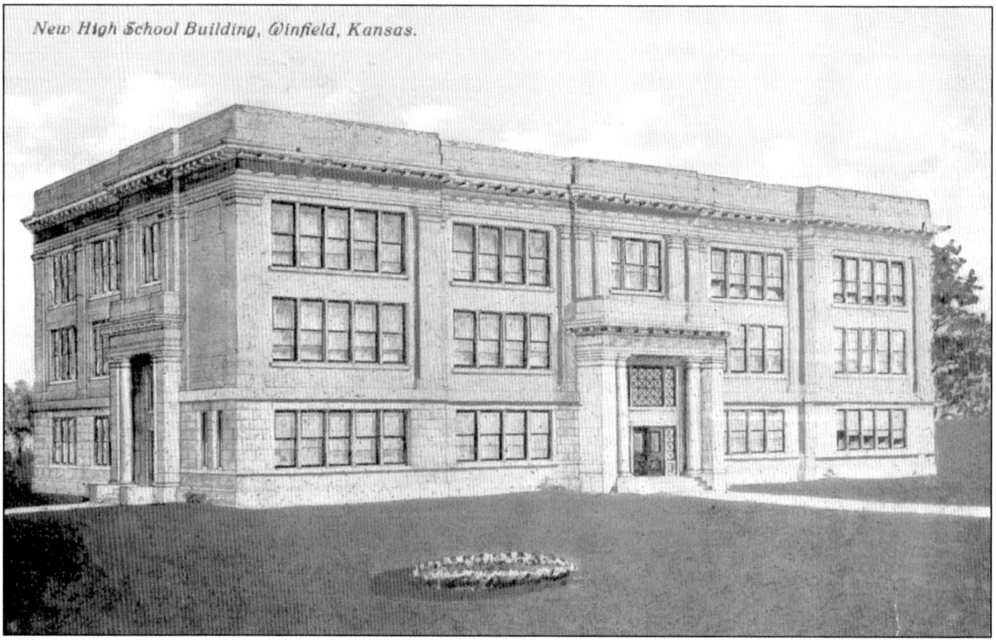


In 1910, the growing student population and public demand for a building better suited to the changing needs of public education led to the construction of a new three-story redbrick building on the same block as the Central School, dedicated for use as a high school. Central School then served as a junior high school for a number of years.

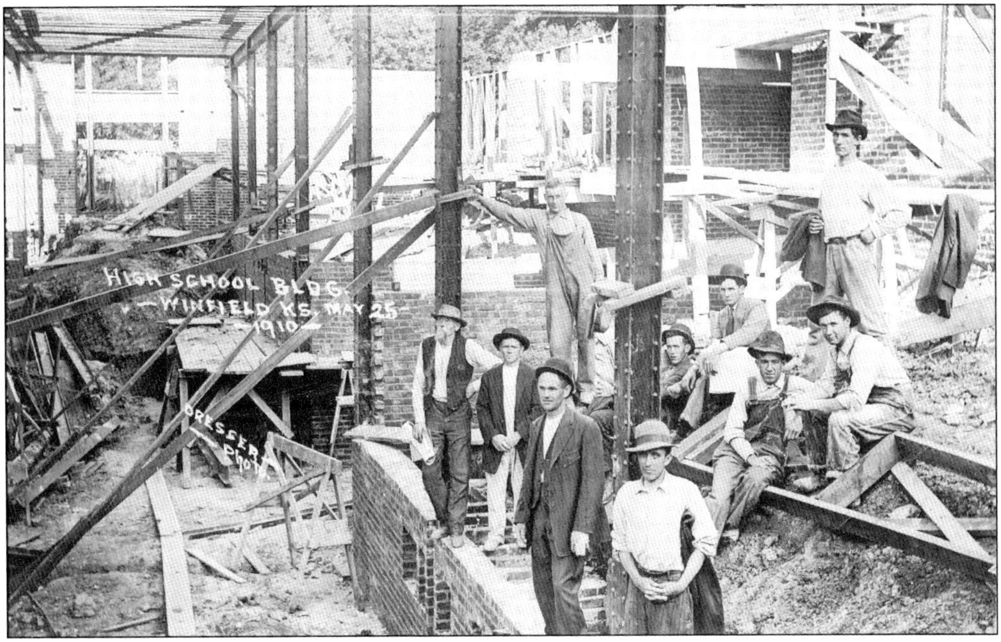


Members of the construction crew for the new Winfield High School pose in the midst of their building project. This building included a gymnasium, an auditorium, and space for many additions to the school day. The *Oracle* school newspaper appeared in 1911, music opportunities increased, and school assemblies, even including the junior high students, met on-site.

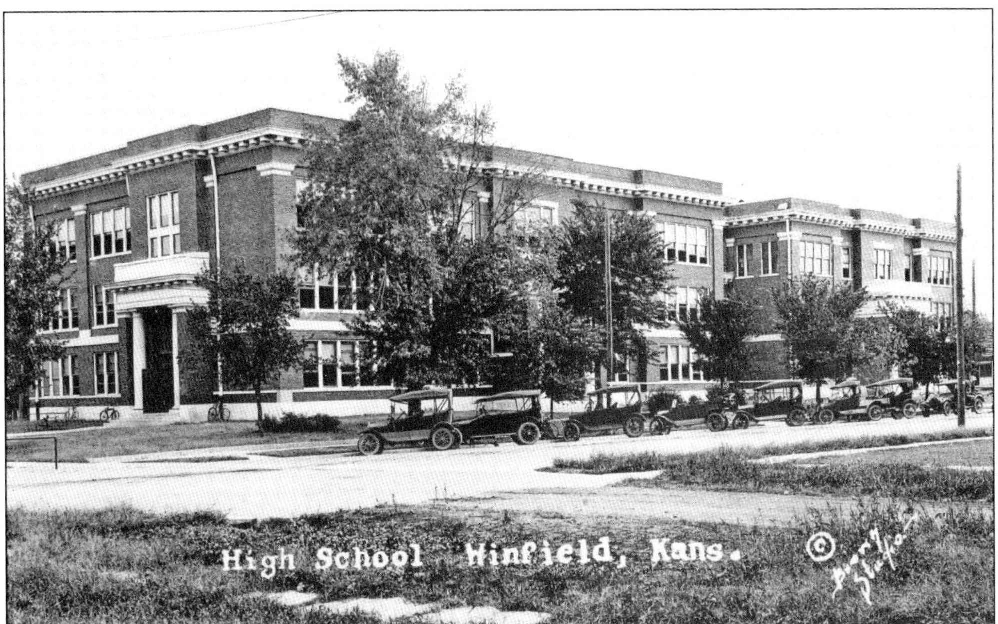


Expansion continued at the high school site as this card postmarked July 1922 shows. In 1916, the community voted bonds for the addition of a "manual high building" to be added to the 1910 building. The redbrick buildings remained in service as Winfield Junior-Senior High until 1972, with the addition of an industrial arts building west of these buildings in 1951.

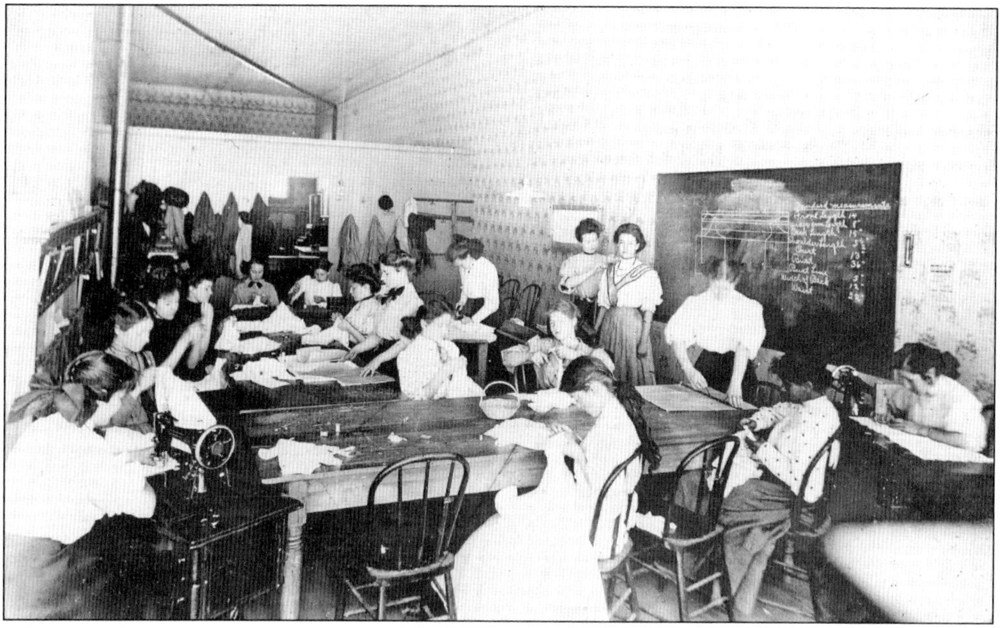

This crowded sewing class with two machines provides a view into a Central School classroom and includes one African American student. This practical class taught girls how to stitch, darn, patch, cut out clothes without a pattern, and make their own dresses. According the chalkboard, the standard measurement for the waist was 22 inches.

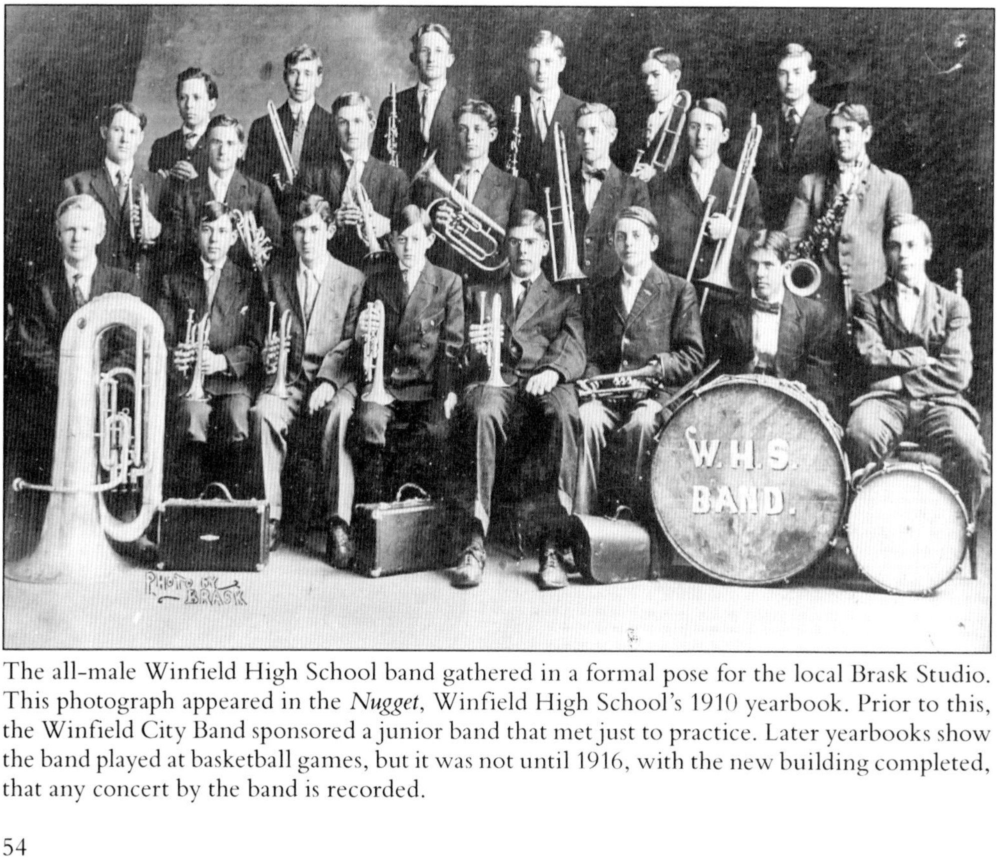


The all-male Winfield High School band gathered in a formal pose for the local Brask Studio. This photograph appeared in the *Nugget*, Winfield High School's 1910 yearbook. Prior to this, the Winfield City Band sponsored a junior band that met just to practice. Later yearbooks show the band played at basketball games, but it was not until 1916, with the new building completed, that any concert by the band is recorded.

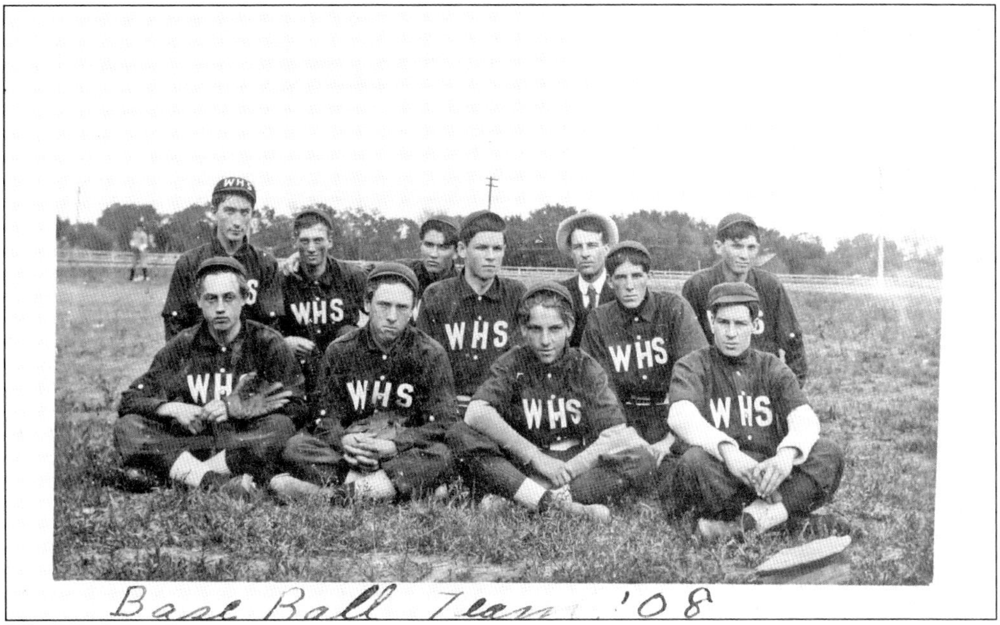


This Winfield High baseball team no doubt strove to emulate the city's championship-winning Reds, but few high schools had teams in 1908. The 1909 team played only one game with another high school. Winfield High School teams enjoyed success with state titles in football in 1919, four state titles for track and field in the 1920s, and a 1922 state tennis championship, which was the first of many for the team.

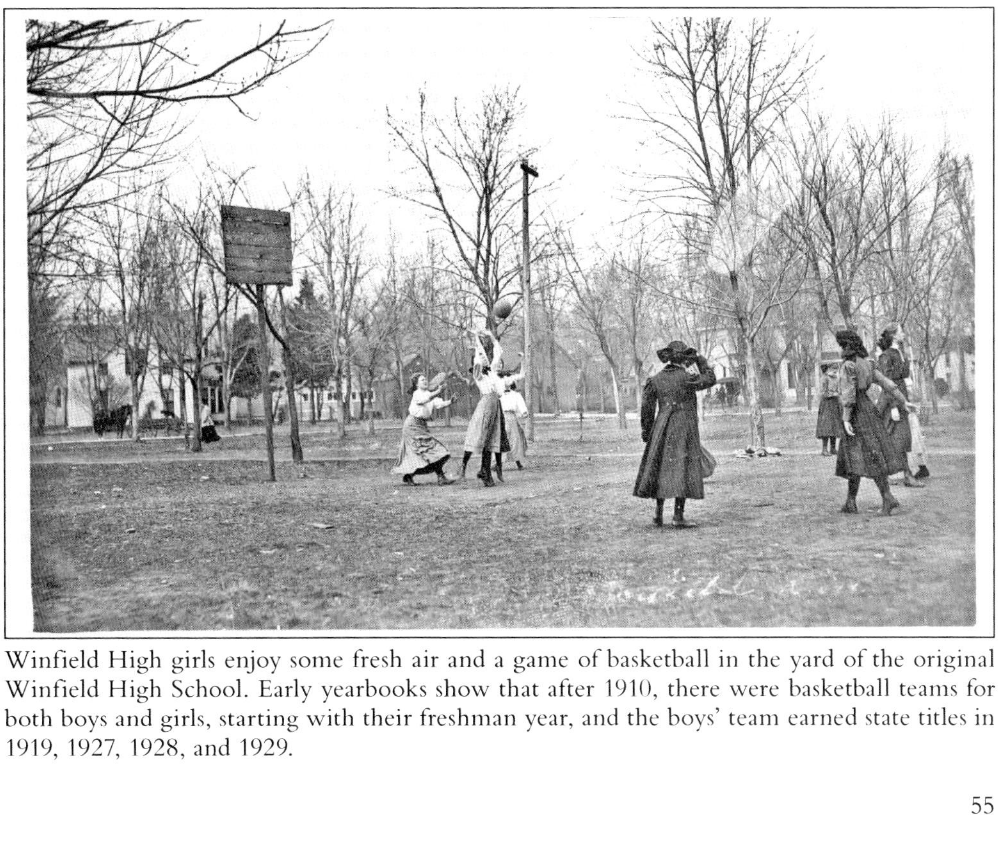

Winfield High girls enjoy some fresh air and a game of basketball in the yard of the original Winfield High School. Early yearbooks show that after 1910, there were basketball teams for both boys and girls, starting with their freshman year, and the boys' team earned state titles in 1919, 1927, 1928, and 1929.

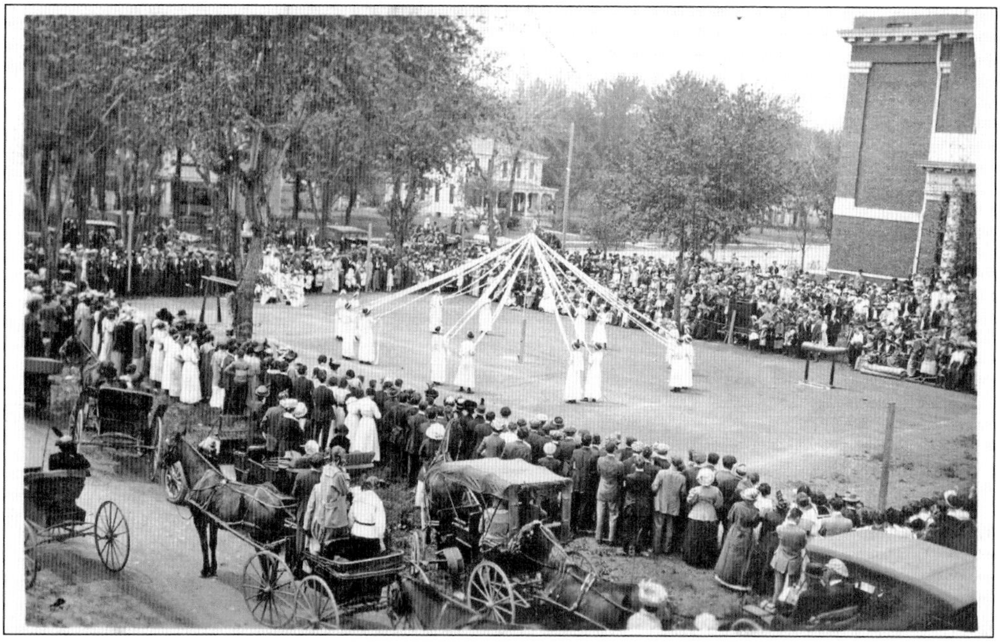

In 1916, the town turned out for a May Fete at Winfield High School, held east of the new manual high building. According to the yearbook that year, the event featured "displays of some of the clever and beautiful work accomplished by WHS girls from all classes under Helen Pritchard's supervision." The event likely grew from Pritchard's physical education classes. Here, girls go round the Maypole.

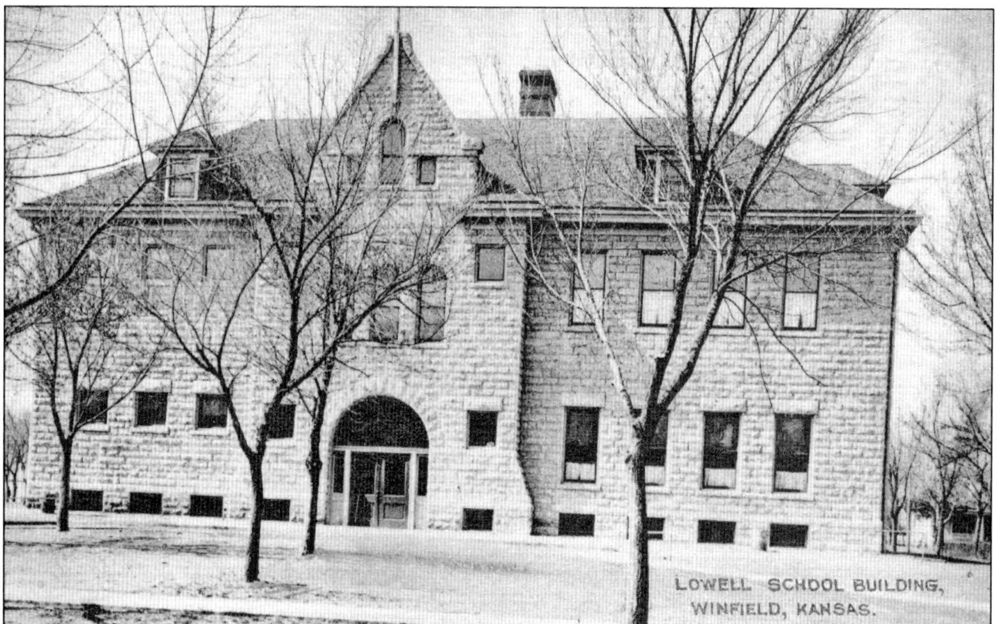


All of Winfield's elementary schools were named for poets and constructed in the four wards of the city. Lowell, pictured here, went up in the south ward in 1893, while Irving began serving the children of the north ward that same year. A new building replaced Lowell in 1958 and Irving in 1963. Both remain open today.

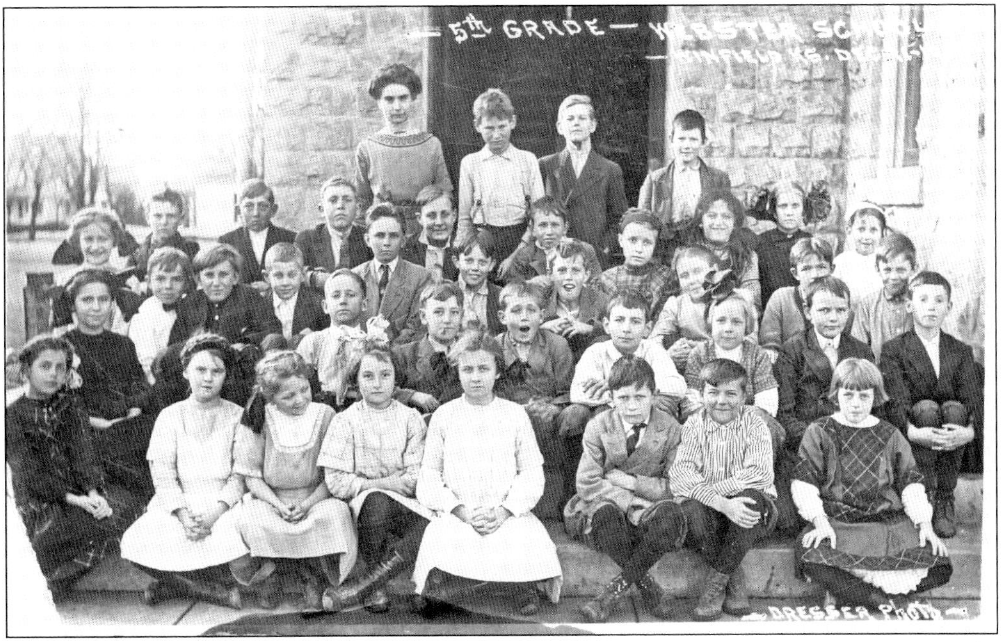


In 1884, Webster and Bryant Elementary Schools were built in the east and west wards, respectively. In this postcard, 38 students sit with their teacher on the steps of Webster Elementary in 1911. When Webster opened, the highest-paid teachers in the district received $50 a month. Webster Elementary remains in use by the district today, and Bryant houses the Cowley County Historical Museum.

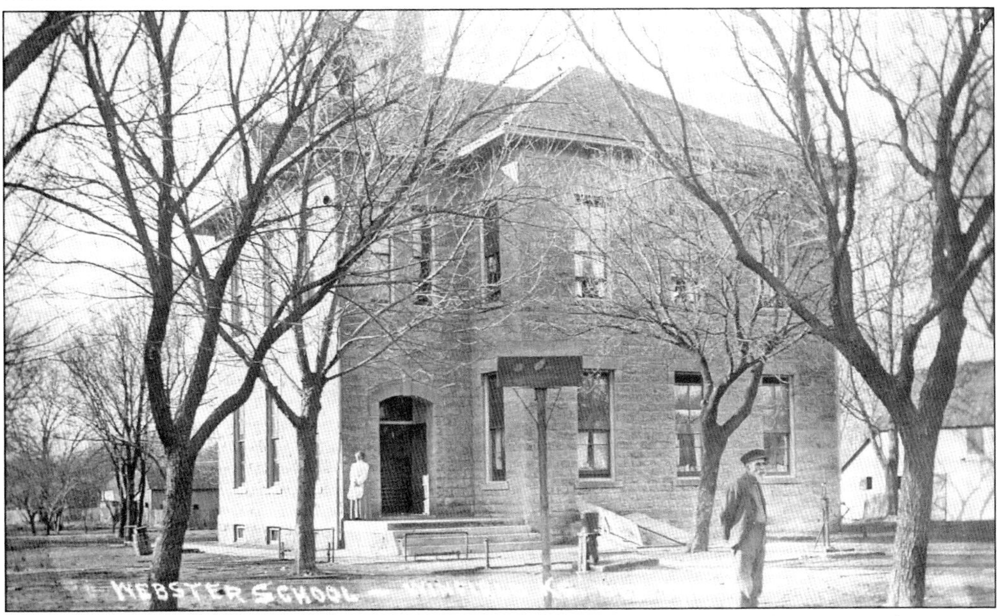


A new building replaced the Webster Elementary pictured here in 1938, and two more elementary schools named after poets joined it over the years. In 1925, Stevenson Elementary went up at 1406 East Eighth Avenue, and Whittier Elementary opened to serve the new neighborhoods growing up around Mound Street in 1955. Of these two schools, only Whittier still serves students today.

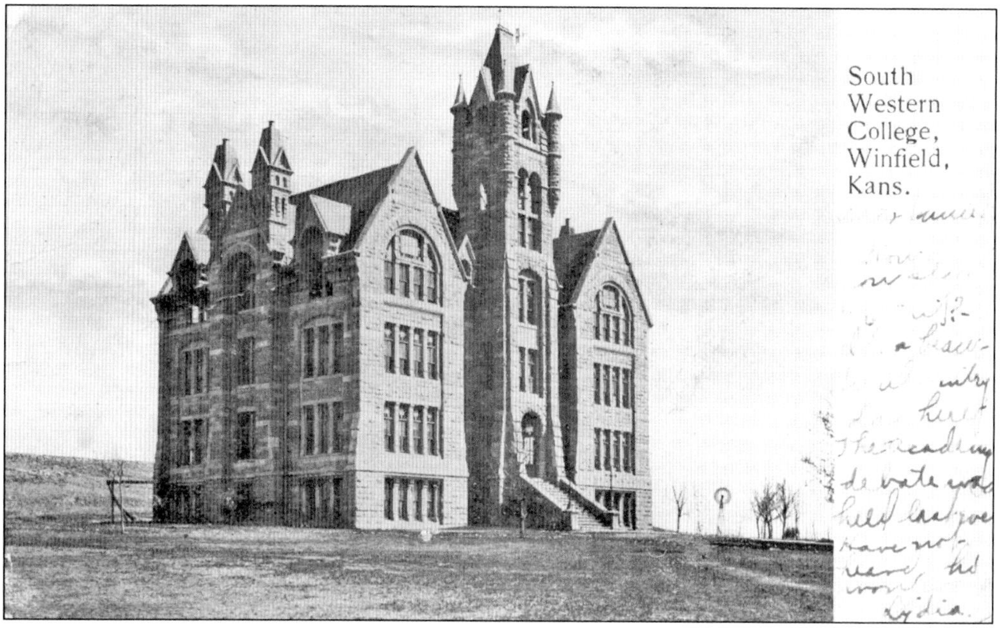


Southwest Kansas College grew out of the annual meeting of the Southwest Kansas Annual Conference of the Methodist Episcopal Church, held in Winfield in 1883. The City of Winfield provided several incentives to bring an institute of higher learning to town, including 41 acres of land, $60,000, and the lumber and stone for a college building. The college's first 43 students gathered on September 7, 1886, in a downtown building.

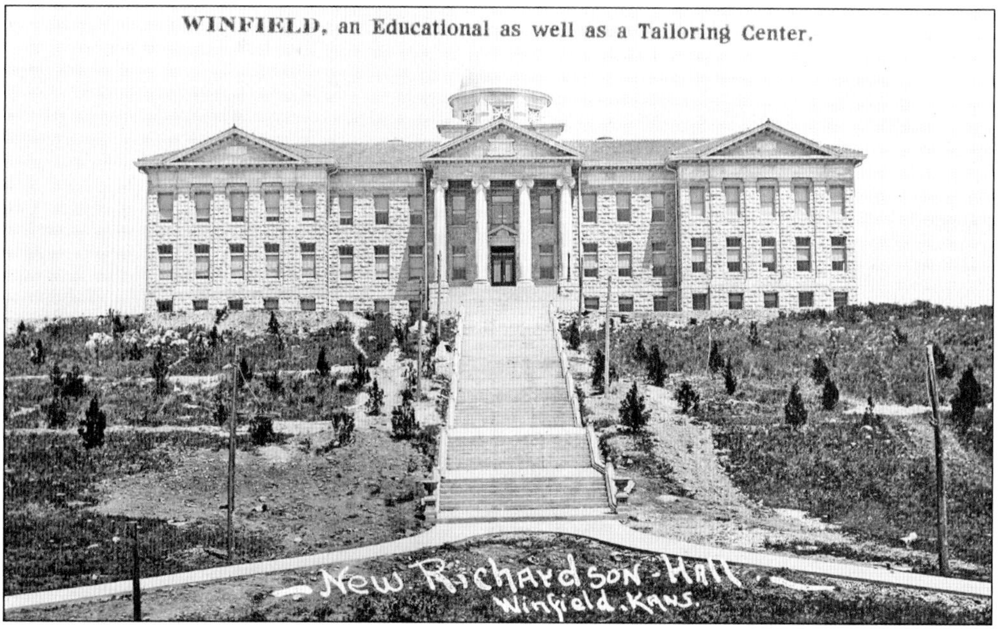


The first college building welcomed students in the fall of 1887. By 1908, a president's home, ladies' boarding hall, and frame gymnasium were added to the campus. Streets around the school received the names of Methodist bishops (Simpson, Janes, Warren, Fowler, and Ames). In 1909, with the board of trustees' approval the previous year, the college's charter changed to the name of Southwestern College. May 31, 1910, saw the dedication of Richardson Hall.

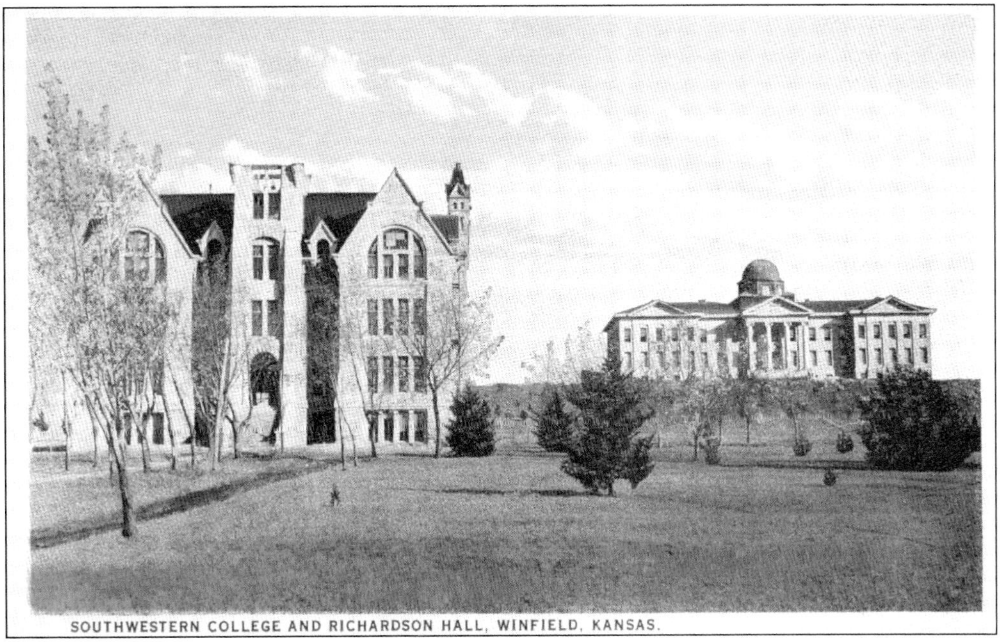


When North Hall (the original college building) received a condemnation order in 1949 and fire struck Richardson Hall a year later, the future of the college was in question. Students, faculty, alumni, and citizens stepped up to save it. With help from the city and private donors, Mossman Hall of Science and Christy Administration Building replaced the two buildings pictured here, and the Memorial Library was built.

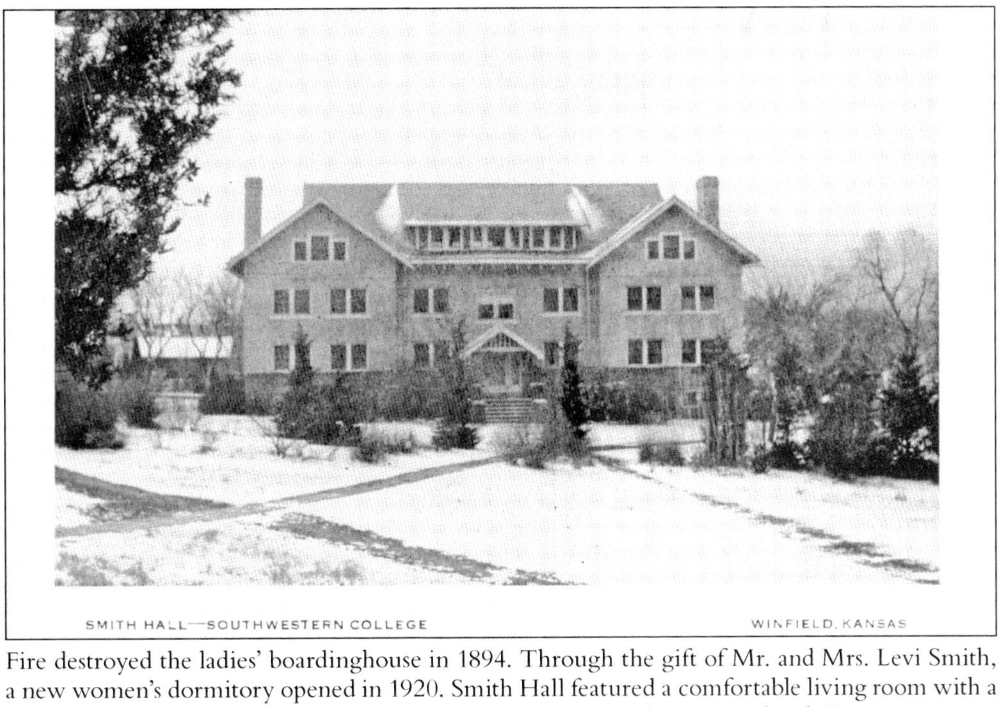


Fire destroyed the ladies' boardinghouse in 1894. Through the gift of Mr. and Mrs. Levi Smith, a new women's dormitory opened in 1920. Smith Hall featured a comfortable living room with a fireplace and a dining facility for the college in the basement and accommodated 60 young women. It was located between Broadhurst and Wallingford Halls on the current Southwestern campus.

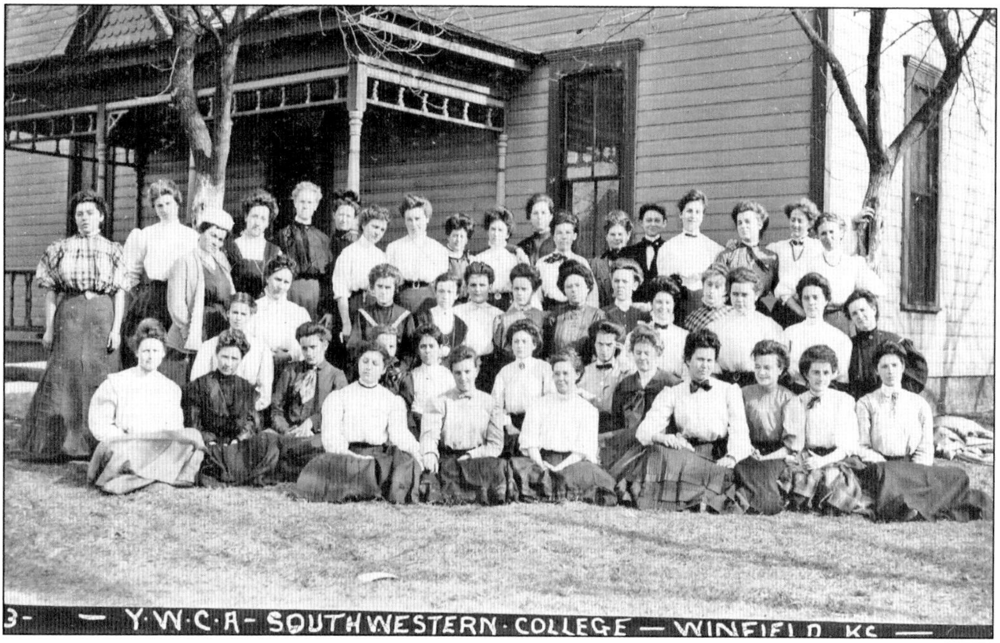


Southwestern had both YWCA and YMCA chapters that began a year apart from each other. The two often held joint receptions and meetings, and both sent members to state and interstate conferences. The YWCA chapter began in 1899 and had 54 members by 1906 and 364 by 1923. The Belles Lettres and the Athenians, literary societies for women and men, respectively, provided another healthy social outlet for Southwestern students.

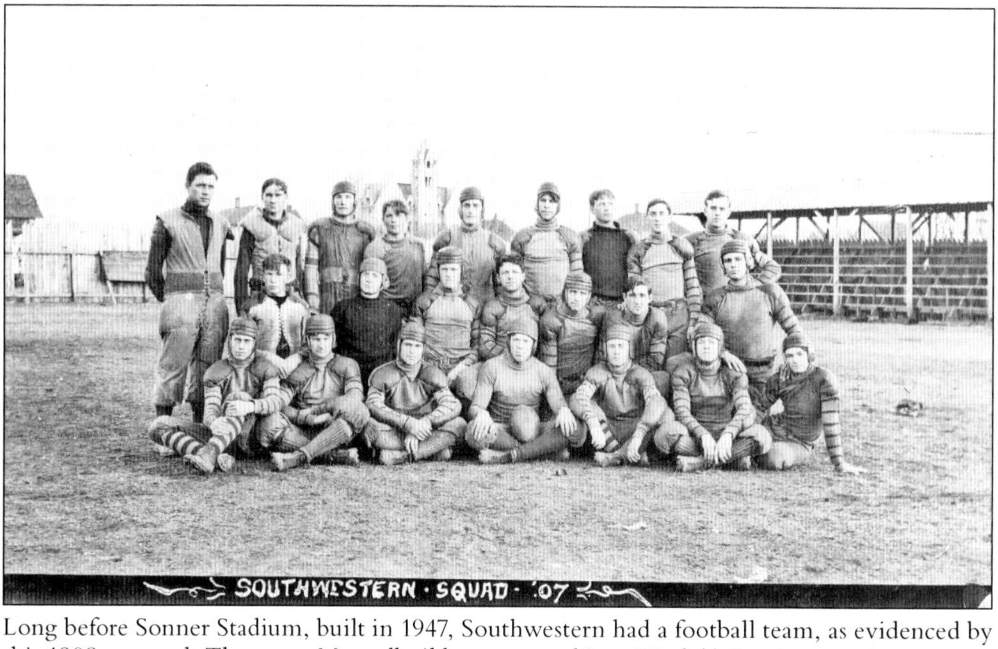


Long before Sonner Stadium, built in 1947, Southwestern had a football team, as evidenced by this 1908 postcard. The name Moundbuilders appeared in a *Winfield Courier* story about a 1910 football game. The Jinx mascot also grew from a football game. To celebrate Southwestern's defeat of Fairmount College (now Wichita State), a student created a tombstone with a black cat at the top and the 41-3 score underneath.

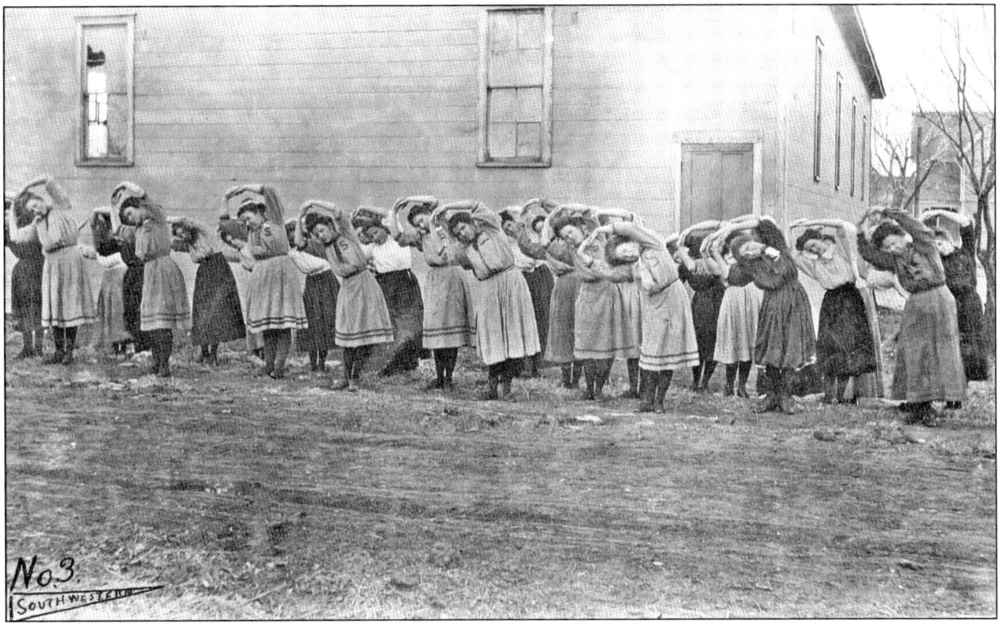


Southwestern College girls engage in calisthenics, likely at the site of "Prexy's Barn," the school's gymnasium, built in 1908. Another form of exercise for Southwestern students was the climbing of Observatory Hill. A 25-foot-tall observatory was built there of native stone in 1898, but dismantled in 1927, without a telescope installed. The hill, planted with native trees by college students, remains at Ninth Avenue and College Street today.

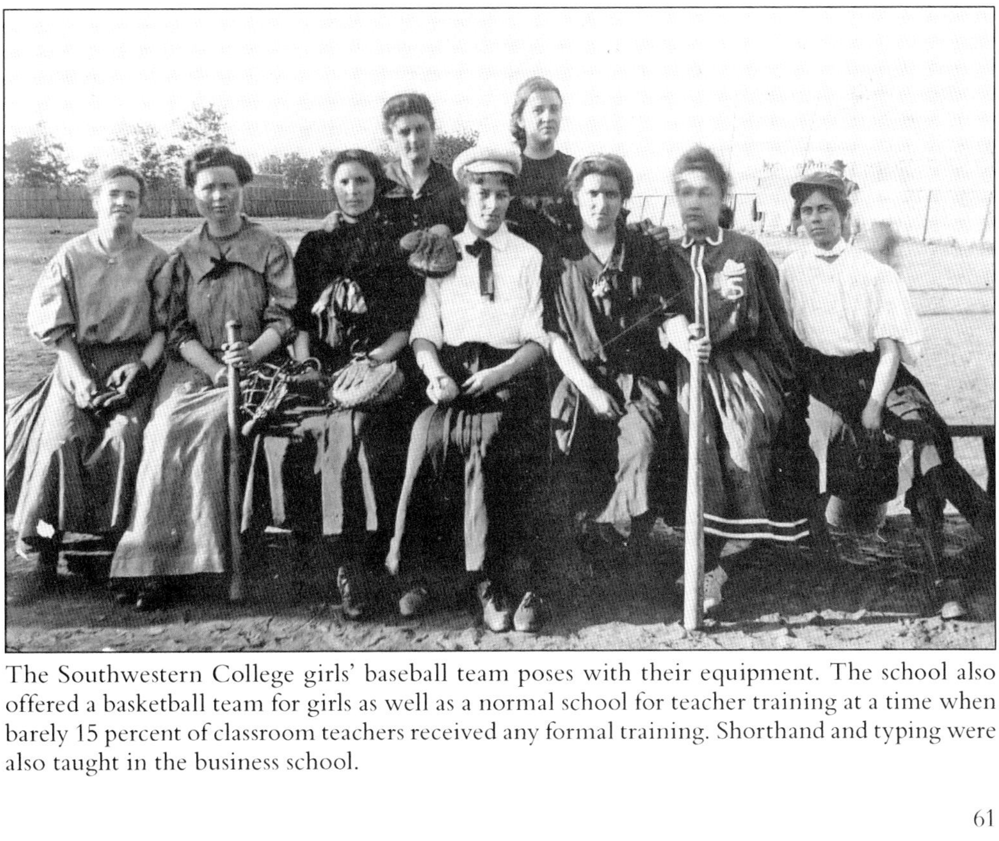

The Southwestern College girls' baseball team poses with their equipment. The school also offered a basketball team for girls as well as a normal school for teacher training at a time when barely 15 percent of classroom teachers received any formal training. Shorthand and typing were also taught in the business school.

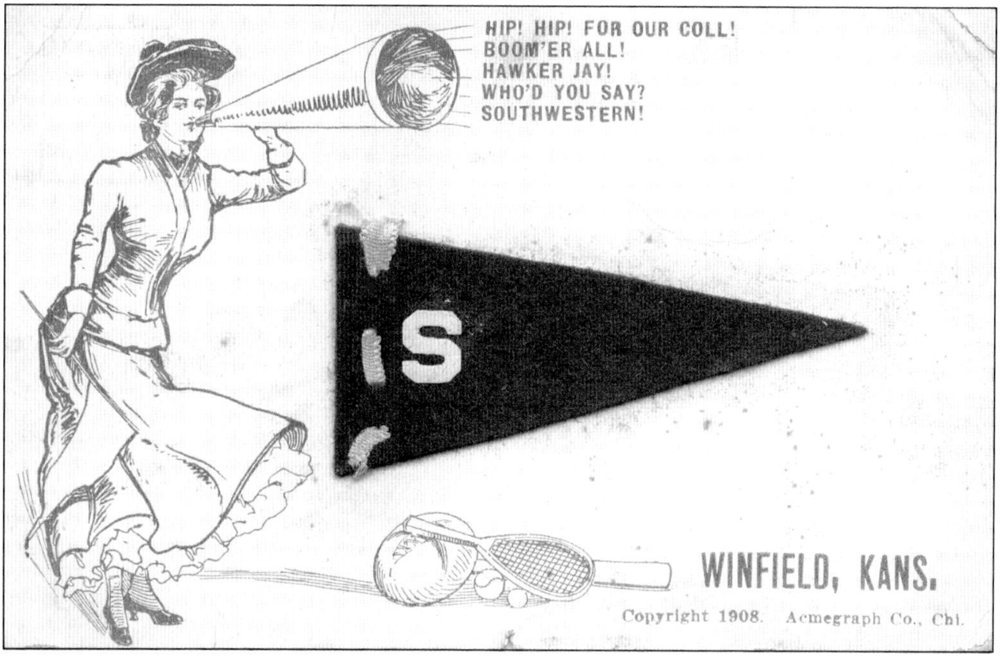


The sender of this 1908 postcard wrote, "The prof's sure know how to soak a fellow down here. I study chemistry, college algebra, English comp., German and astronomy." Other offerings included French, Greek, Latin, oratory, music, art, education, and business instruction at that time. Attendance at chapel was mandatory. A 1926 merger with the Winfield School of Music strengthened the music program.

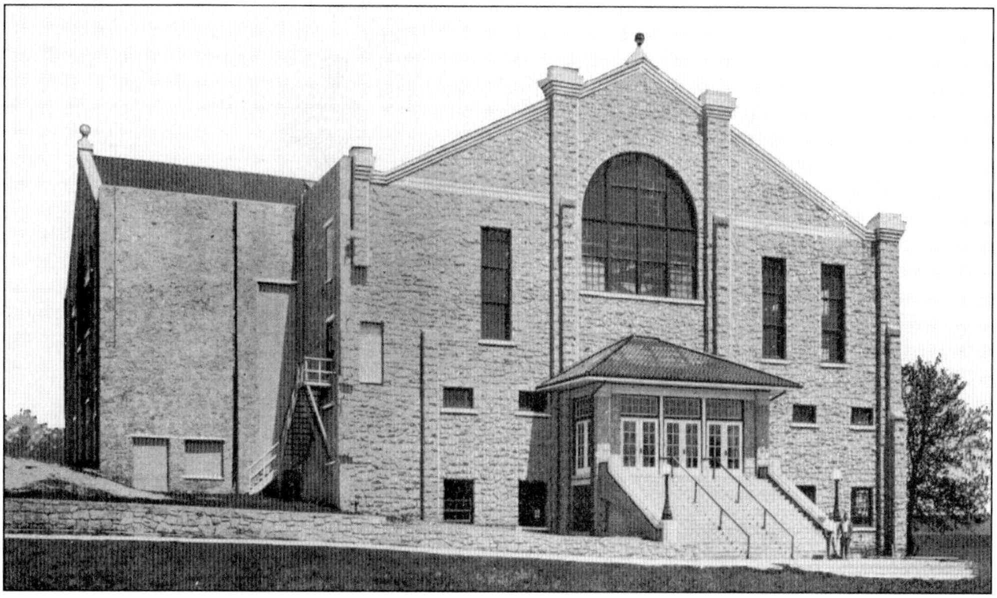

In 1923, Southwestern got a new gymnasium when Stewart Field House was constructed. A poem in the yearbook that year predicted, "Prexy's Barn must soon give way to a fine new gym where the champs will play." It took a few years, but the Moundbuilders' basketball team won the Intercollegiate Athletics Tournament in 1940 and won or tied five Central Intercollegiate Conference championships in years after that.

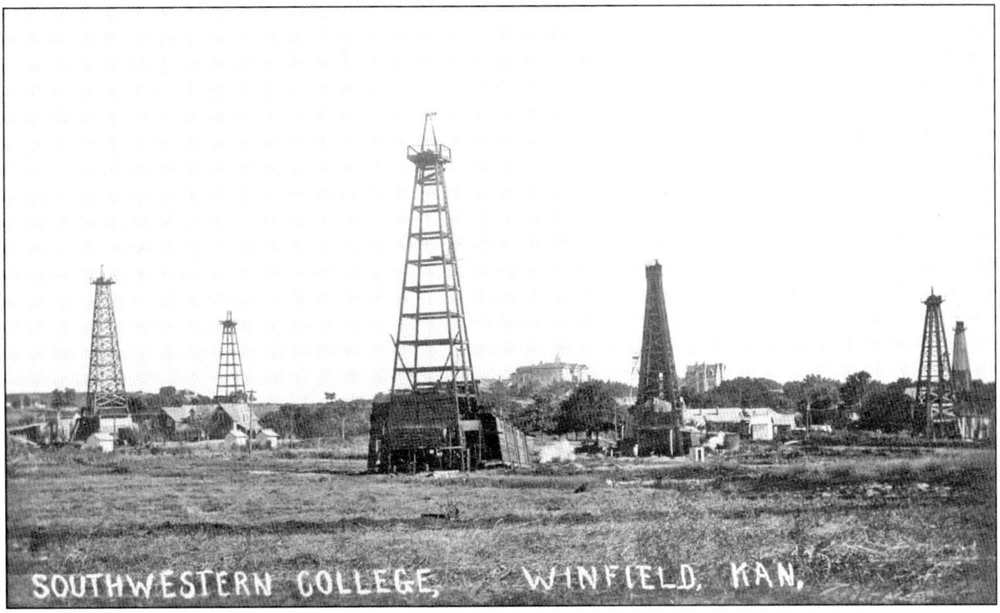


Look closely to see Old North Hall and Richardson Hall in this view of Dibbens oil field, located north of Southwestern College. At one time, this land included 19 oil wells. When purchased by Southwestern College graduate Marilyn McNeish and her husband, George, in 1985, only five wells were active. Those wells were capped in time for the ground-breaking on Cumbernauld Village, a retirement campus that opened in 1989.

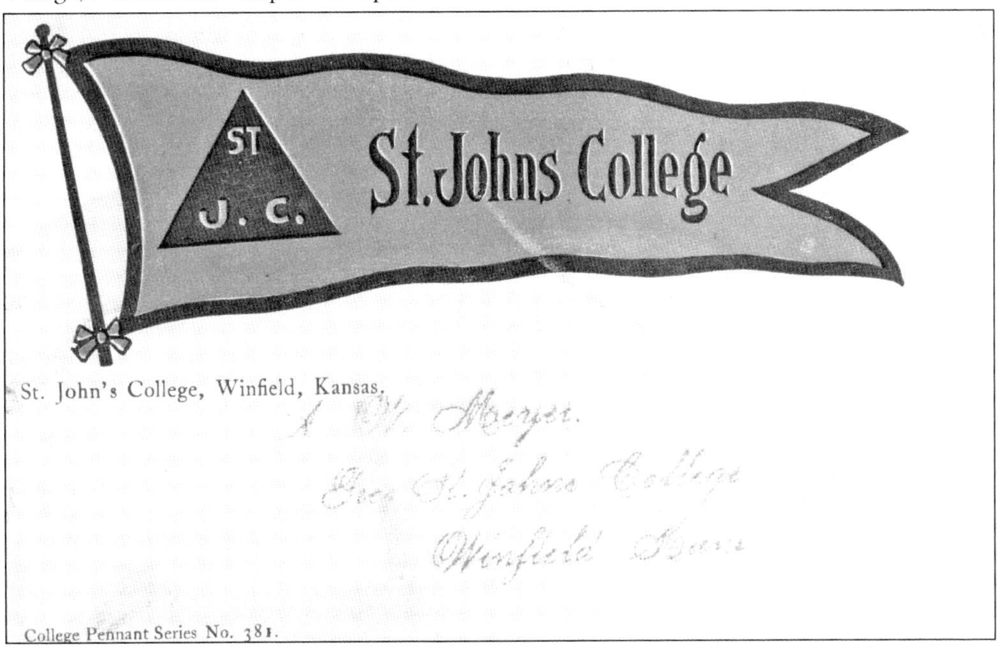


St. John's College began with a gift in 1893 to the Lutheran Synod from Winfield businessman J.P. Baden. In 1908, the college came under the ownership of the Lutheran Church-Missouri Synod. It had the distinction of being the first coeducational college in the synod and served over 9,000 students before its closing in 1986. Rev. A.W. Meyer was its second and longest-tenured president (1895–1927).

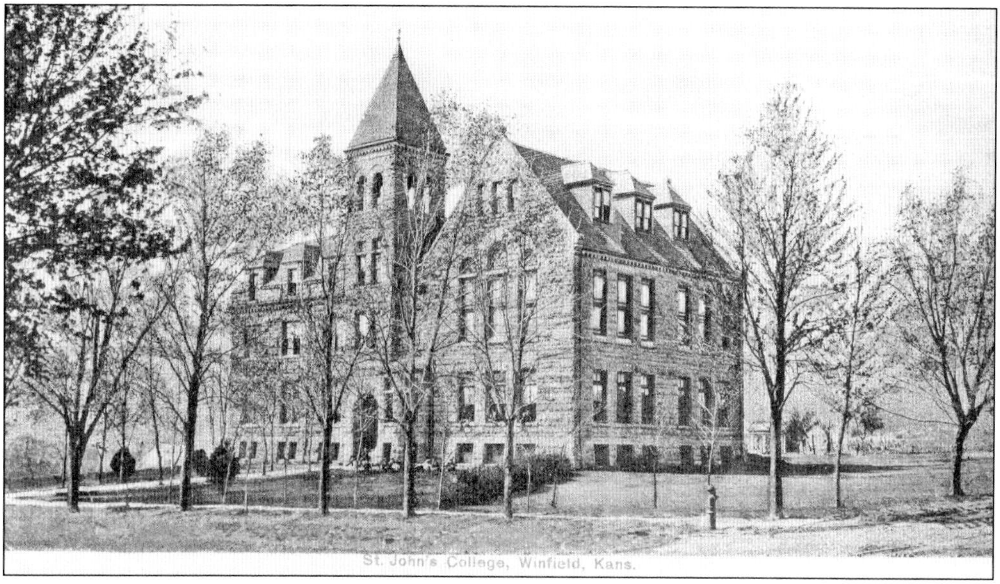


Construction began in June 1893 on the college's first building, Baden Hall. The school opened that month with one professor, Rev. Henry Stoeppelwerth, and met in Baden's downtown mercantile store. Rev. Henry Sieck joined the faculty in December. When dedicated on March 1, 1894, Baden Hall included classrooms, a chapel, library, laboratory, boys' dormitory, storage for musical instruments, kitchen, dining hall, laundry room, administrative offices, and a gymnasium in the basement.

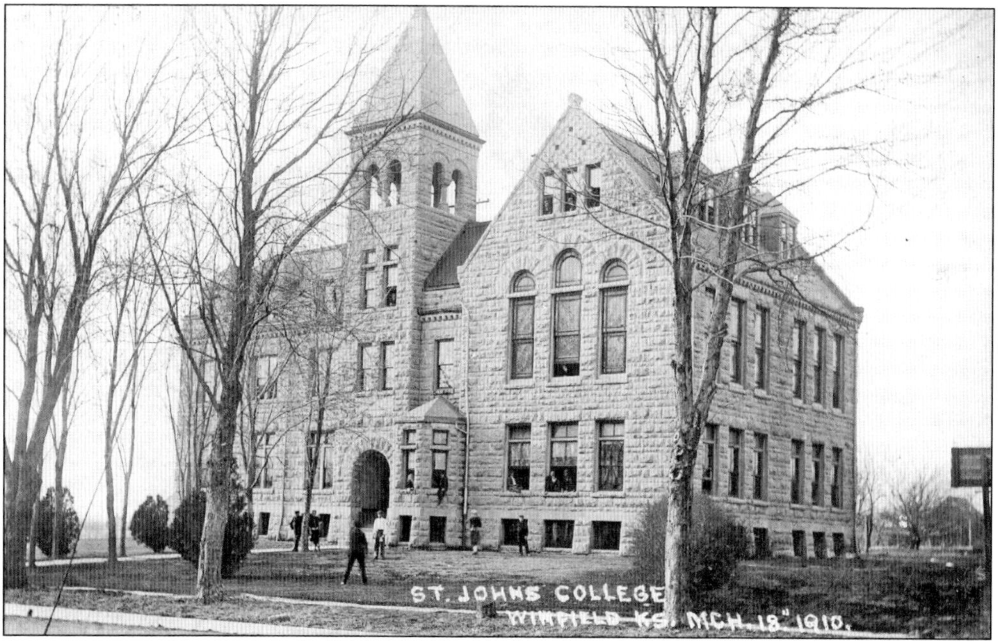


By 1910, St. John's center remained Baden Hall, but its academic offerings had expanded to include these programs of study: preparatory (later to become the Academy), classical, scientific, elocution, and business/secretarial training. Future pastors as well as lay students enrolled in these courses. The Winfield College of Music provided music instruction, with music college students receiving literary instruction at St. John's. Female students roomed in local homes.

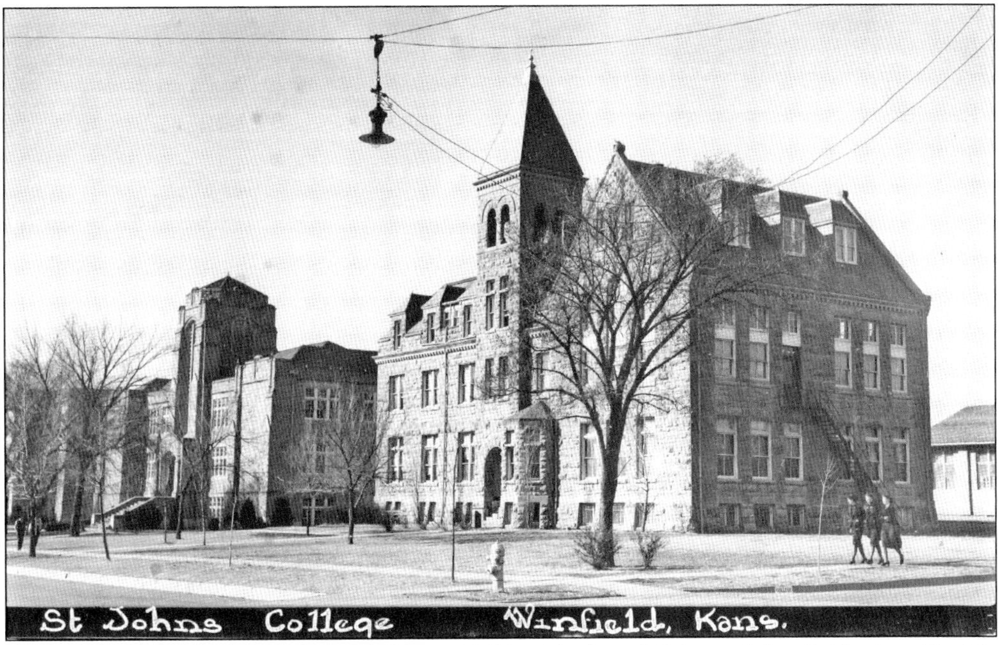


St. John's College grew substantially by 1925 with the addition of the Collegiate Gothic administration building known as Meyer Hall. It provided the same functions as Baden Hall but in a greatly improved fashion, including restrooms on all three levels. This postcard also shows the edges of the gymnasium north of Baden Hall, built in 1914, and the 1916 dormitory west of Meyer Hall.

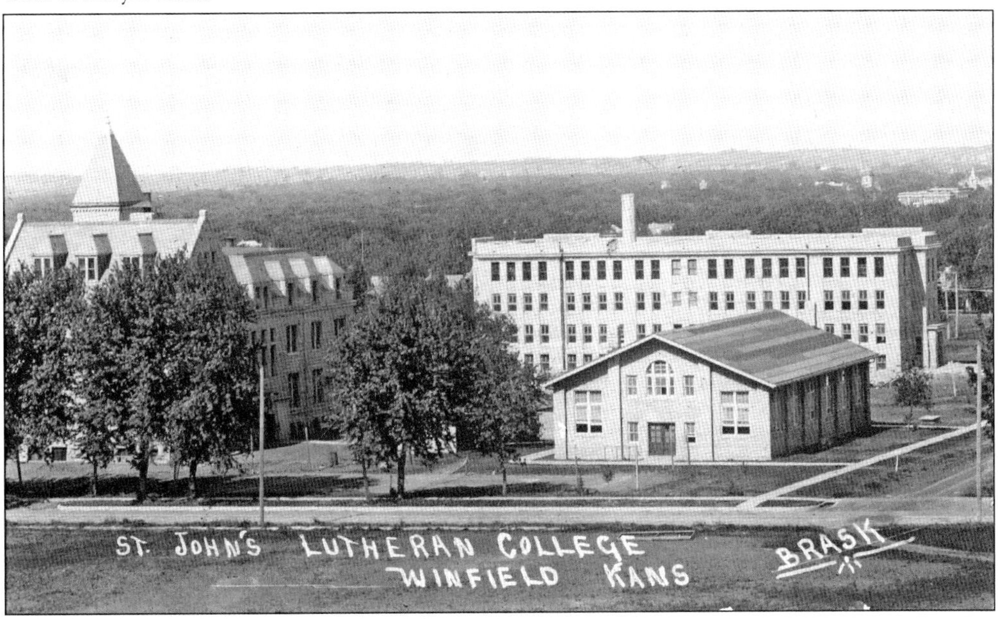


This view, taken from the college athletic field on the east side of College Street, shows a post-1916 campus, with Baden and Meyer Halls towering to the south. In the foreground to the north stands the gymnasium built in 1914, used for two years as a boys' dormitory during the construction of the four-story West Dorm behind it. In 1973, West Dorm received the name Rehwinkel Hall.

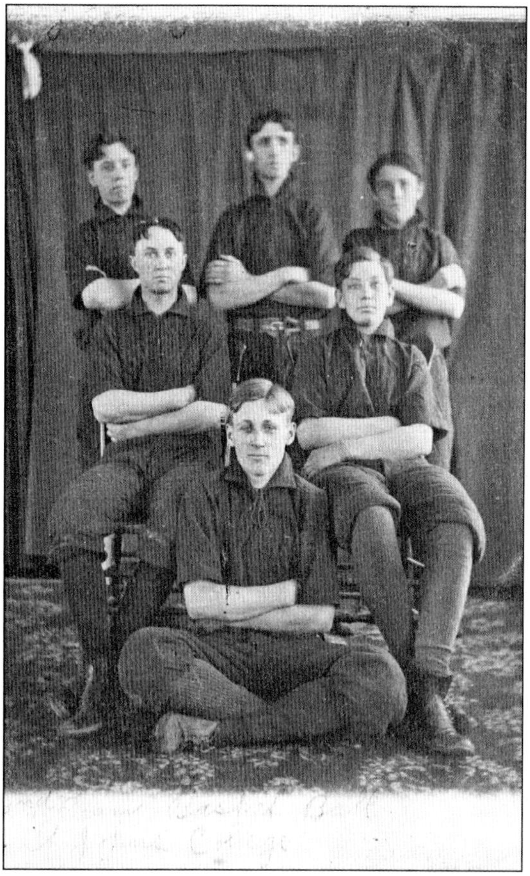

The development of the body as well as the mind was encouraged at St. John's College. With an athletic association organized by the early 1900s and grounds set up for tennis, baseball, and football, students had many choices for activity. This postcard, postmarked 1901, shows a St. John's basketball team, which would have used the well-equipped Baden Hall basement gymnasium as much as its eight-foot ceilings would allow.

A 1940 remodel of St. John's gymnasium added a handball/racquetball court, snack bar, bleacher seating, bookstore, locker rooms, and offices. In 1959, a student body of over 500 led to a new gym across the street. A library took the spot of the old gymnasium in 1961. When the Synod closed the college in 1986, the campus included two dormitories for women, an Academy dorm, and a Campus Community Center.

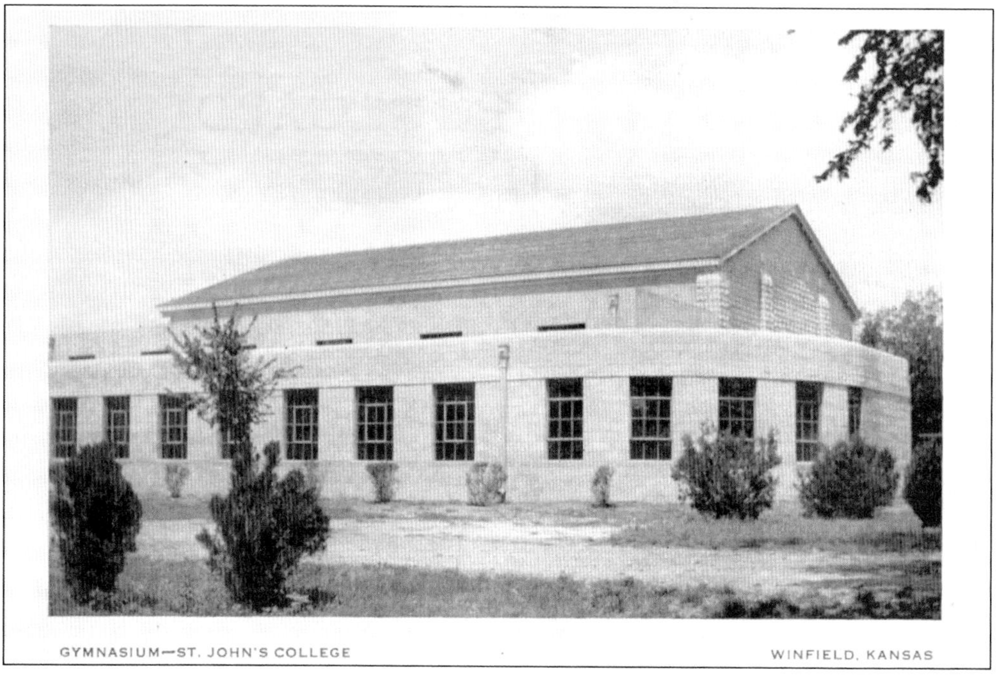

*Five*

# WINFIELD AT WORSHIP

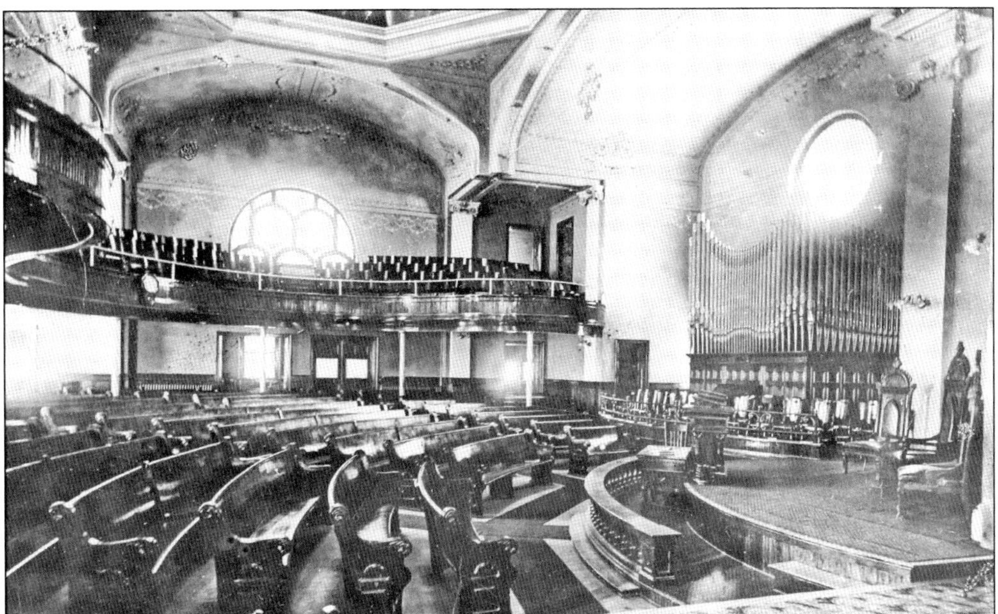


Church bodies began organizing in Winfield as early as 1870, with the Methodist Episcopal being the first in May that year, followed by the First Baptist in November. By the turn of the 20th century, so many of them, including the M.E. church exhibited here, constructed buildings along Millington Street that it came to be called "Church Street."

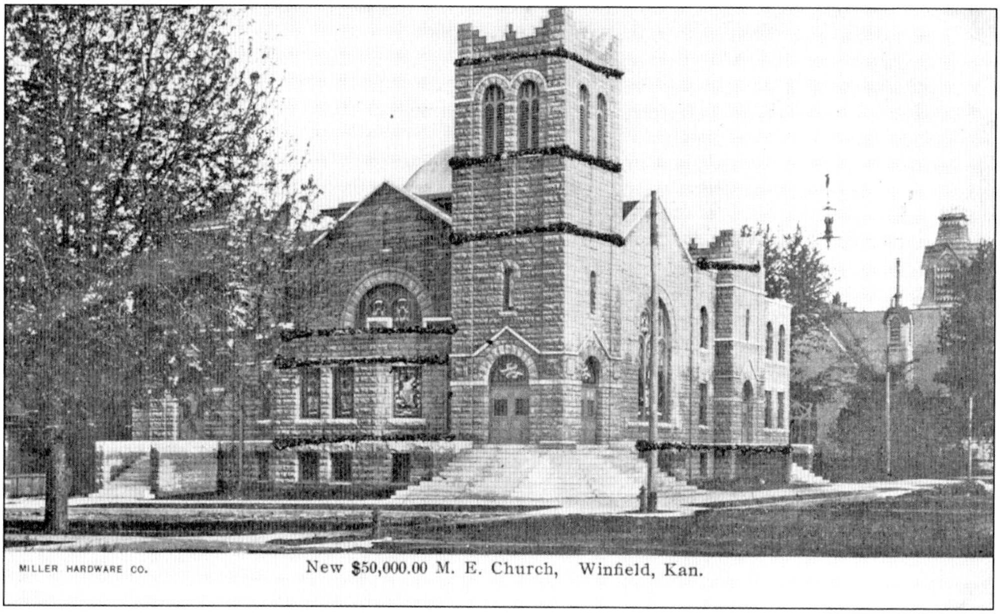


The Winfield Town Company donated a lot on the 200 block of East Ninth Avenue for the first Methodist Episcopal Church. Built from donated materials with the labor of its members, the building served worshippers until 1876, when construction commenced on a stone church with a 100-foot tall steeple at Tenth Avenue and Millington Street. A proud congregation announced the building of its new church on the same corner in 1907.

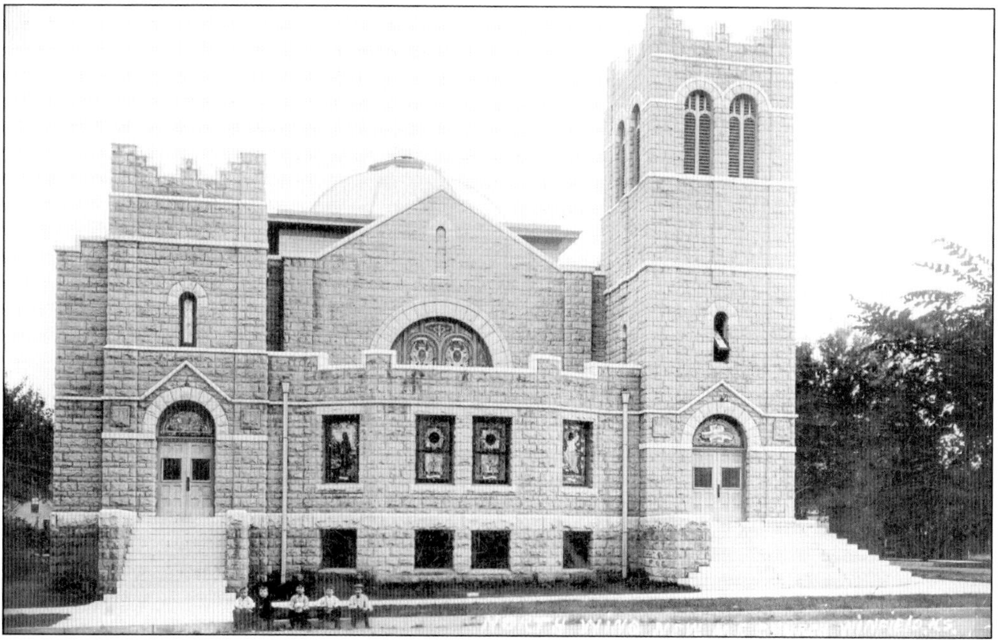

After a windstorm destroyed the steeple of the earlier church following its 1877 dedication, the new First Methodist Church, built on the same site 30 years later, sported a low dome and sturdy local limestone as well as stained-glass windows from the earlier church. This building stood until 1966, when the current church was constructed on its site. Another Methodist congregation built Grace United in 1919 at 320 College Street.

The charter for the First Presbyterian Church in Winfield dates to 1873, with early congregations meeting in the courthouse and other buildings even before that. The building pictured here was located at the northeast corner of Tenth Avenue and Millington Street in 1877, remodeled around the turn of the 20th century, and used by the congregation for 36 years.

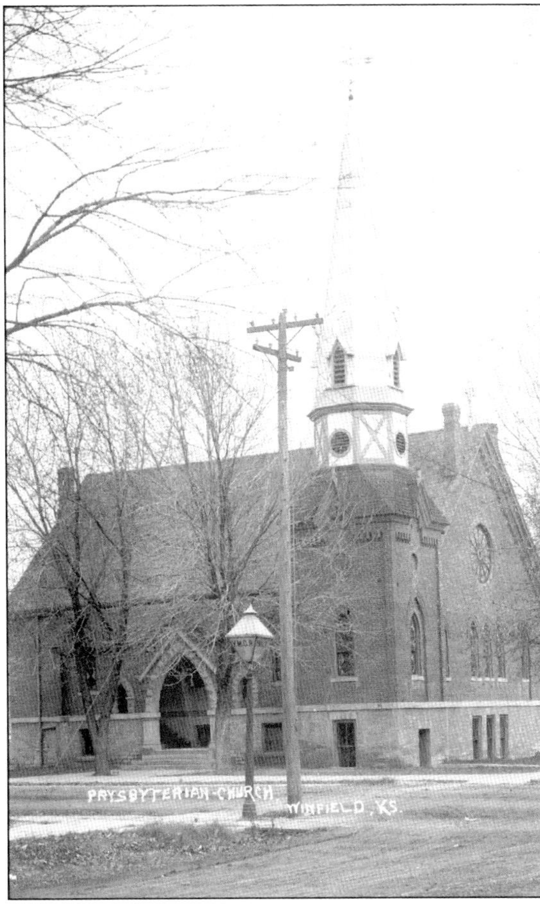


With the old building sold to the government for use as a post office, the cornerstone for a new First Presbyterian Church at Eleventh Avenue and Millington Street was laid July 14, 1912, with the church dedicated on May 3, 1914. The addition of an educational building and an elevator in 1954 and a remodeling in 1975 brought this church into continued use in 21st century. The church celebrated its centennial in 1973.

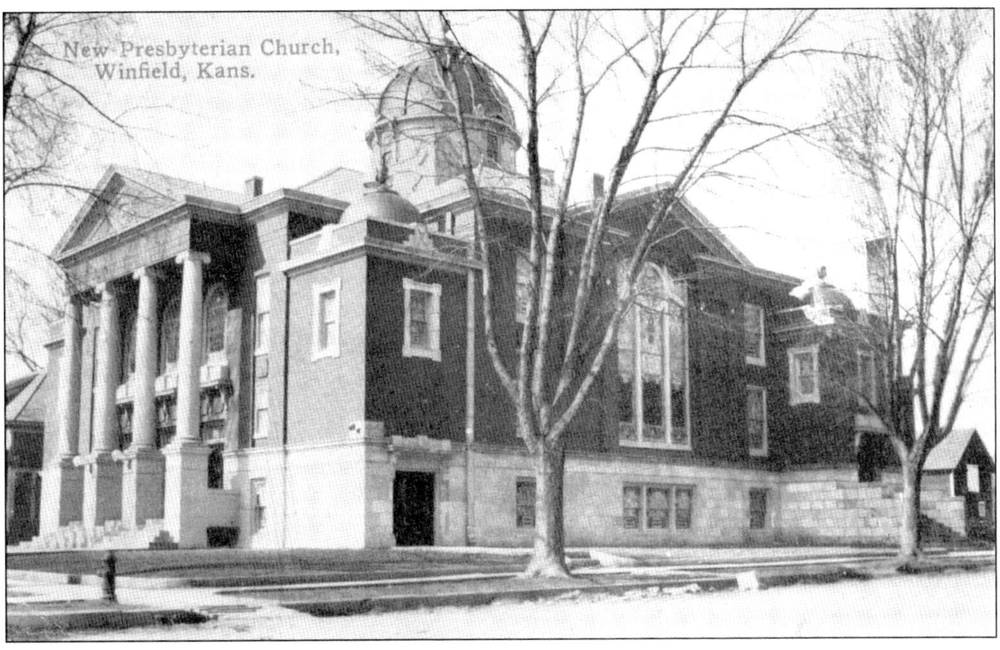

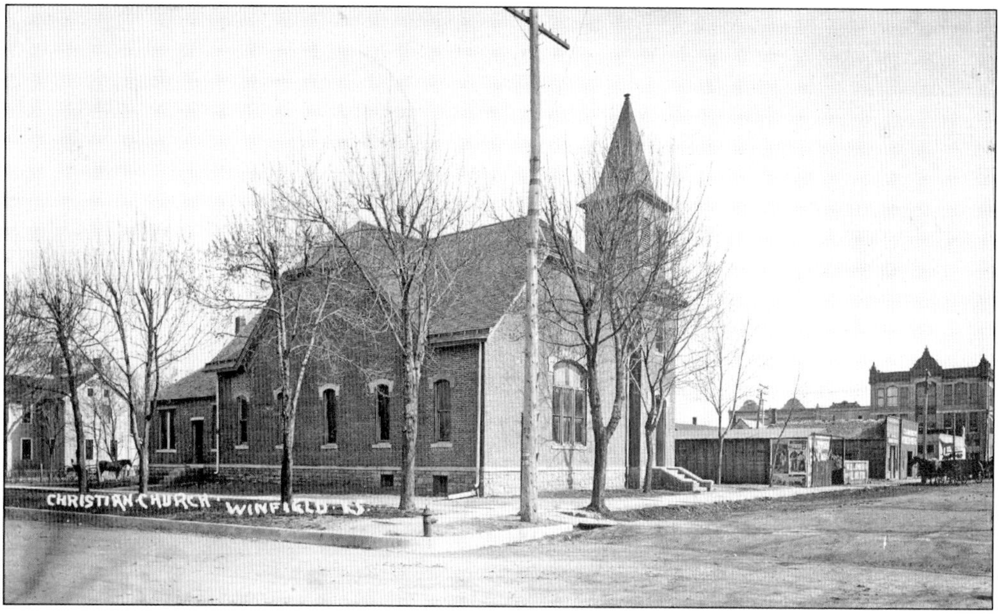


The First Christian Church began in Winfield through the efforts of a circuit-riding preacher meeting with people in a downtown store. By 1873, a wood-frame church was built at Thirteenth Avenue and Millington Street. Within 10 years, an increase in members led to the construction of the redbrick building at Eighth and Millington Streets pictured here. After a tornado struck in 1893 and fire in 1895, the congregation rebuilt.

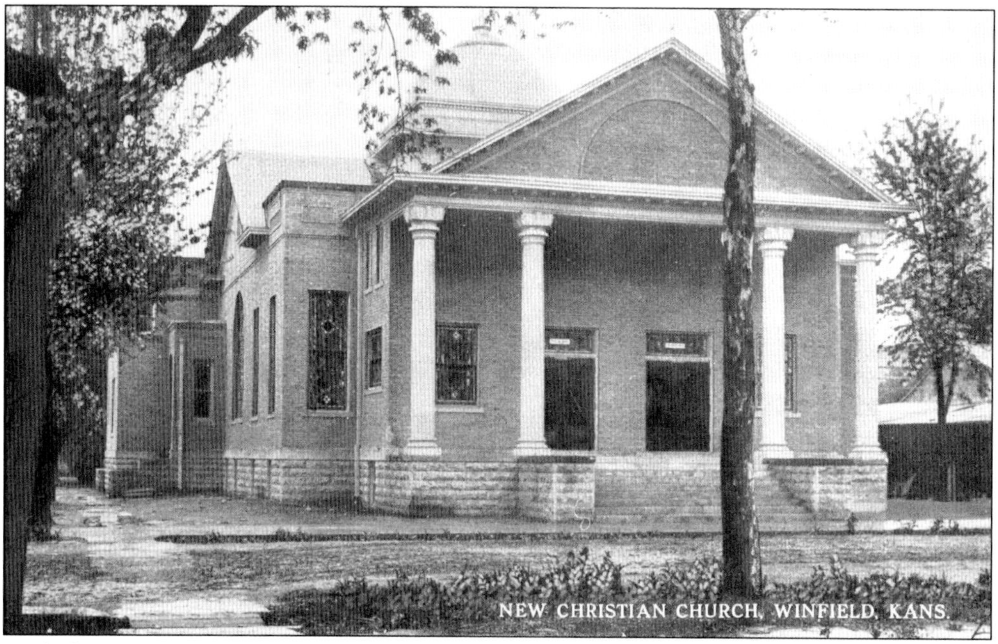


With the congregation reaching over 400 members, a new yellow-brick First Christian Church grew up in 1910 on the site of the 1883 redbrick one. This church featured a circular sanctuary and a balcony but never quite recovered from a 1944 flood. Its Christ the Good Shepherd stained-glass window survives in the chapel at the newest First Christian Church, which was built in 1958 at Ninth Avenue and Alexander Street.

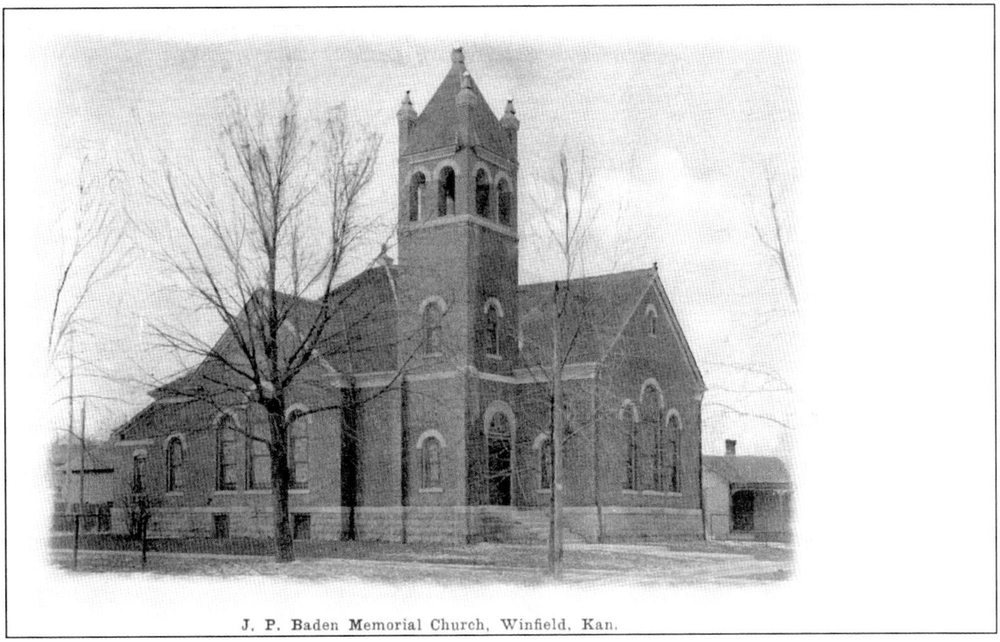


Local businessman J.P. Baden brought the Lutheran faith to Winfield in 1879, holding services in his own home. Later, the congregation met in downtown buildings, including Baden's own at Eighth Avenue and Main Street, leading to the building of a church in 1888 at Seventh Avenue and Andrews Street. Baden's death in 1900 and a growing membership led Baden's widow to donate the money for a new church, built in 1905.

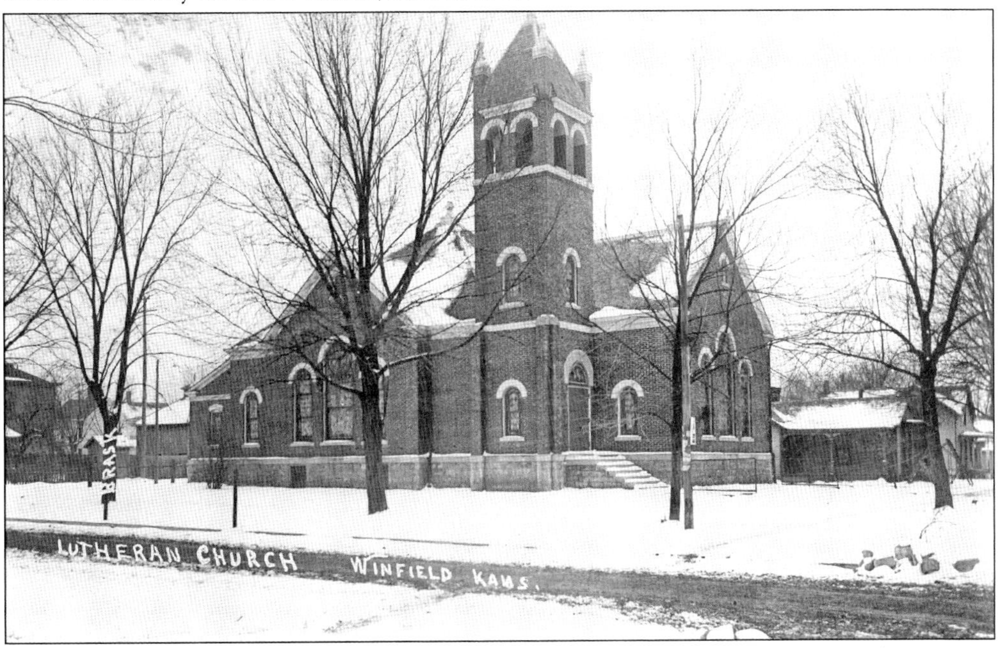


The 1905 church at Eighth and Loomis Streets originally bore the name of its donor, but in 1930 the name became Trinity Lutheran Church. Flood damage and growing membership led to remodeling over the next 25 years. In 1961, construction began on the current church at Ninth Avenue and Mound Street, and the 1905 building was sold to the local Church of Christ.

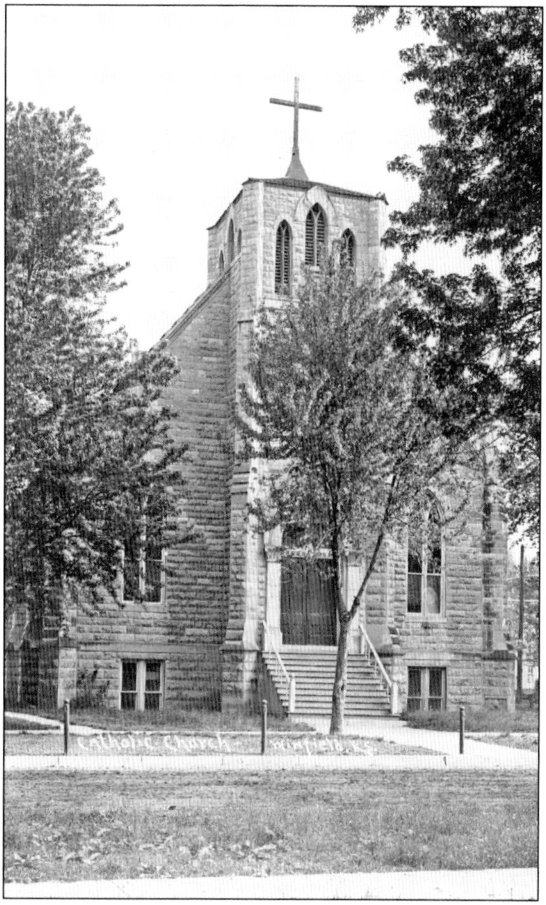


Holy Name Catholic Church began through the ministrations of Jesuit priests, including Fr. Paul Ponziglione, who served as a missionary to Indians. Winfield booster J.C. Fuller offered his home for an early meeting place, and he later donated land on the 400 block of East Eighth Avenue for a small church, which was replaced in 1887 by the limestone building pictured here. Following a 1921 fire, the redbrick church currently in use was built.

Col. H.C. Loomis started the United Brethren Church in 1881. Early members gathered in a meeting room at the courthouse until a small church on South Church Street arose in 1890. By the turn of the century, membership had increased considerably, leading to the construction of the church pictured here. In 1922, a larger structure replaced this one. In the 1960s, this congregation merged with the United Methodist Church.

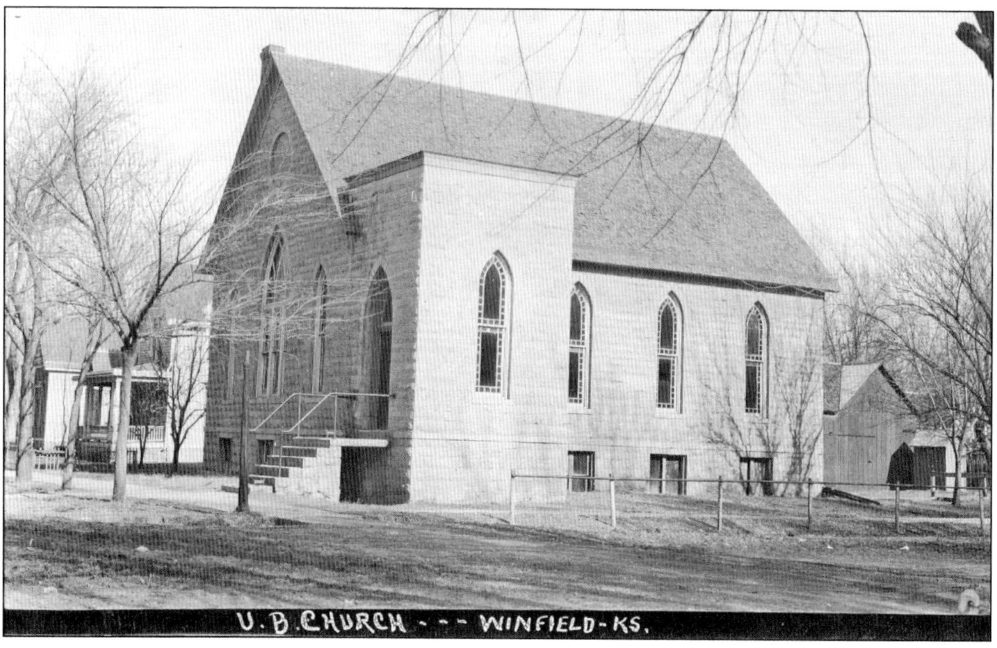

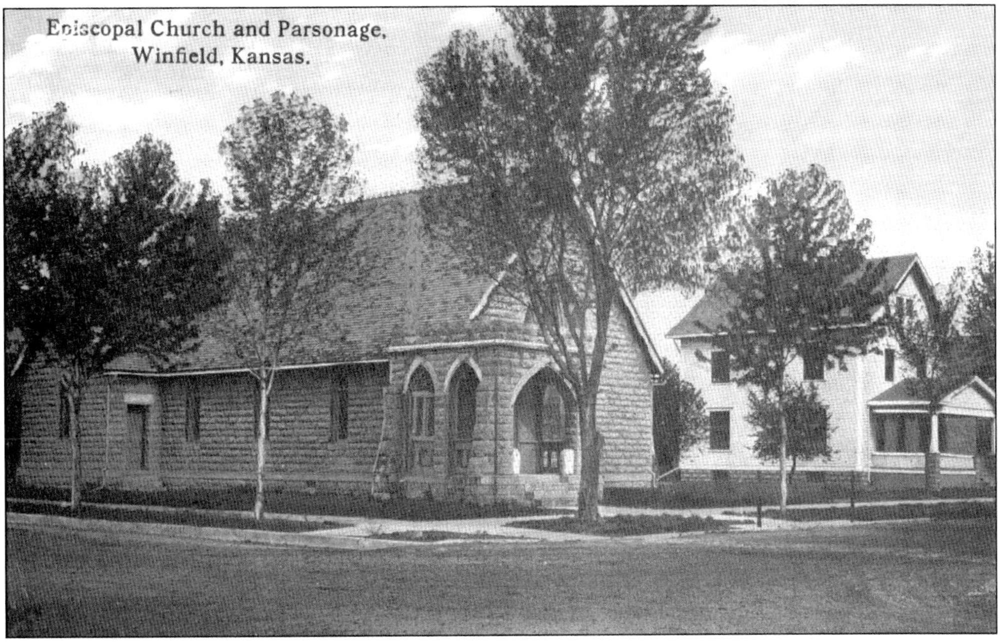


Despite never leaving the corner of Eighth Avenue and Millington Street, Grace Episcopal Church experienced many changes in its early years. The organization of the parish occurred in 1878, with the first church built nine years later. Fire and a tornado struck this frame structure, leading to construction of the limestone church pictured here in 1898. Fire damaged its roof in 1906, and floods struck its interior in 1923 and 1928.

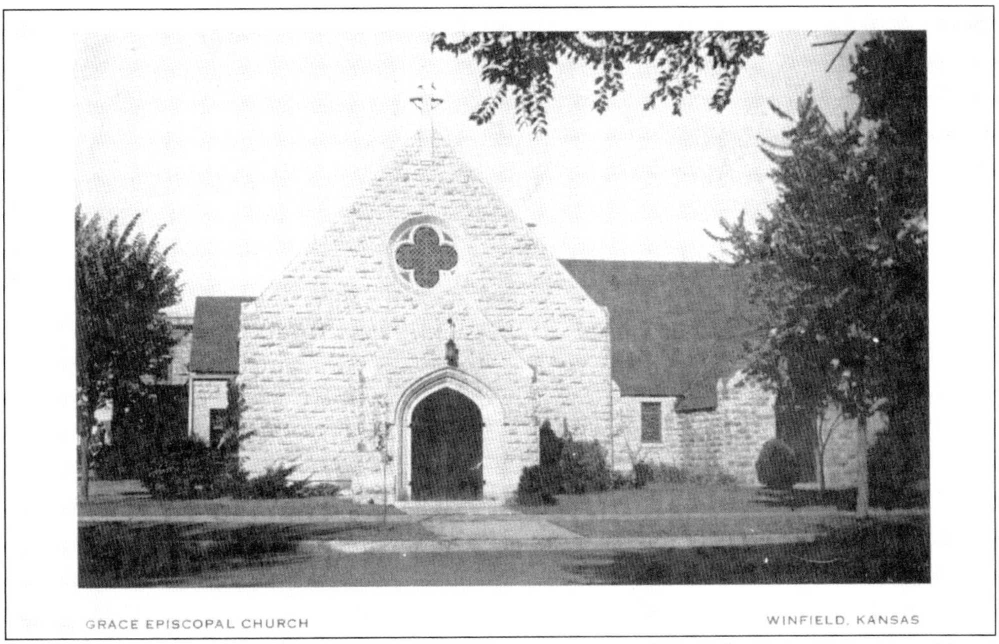


A 1934 fire left only the stone walls of the church and its guildhall, built in 1918. Noted local architect William Caton restored the church, retaining the guildhall on the north, with Silverdale limestone, solid wood beams, and hand-forged ironwork in 1935. An education wing replaced the old parsonage used for Sunday school classes in the 1990s, and the house moved off-site.

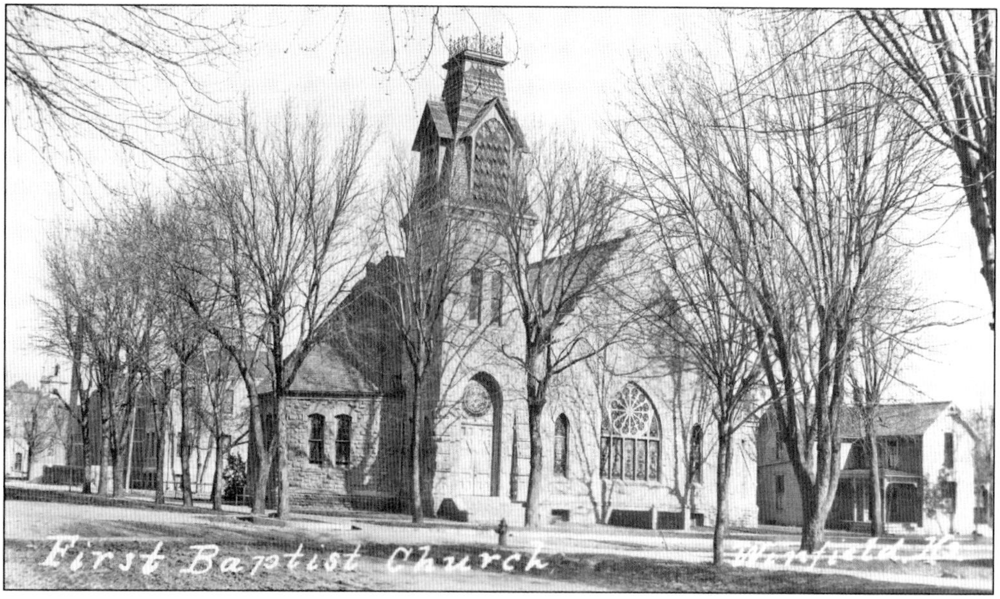


Winfield's First Baptist Church formed following a visit from Rev. Winfield Scott in 1870, and by 1872 he had built a stone church between Seventh and Eighth Avenues on North Millington Street. In 1882, the church was built at its current site of Eleventh Avenue and Millington Street. Wings added to this building in 1927 and 1952 as well as a gym and a kitchen in 1962 allow for its continued use.

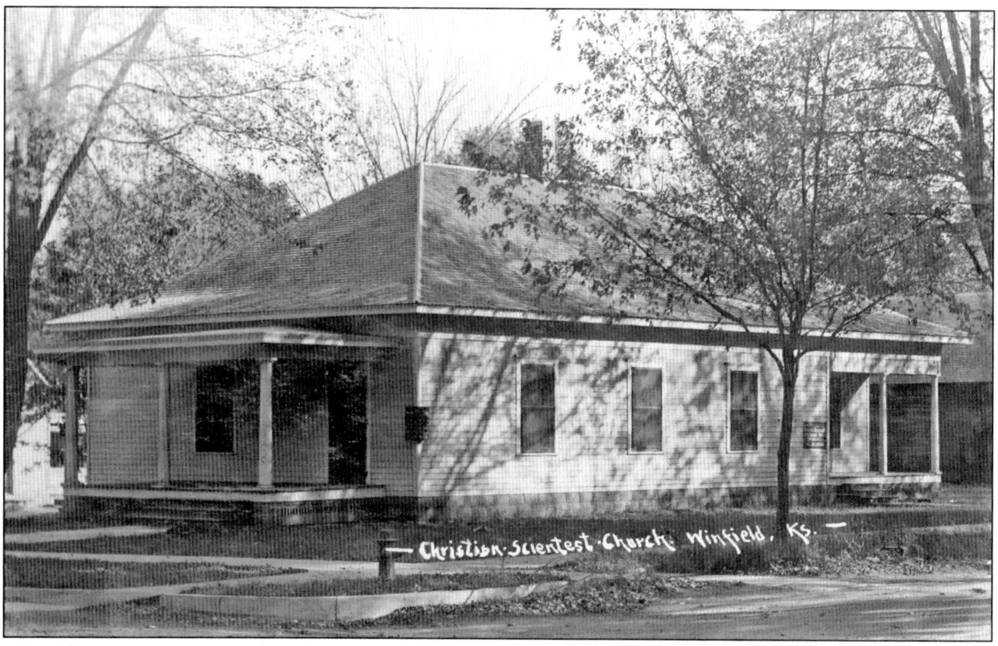


The Christian Science Church began meeting in local homes in 1884. By 1899, it moved to the Hackney Building on East Ninth Avenue for Sunday school and a reading room. Once chartered in 1902, it met at 110 ½ East Ninth Avenue until 1909. The church pictured here at the southeast corner of Eleventh Avenue and Millington Street was dedicated in 1914 and remodeled in 1942, but it is now a private residence.

# *Six*

# Winfield on the Move

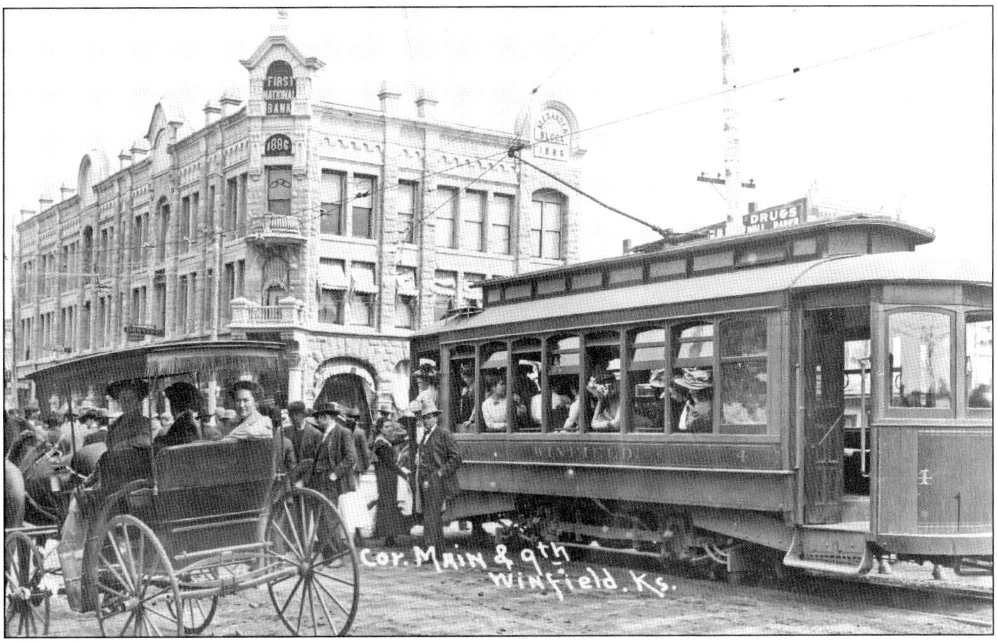


Early Winfield residents could choose from a wide variety of transportation modes. Besides walking, bicycling, or horseback riding, they could hop on one of the buggies, wagons, trollies, or trains dotting the Winfield landscape. The arrival of the interurban system in 1909 increased the speed of local travel. The advent of automobiles brought real change to Winfield streets and an end to several earlier modes of transportation.

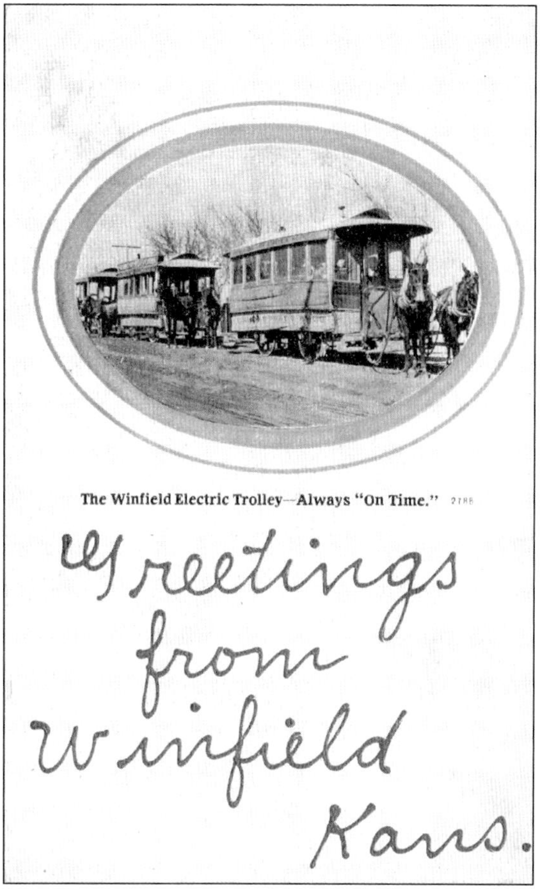


The Winfield Electric Trolley—Always "On Time." 2788

Winfield's mule-drawn streetcars added charm and appeal to the city's image, and they became a tourist attraction from 1886 to 1909, as they provided an entertaining and progressive way around town for visitors and residents alike. Later cars included electric stoves for heating. The 1905 Southwestern College *Moundbuilder* reports a "wait in Craig's bookstore while the electricity is turned on" after purchasing a ticket for a trolley ride.

Public transportation first came to Winfield in 1886 when the Union Street Railway received its charter to provide trolleys powered by mules. The car in the foreground of this view at the intersection of Ninth Avenue and Main Street displays the Union Street Railway sign above its wheels, while the one in the middle designates "hotels, colleges, depots and hospitals" as its route and advertises the upcoming Dockstader minstrel show on its side.

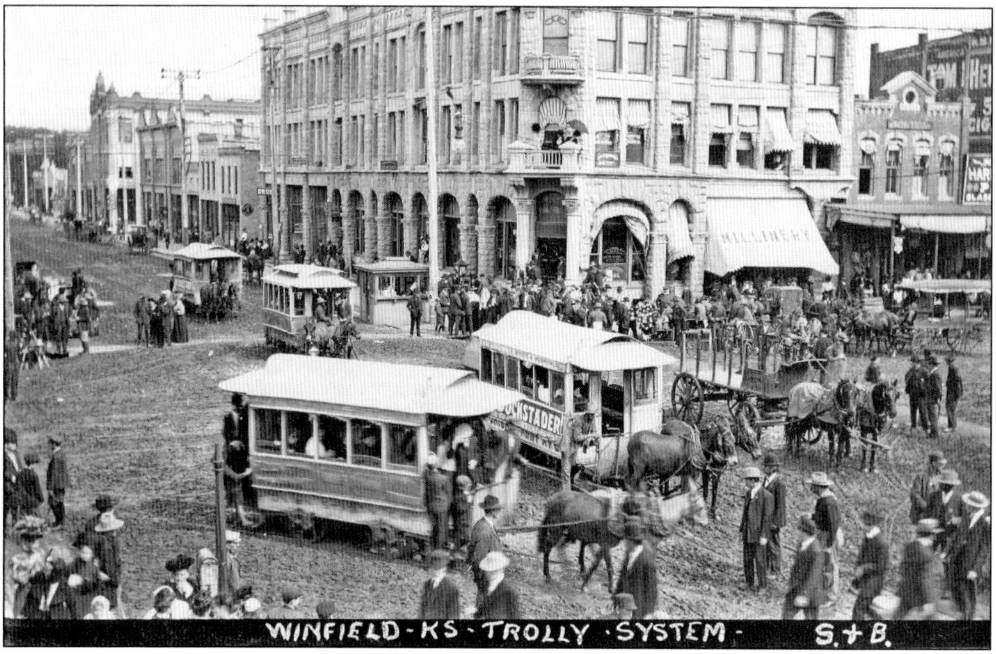


WINFIELD-KS-TROLLY·SYSTEM- S.+B.

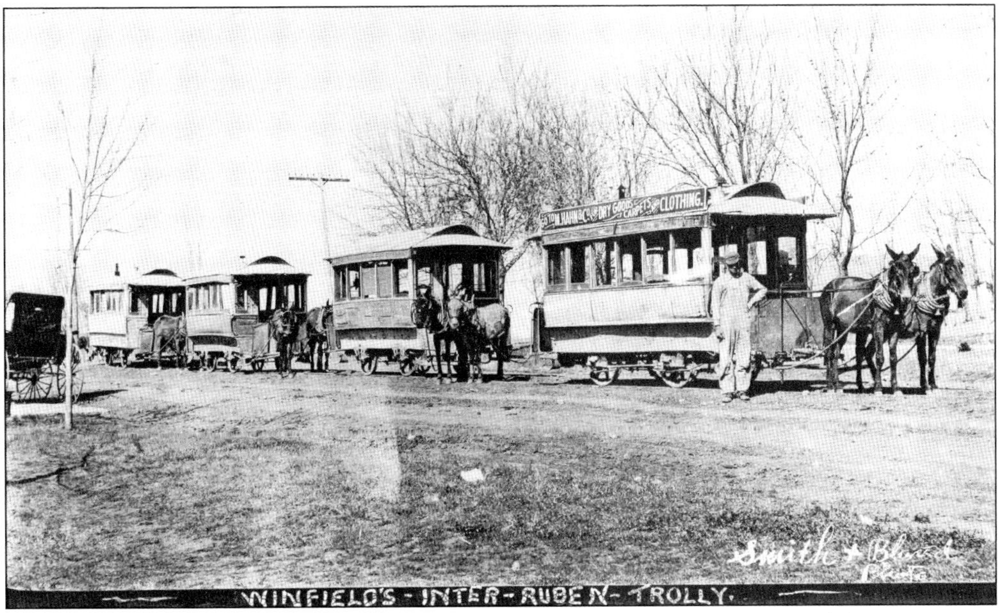


The Union Street Railway headquartered at 710 North Main Street, west of the entrance to Island Park. By 1900, the railway boasted 21 mules, 25 employees, six cars, and 10 miles of track. By 1888, tracks went in all four directions from Ninth Avenue and Main Street, allowing access to many places off Main Street, including Island Park, the fairgrounds, Southwestern College, St. John's College, and all railroad depots.

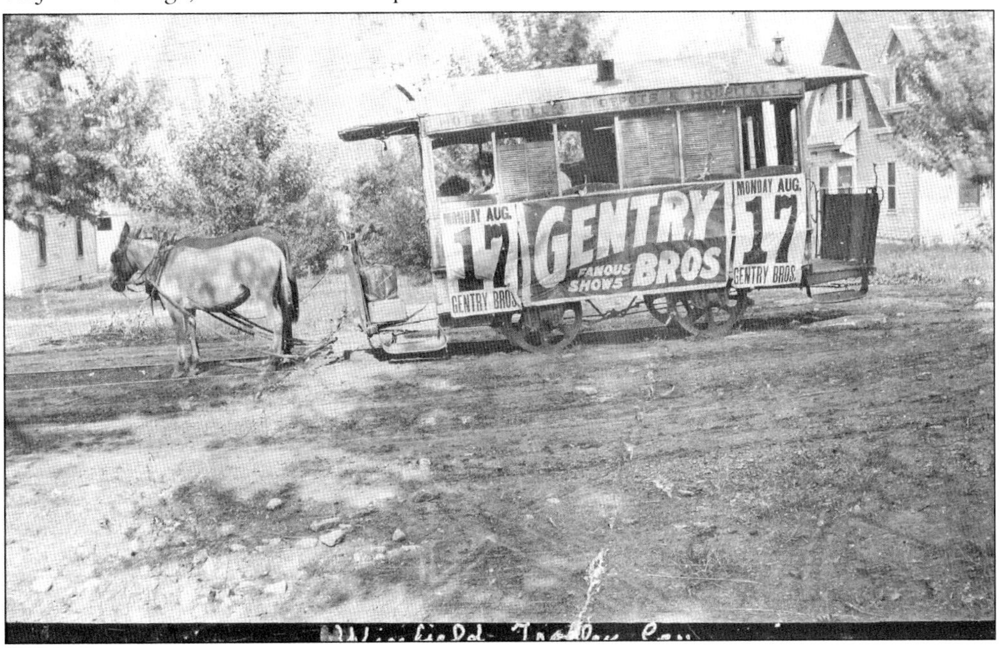


While they did keep a regular schedule, trolleys took extra runs during special events such as Chautauqua assemblies and fairs to allow easy access to the events advertised on their cars. The patient mules waited for people to shop downtown or at their doorstep as they prepared to leave their home. Children and adults alike enjoyed riding on the cars for the view and just for the fun of it.

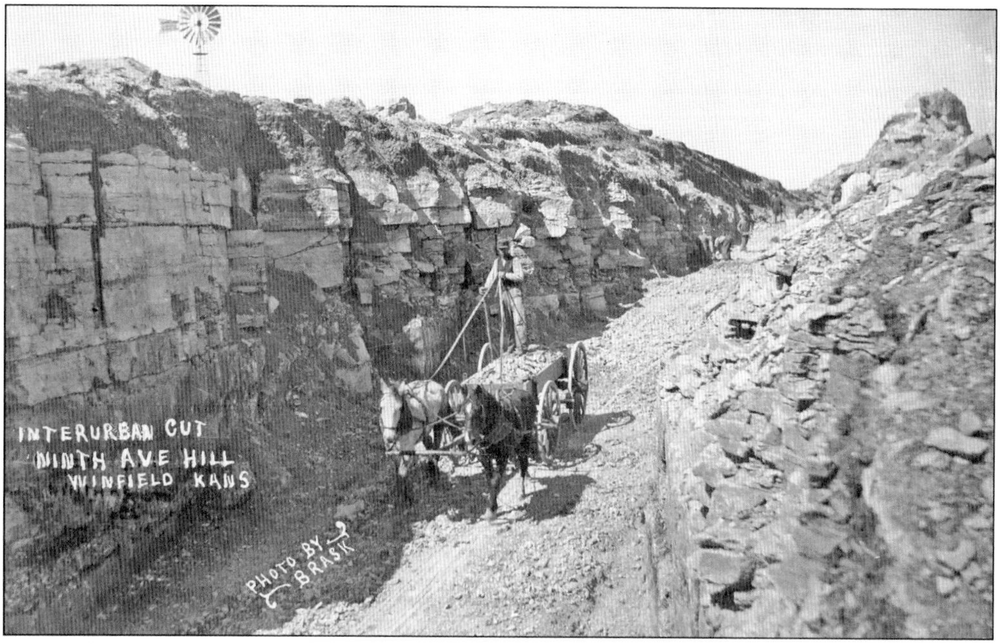


Laying the 10 miles of track for the trolley was most difficult on the line that went east on Ninth Avenue from Main Street and turned north onto College Street to stop at St. John's College and then out to Southwestern College. Lines also went north on Main Street to Island Park, west on Ninth Avenue to the fairgrounds, south on Main Street to Fourteenth Avenue, and then west to the Santa Fe Depot and fairgrounds.

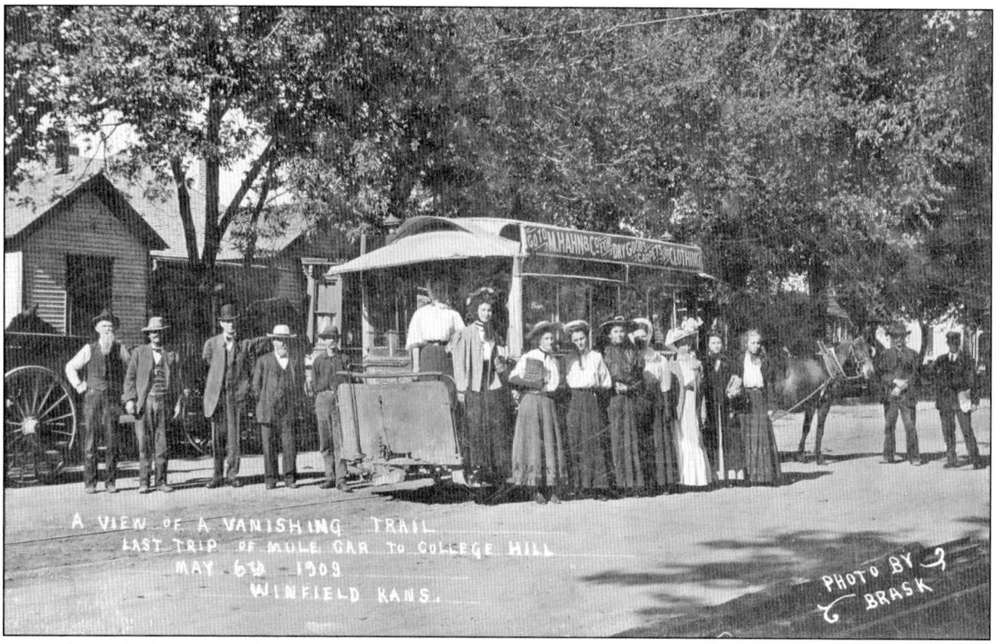


Schoolgirls holding books stand witness to a mule-drawn trolley's last trip up College Hill on May 6, 1909, on a trail that was indeed vanishing. Electric interurban transportation was on its way to Cowley County that year, so nostalgia tinged the city's view of the mule cars as Winfield moved ahead in the new century.

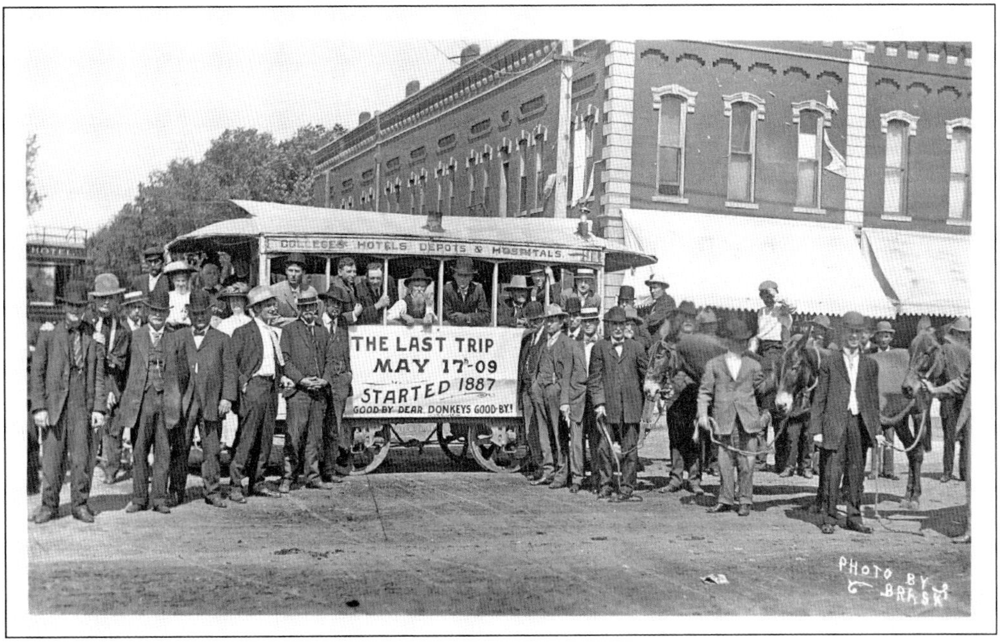


A crowd gathers at the corner of Tenth Avenue and Main Street on May 17, 1909, to commemorate the end of 22 years of mule-car service in Winfield. "Goodbye, dear donkeys, goodbye" was the sentiment as citizens anticipated the faster and more far-reaching public transportation that would come to Winfield that same year.

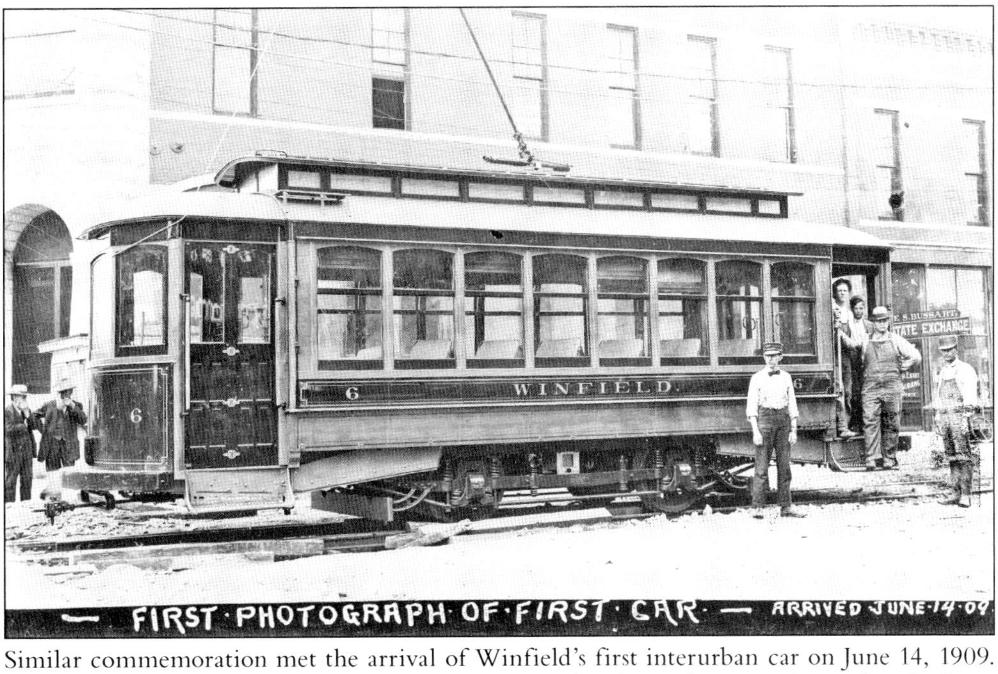


Similar commemoration met the arrival of Winfield's first interurban car on June 14, 1909. Local druggist W.H. Somermeier and others partnered with Southwestern Interurban Railway to bring freight and passenger service not only to Winfield but on to Hackney and Arkansas City, Kansas. Electricity powered the large and comfortable cars through poles and wheels that rolled on overhead cables. Cars added in 1911 featured improved heating systems and toilets.

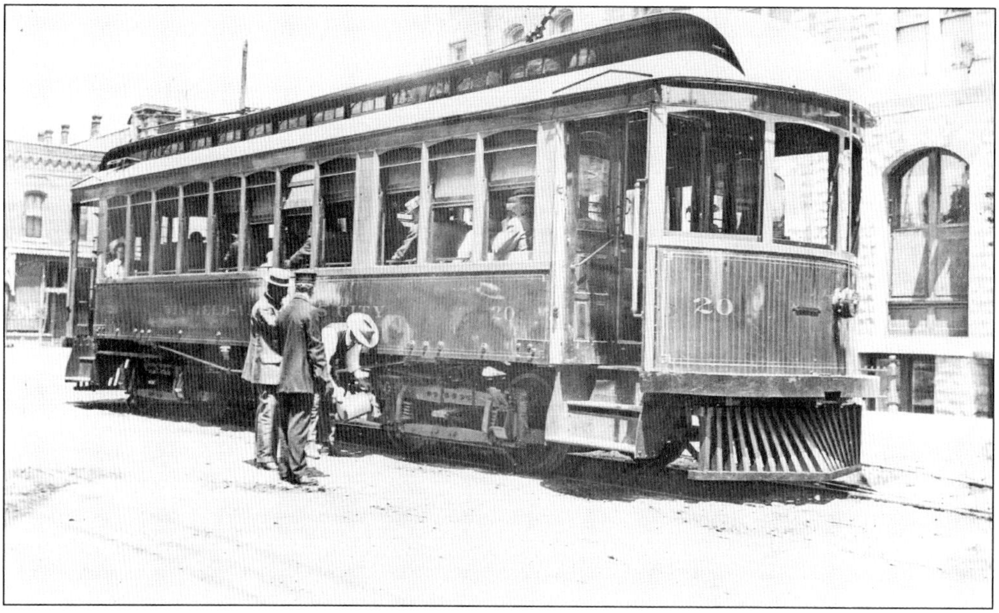

Passenger service composed over half of the interurban system's business. Early cars seated 30, but later editions held up to 75 people. Tickets were 25¢ to Arkansas City or 45¢ roundtrip with shorter distances prorated. Cars ran hourly between 6:00 a.m. and 11:00 p.m., making 18 runs daily. Special runs accommodated fairs, Chautauquas, and even school events between cities. Note the cowcatcher on the car pictured here.

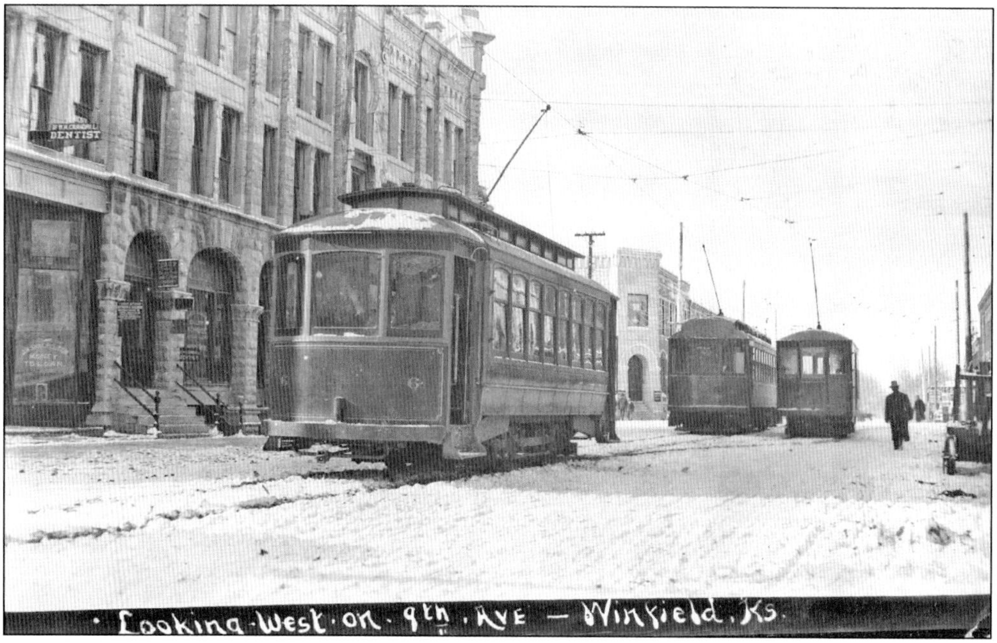


Four stops on the interurban line featured shelters for use in inclement weather, but they were all at stops between Winfield and Arkansas City, Kansas. Buildings, such as the north side of the First National Bank seen here, would have provided shelter for local workers, shoppers, students, and tourists waiting for the interurban. This card, postmarked 1914, also shows the web of electrical lines that ran the cars.

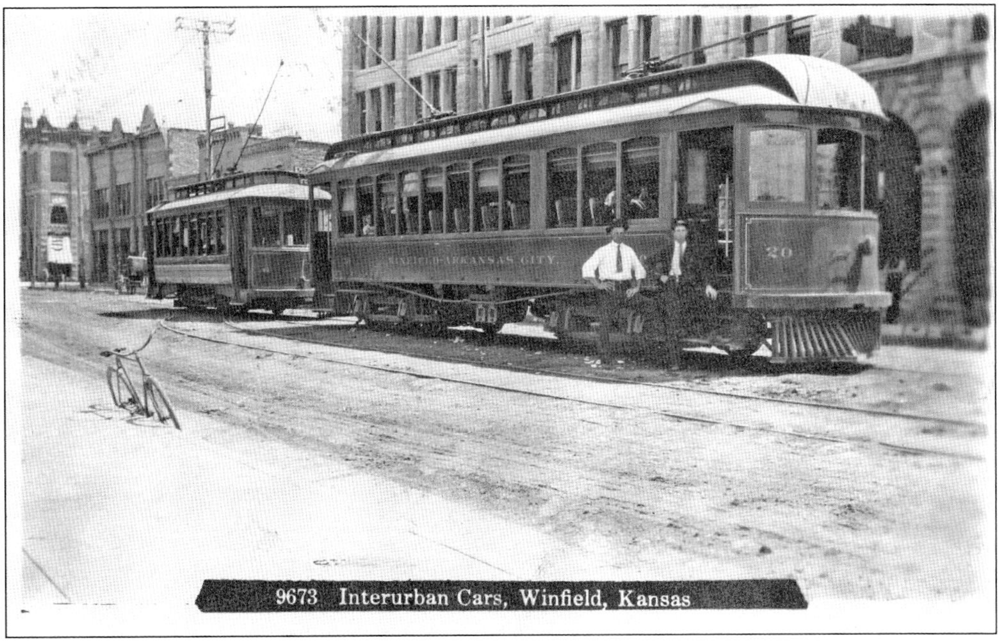


During its 17 years in Winfield, the interurban hauled freight in a boxcar once a day, every day. At its height, investors in the railway received up to a 14 percent return, and talk circulated about expanding into Oklahoma or up to Wichita, Kansas, but by 1919 improved roads and motor vehicles threatened the interurban way of travel. In 1926, Winfield made the switch to motorbuses, and the interurban era ended.

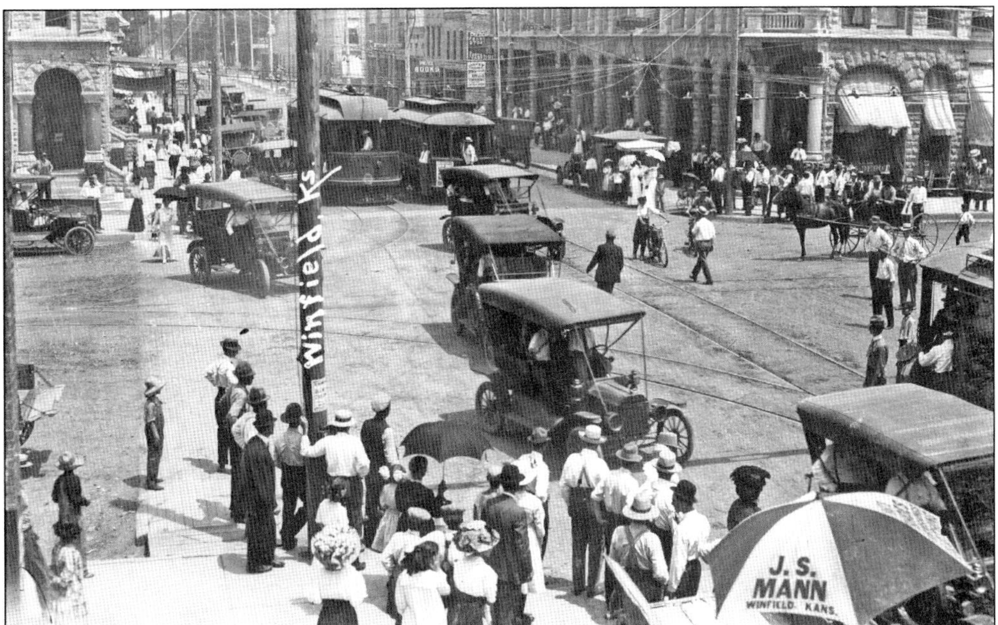


This view illustrates the changing modes of transportation in a growing Winfield. Women in fine hats and summer white dresses, men in straw hats and overalls, a bicyclist, and a horse-drawn wagon vie for space at the popular corner of Ninth Avenue and Main Street. By this time, interurban service had been reduced, and fares increased in a losing battle with progress.

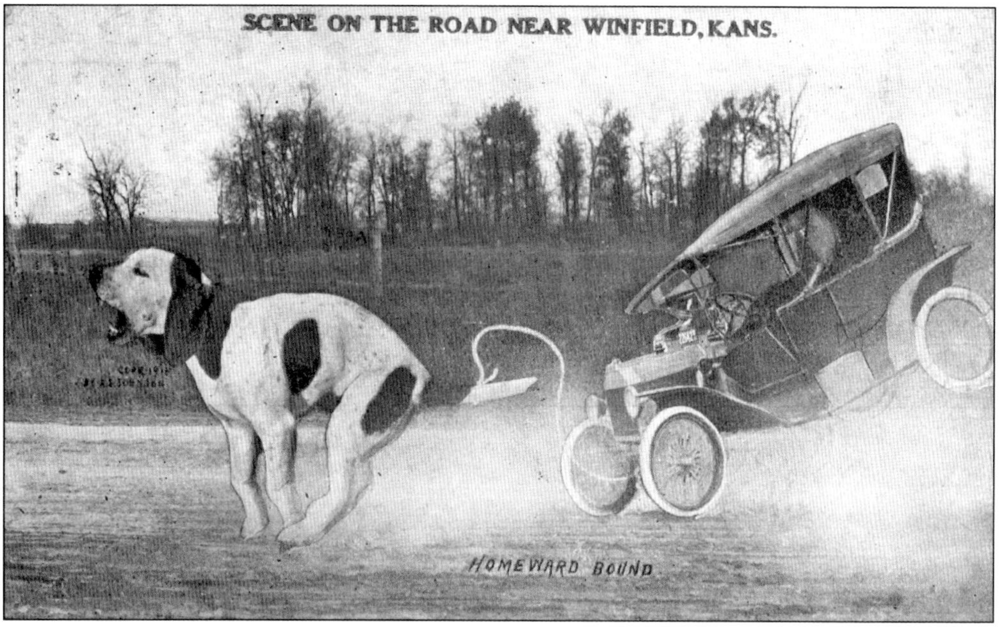


This humorous card dated 1910 reflects the state of local roads and reliability of early automobiles. For those without cars after the dismantling of the interurban system, Winfield's bus system, which changed ownership several times over the years, provided a travel option until 1965. Early tickets were only 5¢.

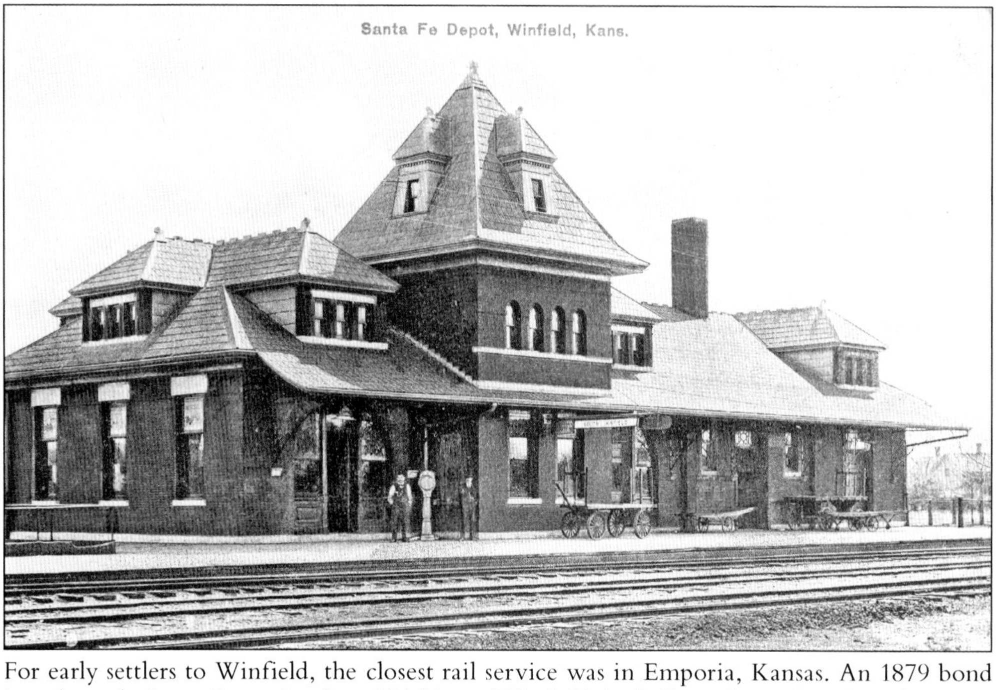


For early settlers to Winfield, the closest rail service was in Emporia, Kansas. An 1879 bond issue brought Santa Fe service from Wichita to Winfield, including telegraph and mail service. Winfield's first train arrived on September 30, 1879, greeted by crowds and celebrated with a parade, a barbeque, and a baseball game at the fairgrounds. Construction on the handsome redbrick depot on West Fourteenth Avenue near the fairgrounds pictured here began in 1886.

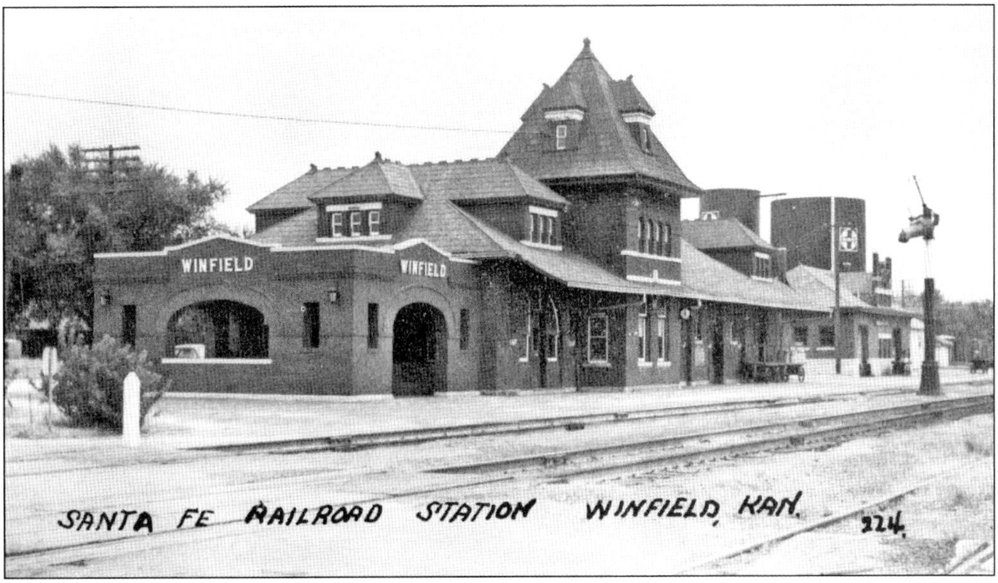


The depot provided sleeping rooms upstairs and waiting rooms for men and women. In 1937, a Santa Fe streamliner train began daily stops in Winfield, running between Kansas City and Oklahoma City, Oklahoma. The Santa Fe discontinued service to this station in 1971, and no amount of community support saved it from razing. Images of it join those of the mule trolleys and interurbans to remind Winfield of what once was.

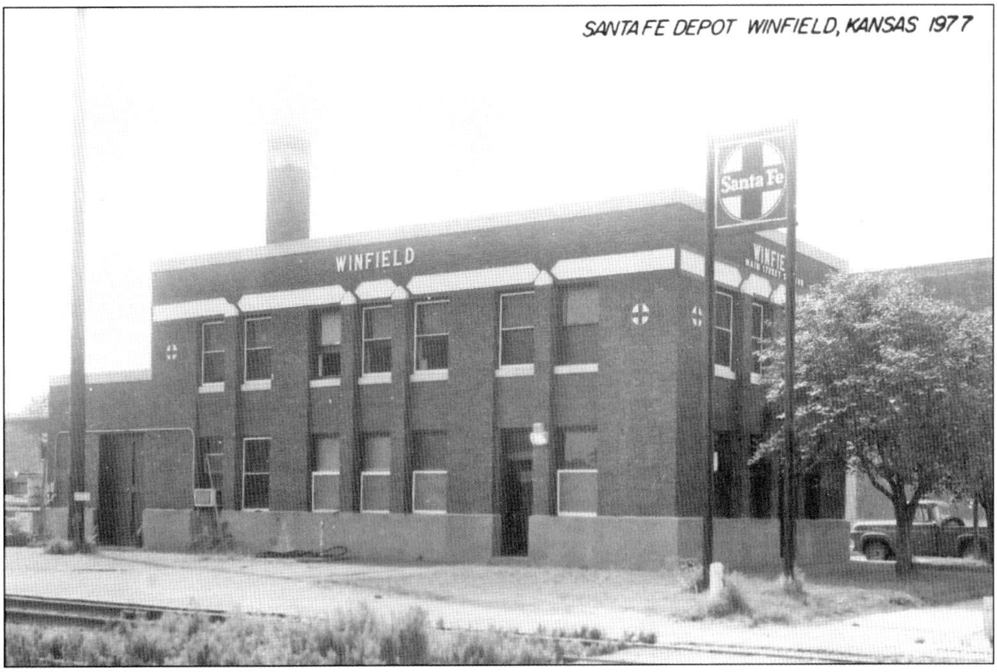


This redbrick building, still standing on the east side of Main Street and Fifth Avenue, opened in 1926 and cost the Atchison, Topeka, & Santa Fe over $100,000. When first built, it housed a passenger depot and local Santa Fe offices, but its main purpose was the handling of freight. When it opened, the Santa Fe employed 106 men, making it one of the largest employers at the time.

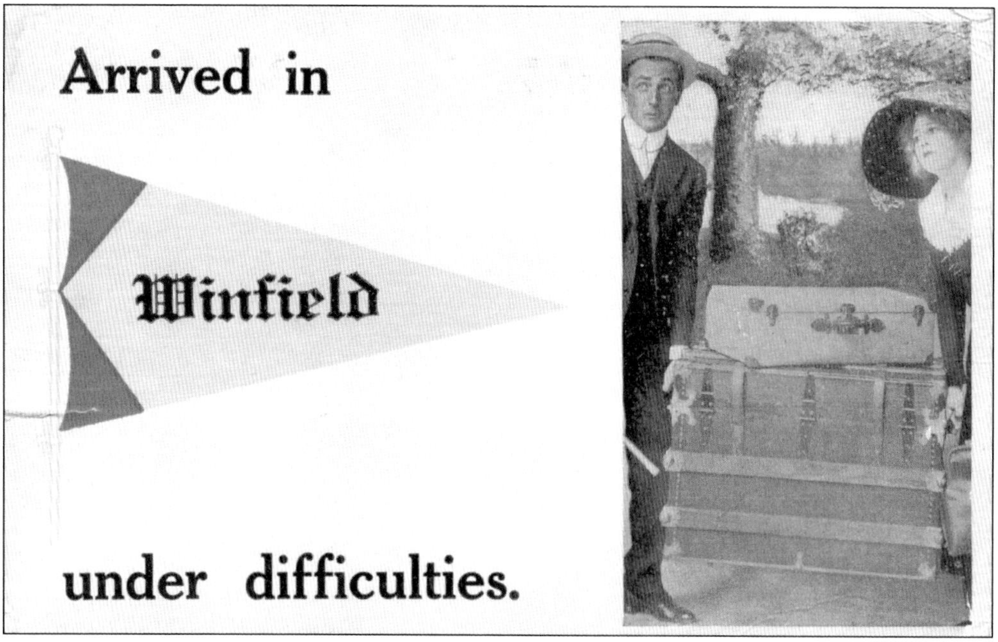


This postcard sent in 1916 to an Army sergeant in Texas likely provided a chuckle about his hometown. Due to the confluence of highways and train service, all roads led to Winfield. Tracks for three railroads (the Southern Kansas/ATSF, Missouri Pacific, and Frisco) intersected on West Fifth Avenue. Even now, the corner of Ninth Avenue and Main Street marks the confluence of US 160 and US 77.

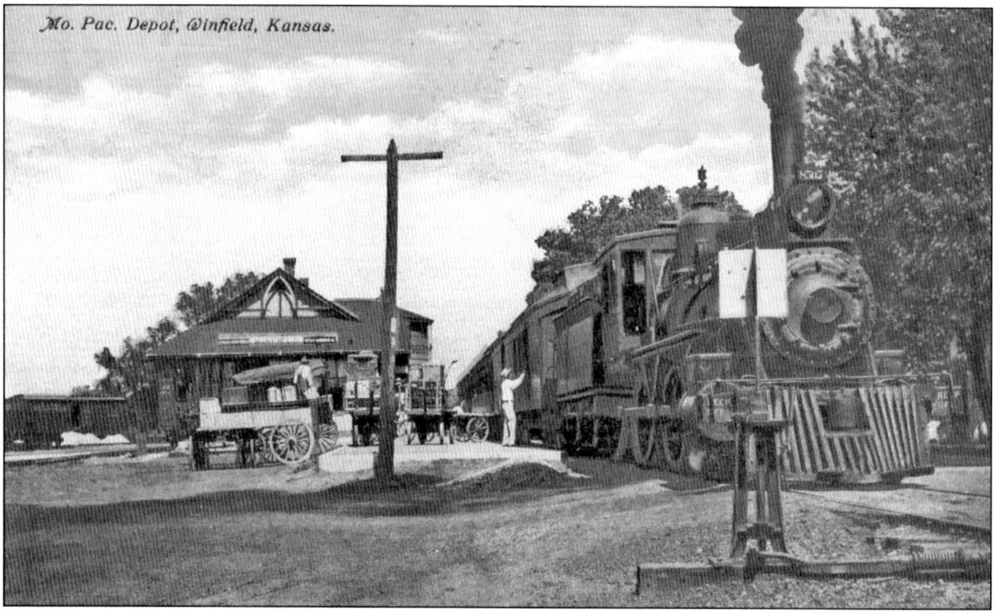


This postcard, sent in 1911 by a Winfield woman to her sister in Washington, DC, shows the original Missouri Pacific Railroad depot, located near Sixth Avenue and Loomis Street. This railroad, the last line to reach Winfield, arrived in May 1887. In 1916, with a push from the railroad committee of the Commercial Club, a redbrick depot with a tile roof, two waiting rooms, and a baggage room was built.

# *Seven*

# WINFIELD AT LEISURE

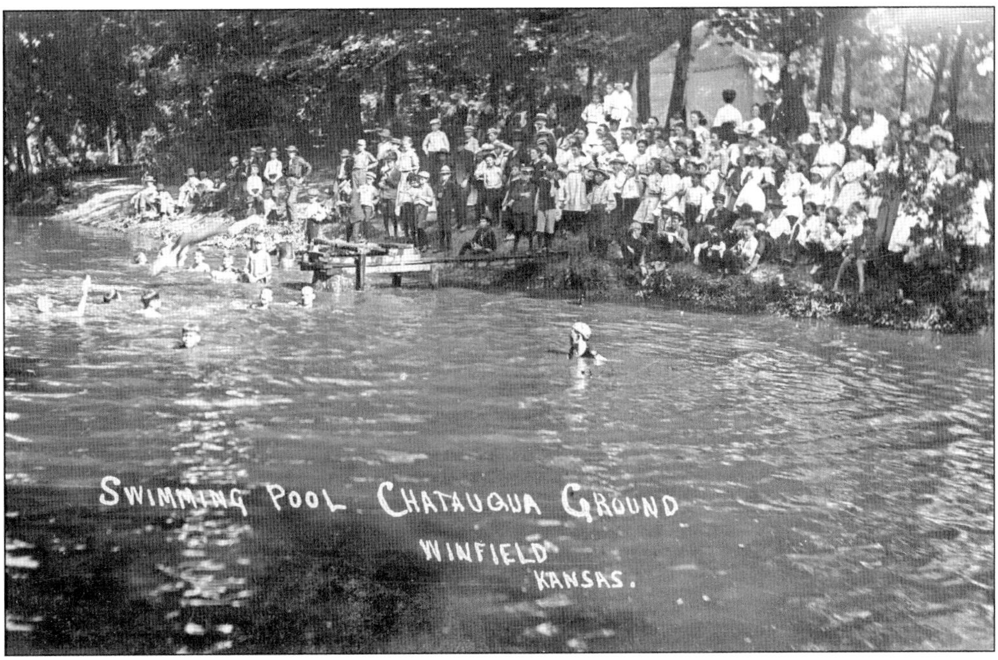


The Chautauqua assemblies, held each summer in Winfield from 1887 to 1924, brought up to 10,000 people at a time to Winfield, many of whom planned their vacation around the event. Stressing education and spiritual growth for adults, the programming for children included swimming and, in 1902, a visit from the founder of basketball, James Naismith, who oversaw the boys' club that year. Even Winfield's play was purposeful.

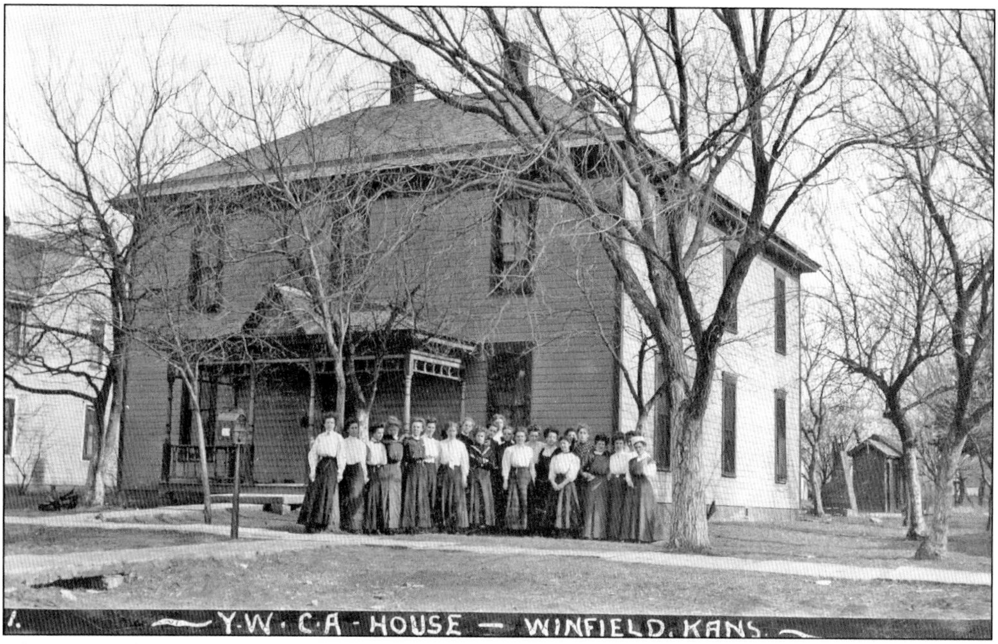


The YWCA house served primarily Southwestern College girls, blending fun with faith. Members could choose from many activities, including weekly devotional meetings, noon prayer meetings, mission study, Bible study, and visiting the sick. The financial committee sold homemade candy as well as college pennants and cushions, and the membership committee faithfully met trains to welcome female students to Winfield.

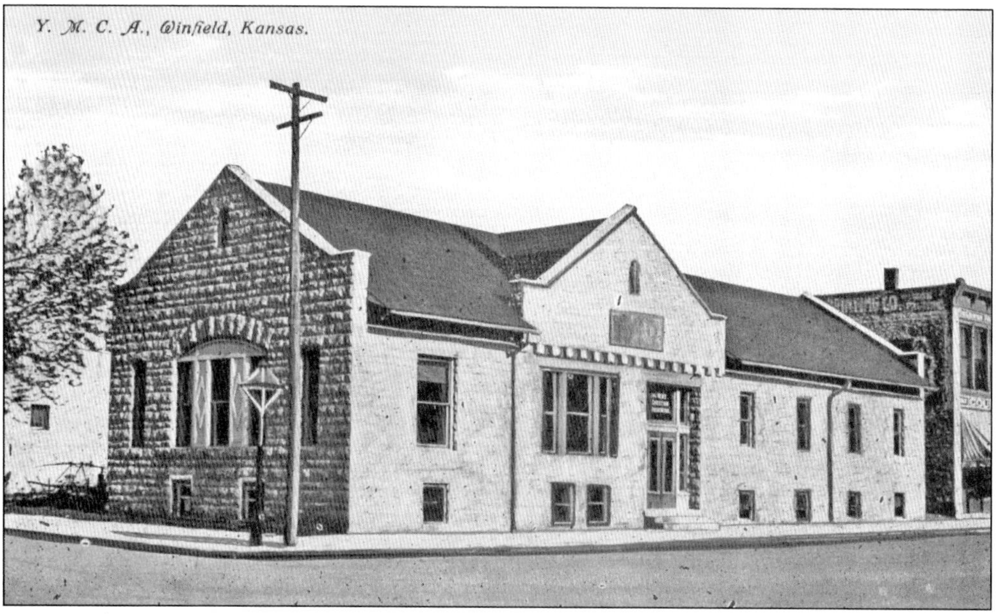


In 1903, the city YMCA opened. Built of cut stone, it stood at the corner of Tenth Avenue and Millington Street. The basement housed a bowling alley, lockers, and baths, while the main floor featured a gymnasium, meeting rooms, a well-stocked reading room, and offices. When support for the YMCA waned, the building became the Commercial Club but was later razed for the creation of a parking lot that remains today.

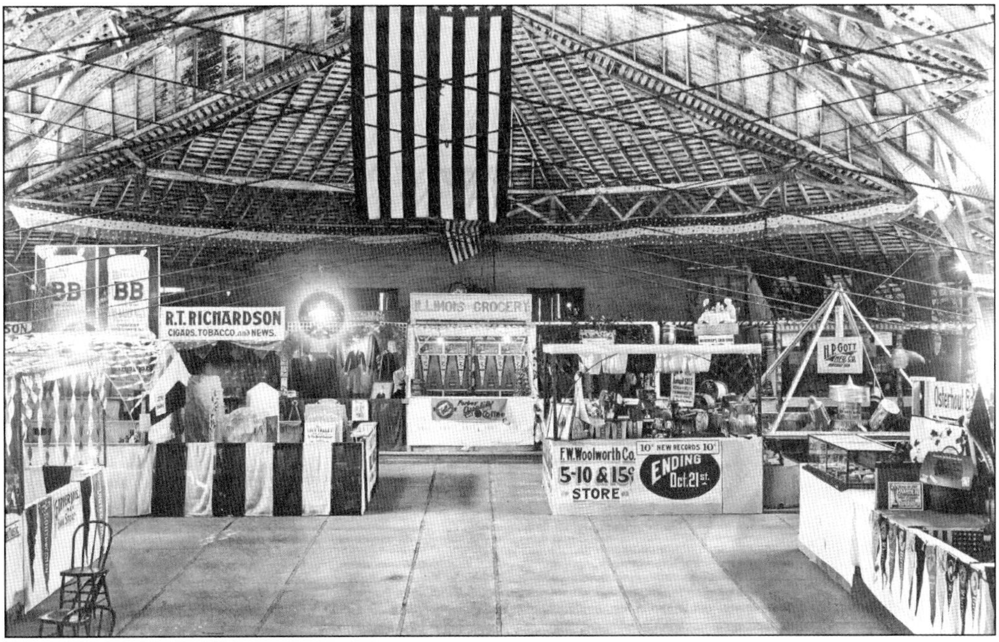


October 4–7, 1916, marked the first Fall Festival in Winfield. The October 5, 1916, *Winfield Daily Free Press* reported, "More than 10,000 people thronged Island Park yesterday." The free event, which grew from the annual Farmers and Merchants Picnic, featured displays from local farms and businesses as well as bands and contests for all age groups, from dolls and fiddling to pie and melon eating.

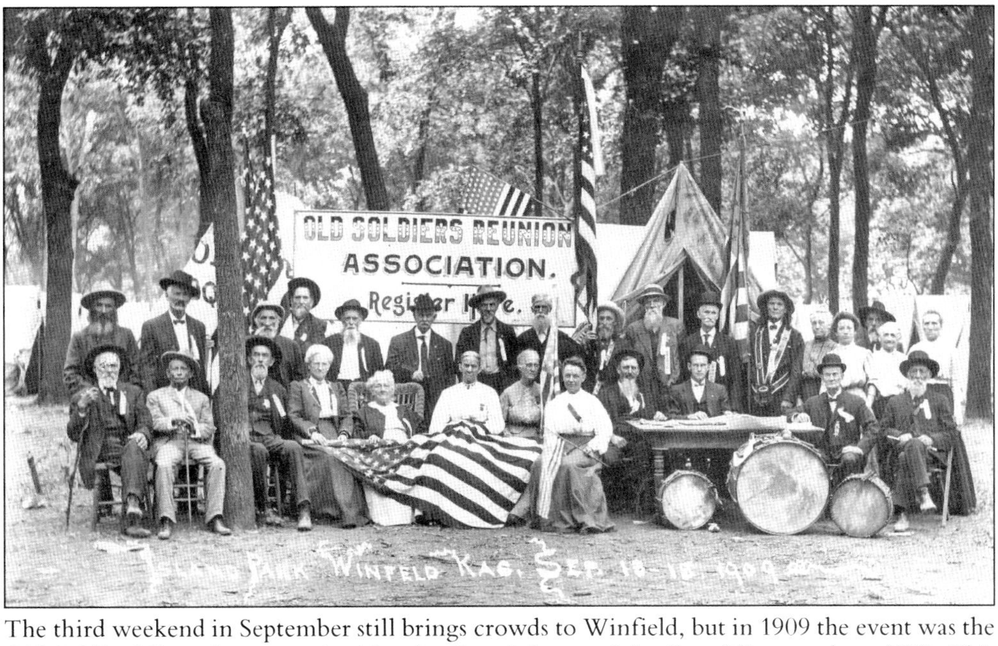


The third weekend in September still brings crowds to Winfield, but in 1909 the event was the Old Soldiers' Reunion, organized by the Grand Army of the Republic as early as 1881. This association, formed to remember the Civil War dead and assist the veterans and their families, held gatherings, encampments, and parades throughout the year, particularly on Memorial Day and the Fourth of July.

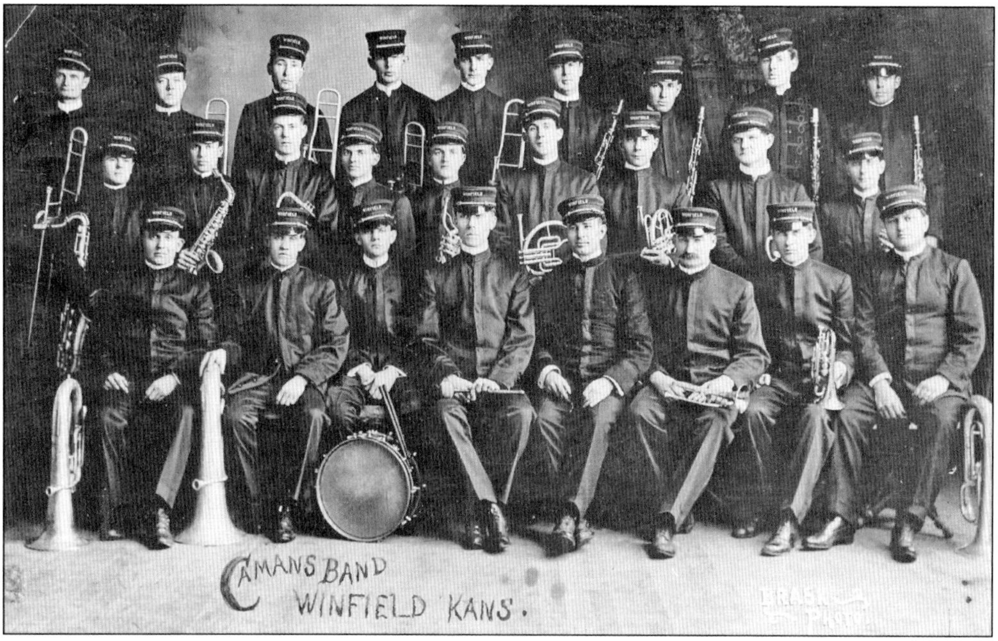


Caman's Winfield Military Band Association formed in 1895 from the remnants of "Caton's Dozen." Under the direction of W.H. Caman and leadership from Harry A. Caton, it performed outside of Kansas. It evolved into the Winfield City Band and began admitting women in 1937. The band played at Ninth Avenue and Main Street, Island Park, Memorial Park, and finally on the lawn of Meyer Hall, where it still entertains today.

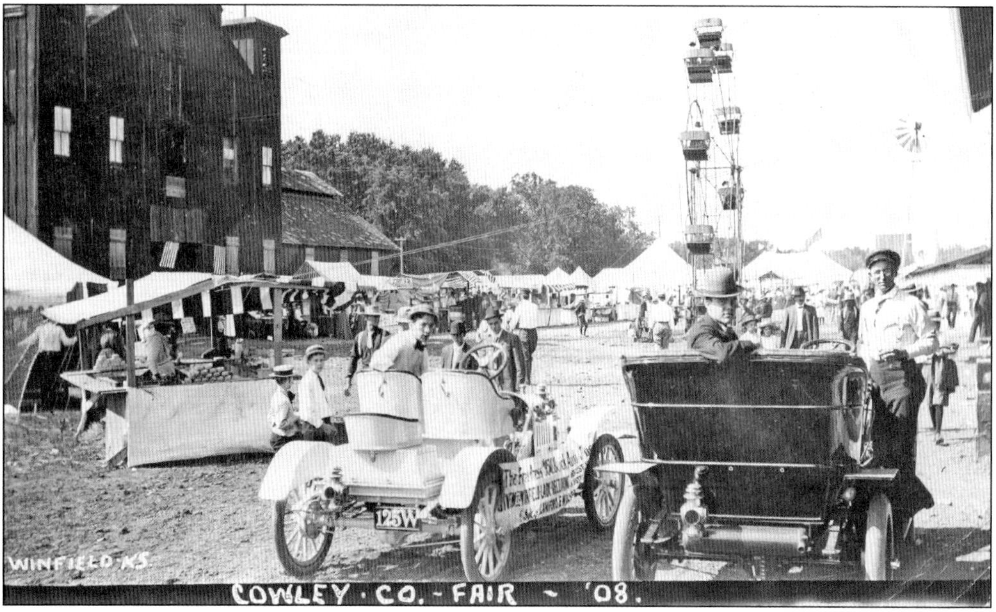


County fairs were held as early as 1872, but they did not become regular events until the current fairgrounds on the west side of town were purchased in 1883. Horse and car racing, circuses, and baseball games joined fairs in events held on the grounds. A grandstand was built in 1916 and updated over the years. In 1971, the Walnut Valley Festival began its long-running history at the fairgrounds, come rain or high water.

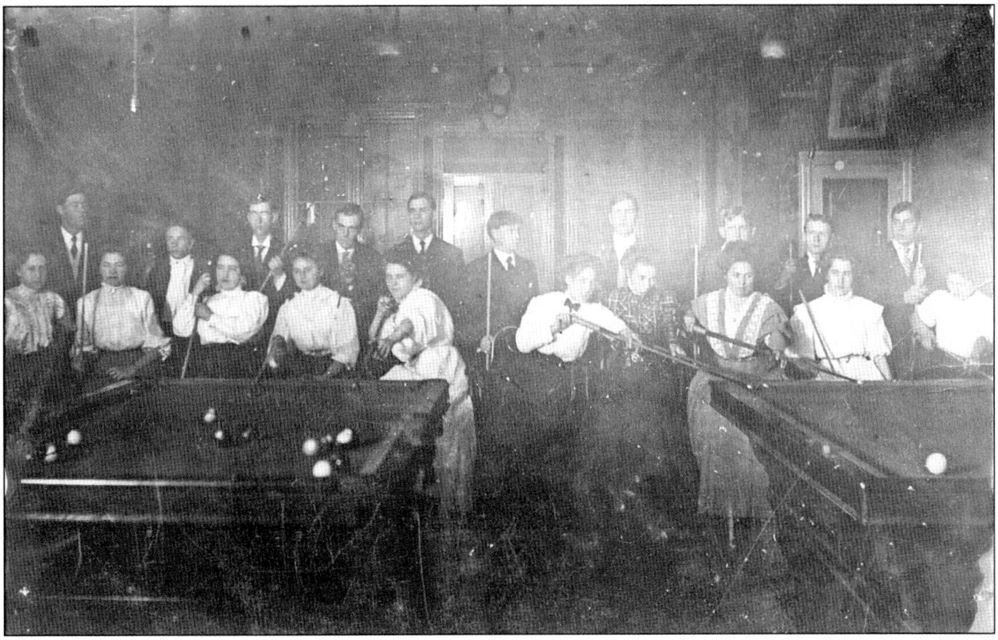

Indoor activities in early-day Winfield included a game of pool at McClain's, located at 902 Main Street, one of many places in town to play. By 1914, discussion on the propriety of pool halls began, and in 1915 an ordinance closed pool halls by 10:00 p.m. on weeknights. An ordinance closed public pool halls for good in Winfield in 1916, but discussion continued for years after.

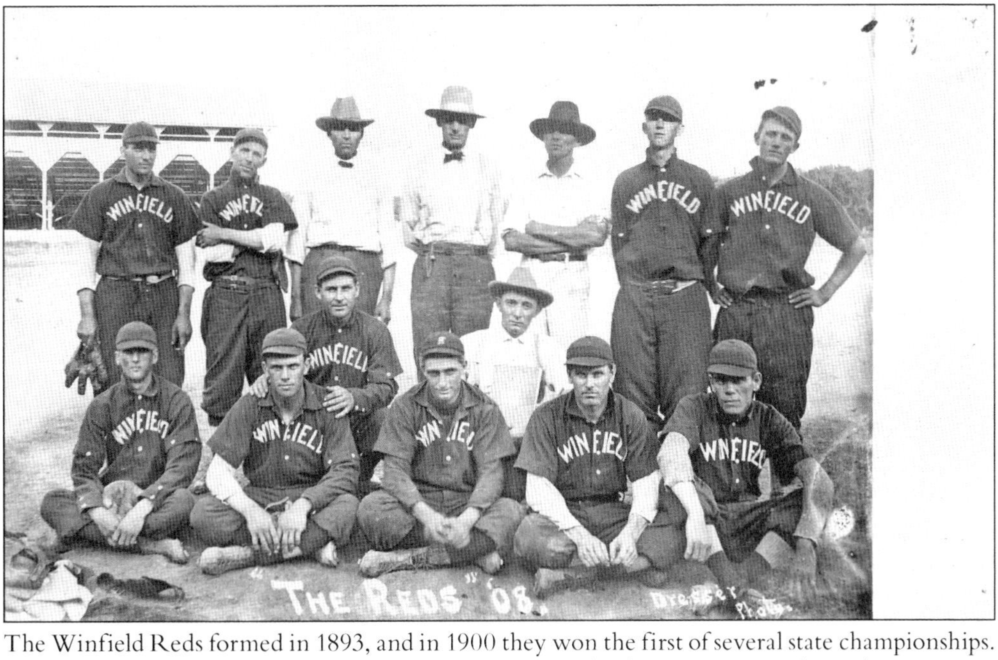


The Winfield Reds formed in 1893, and in 1900 they won the first of several state championships. This postcard lists the names of the 1908 team on its back. Newspapers show the team was still around in 1915, playing warm-up games with the Southwestern boys' team prior to their season opener.

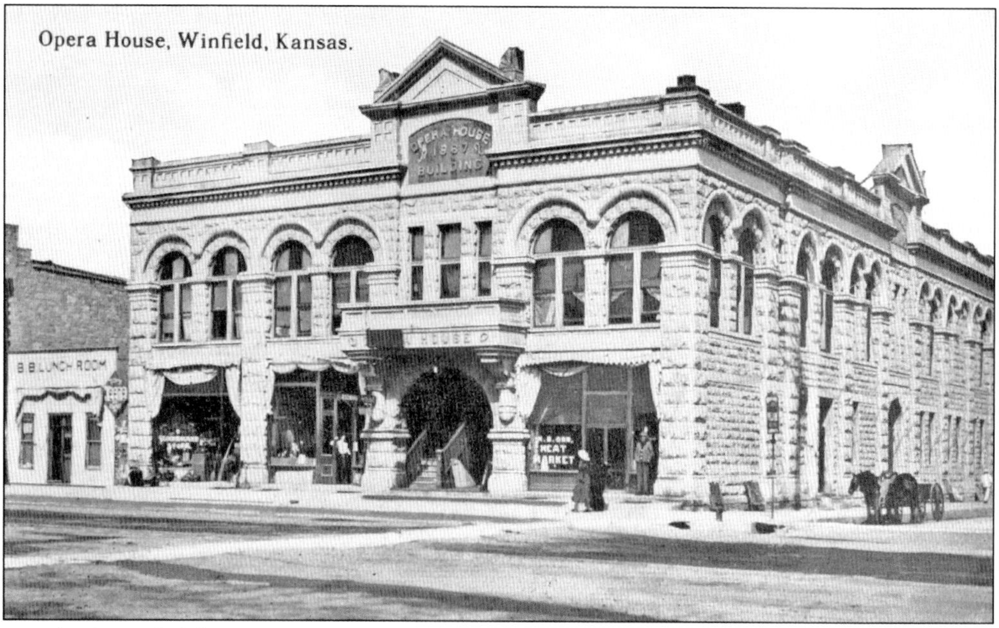


Word of Winfield's opera house spread around the state when it opened in 1888. Costing $60,000 to build, it boasted a crystal chandelier with 64 gas burners and seated 610 on the floor and 80 more in the balcony. Box seating around the huge stage featured plush chairs. Schools held graduations here until 1916, and the Winfield College of Music, which opened in 1899, used its second floor.

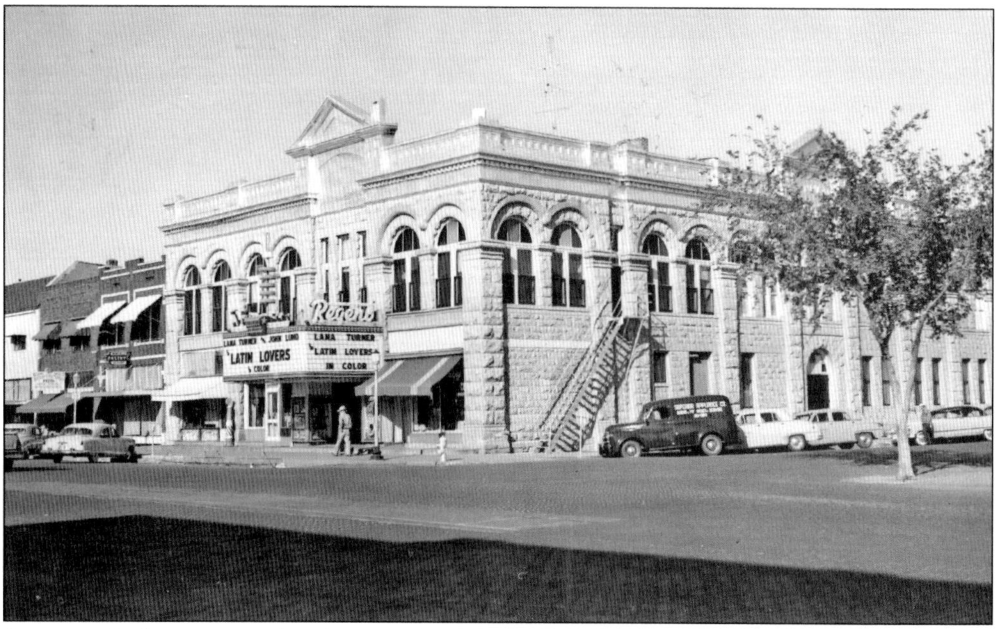


Once movies became popular, the opera house provided a home for the Regent Theatre. A major remodel in 1925 removed much of the showy detail, and fans gave way to air-conditioning in 1951. The building continued to be used for music programs and for Miss Winfield pageants, but it was demolished in 1962. Theaters standing before the Regent included the Novelty, the Jewel, and the Airdome.

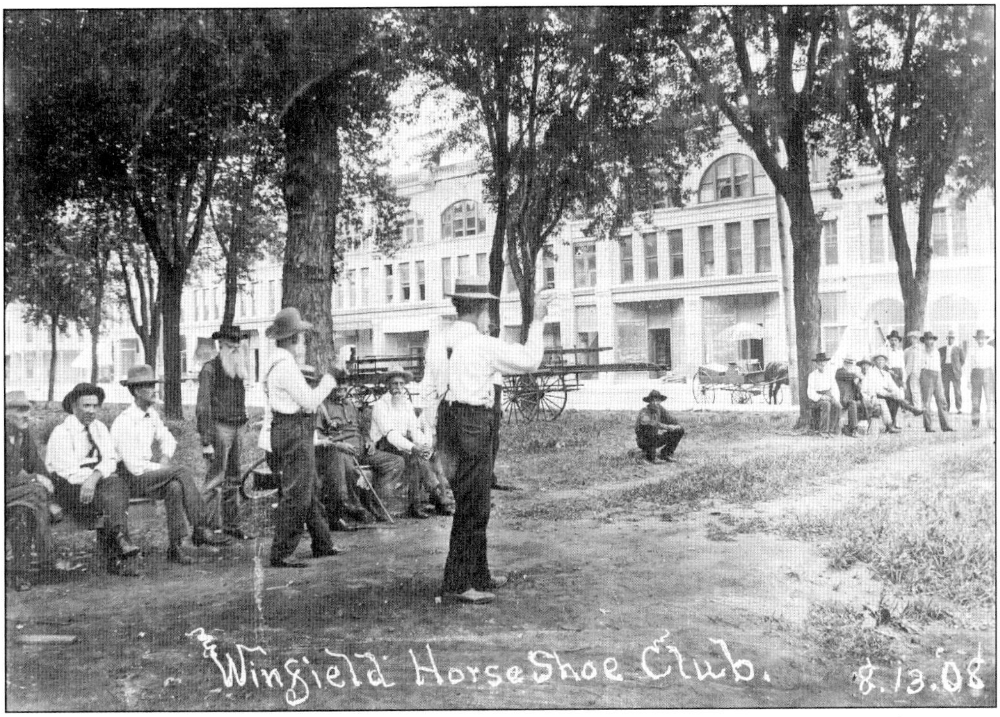


In 1908, the location of the Cowley County Courthouse on its block facing Tenth Avenue between Loomis and Fuller Streets allowed ample space for the Winfield Horseshoe Club to play across the street from the Hackney Block on Ninth Avenue. In September 1910, it moved to Island Park for a reunion week. Winfield's oldest athletic club moved to the grounds west of the Commercial Club on Millington Street in the 1920s.

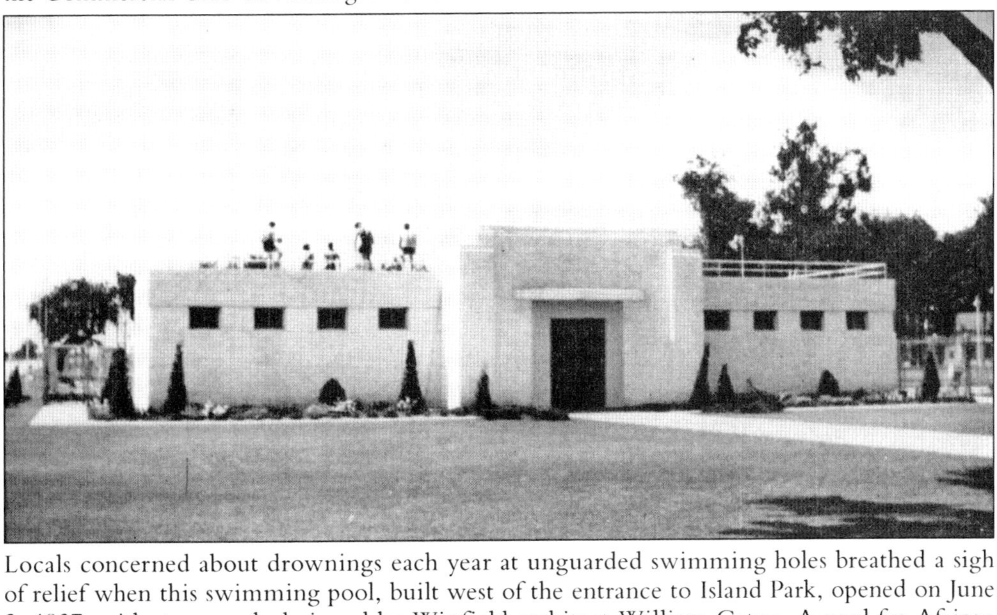

Locals concerned about drownings each year at unguarded swimming holes breathed a sigh of relief when this swimming pool, built west of the entrance to Island Park, opened on June 2, 1937, with stonework designed by Winfield architect William Caton. A pool for African American citizens opened that same year across the street, to the east. That pool closed in 1950, and its site now houses the Winfield Aquatic Center.

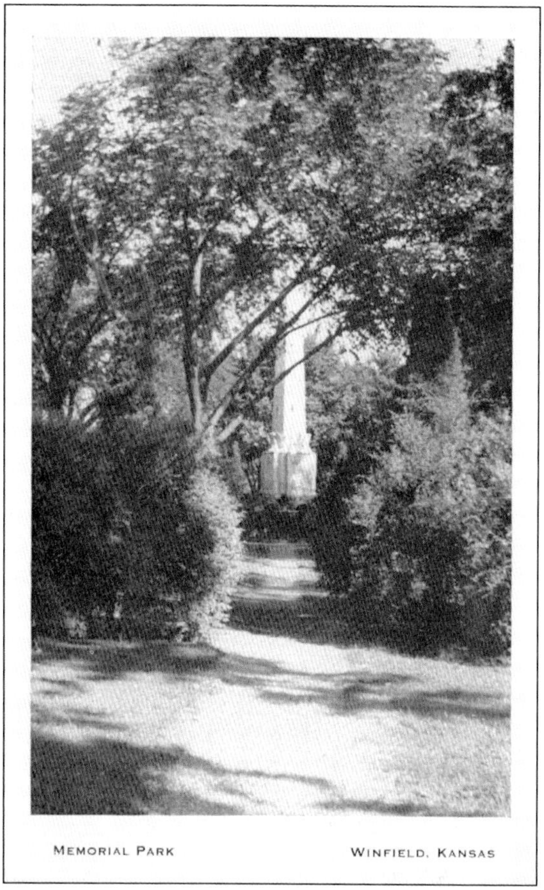

MEMORIAL PARK WINFIELD, KANSAS

In 1920, Winfield voters authorized the building of a soldiers' memorial on the block between Fuller and Andrews Streets on Ninth Avenue. This required the razing of the homes of D.A. Millington at Tenth Avenue and Andrews and W.C. Robinson at Ninth Avenue and Fuller Street, both then belonging to Robinson. The war memorial dedication occurred on Veterans Day 1925. A Vietnam War memorial was constructed in 1989 on the west side of the park.

This card features Riverside Park on the banks of the Walnut River, one of several picnic areas in early Winfield. A unique operation sponsored in 1900 by Caman's Band in Pastime Park, outside of Winfield, offered steamboat rides on the Walnut River, but the enterprise lasted only one year. Hiatt's Park, north of the Walnut River off Fourteenth Avenue, provided natural springs with its picnic areas, but it closed in 1914 after three years of operation.

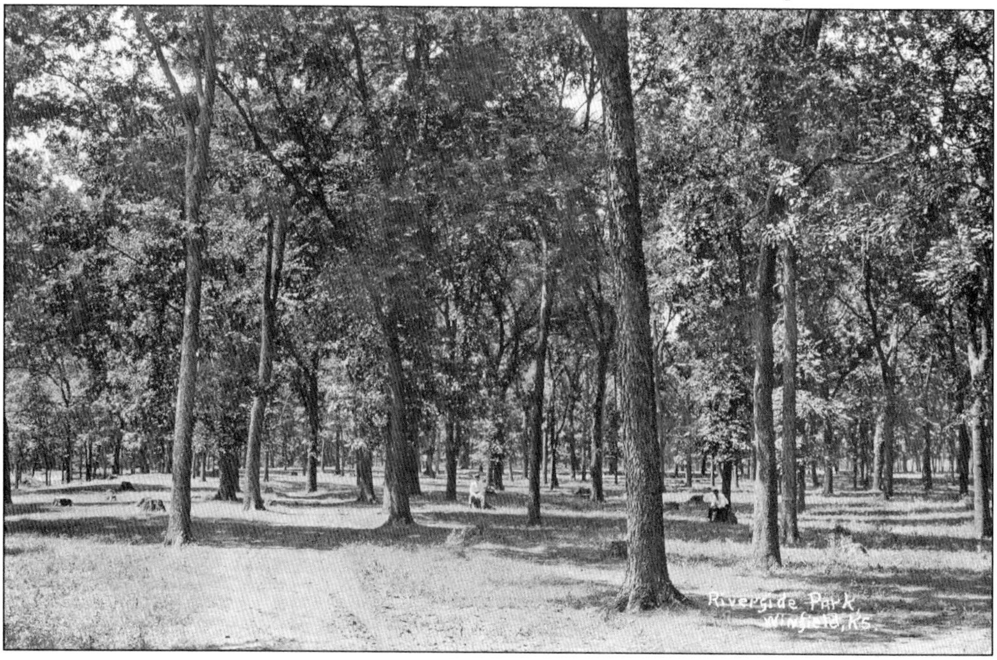

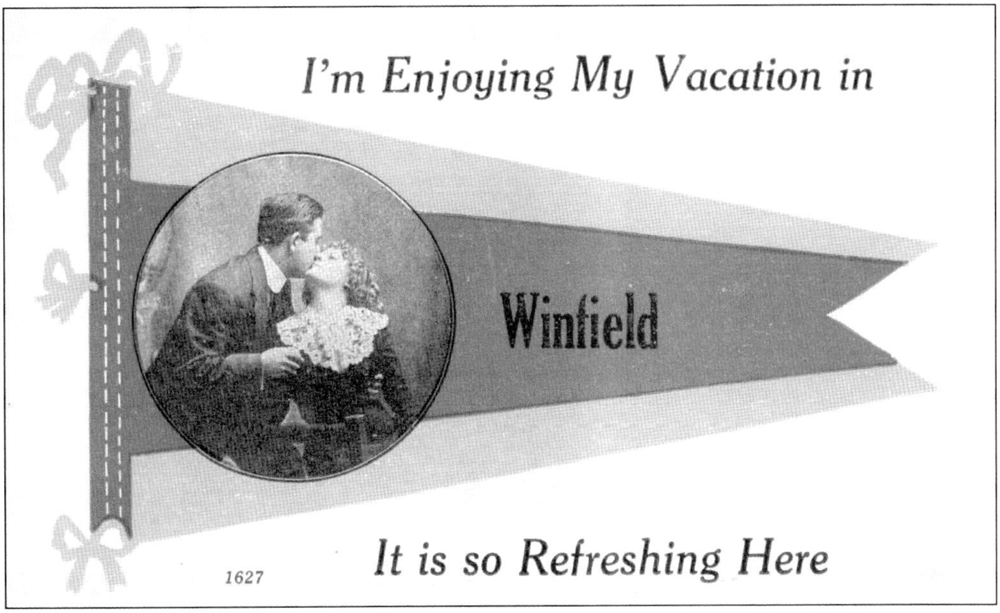


For the person sending this postcard in 1915, a visit to Winfield would likely have involved attending the Chautauqua assembly. This movement began in 1874 with a series of programs for Sunday school teachers held at Lake Chautauqua, New York. By 1876, similar assemblies began outside New York. By 1878, the Chautauqua assembly came to Kansas, and in June 1887 Winfield hosted its first assembly in what is now Island Park.

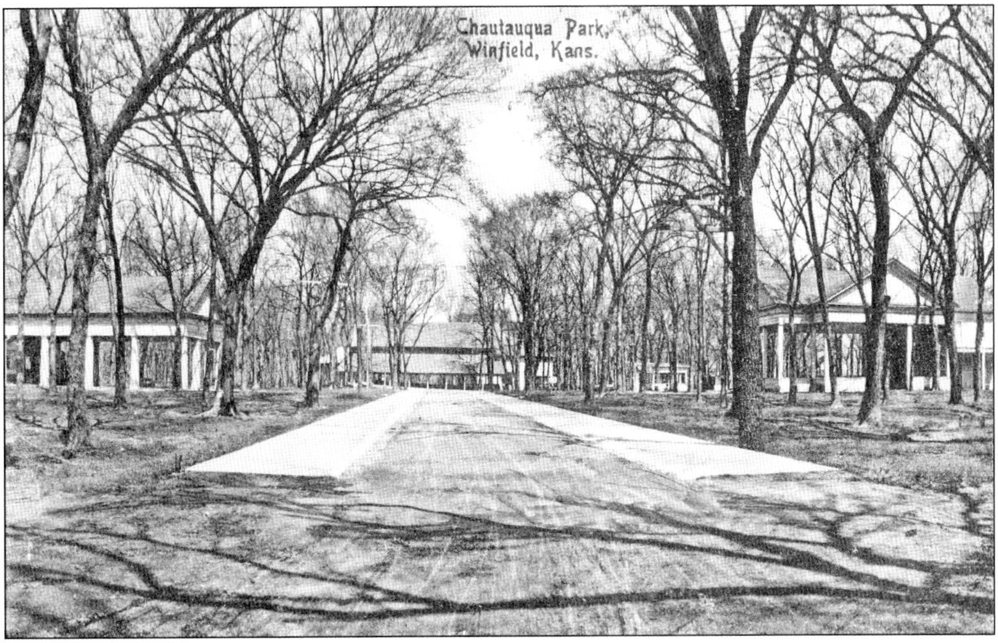


In 1887, Island Park was the property of the North Side Town Company and underwent improvement for the first annual Chautauqua assembly. The tabernacle, built in 1887, can be seen in the background. The Hall of Philosophy, added in 1902, is on the west. To the east was the lecture hall, constructed in 1903 along with tennis courts and a croquet field on the park grounds.

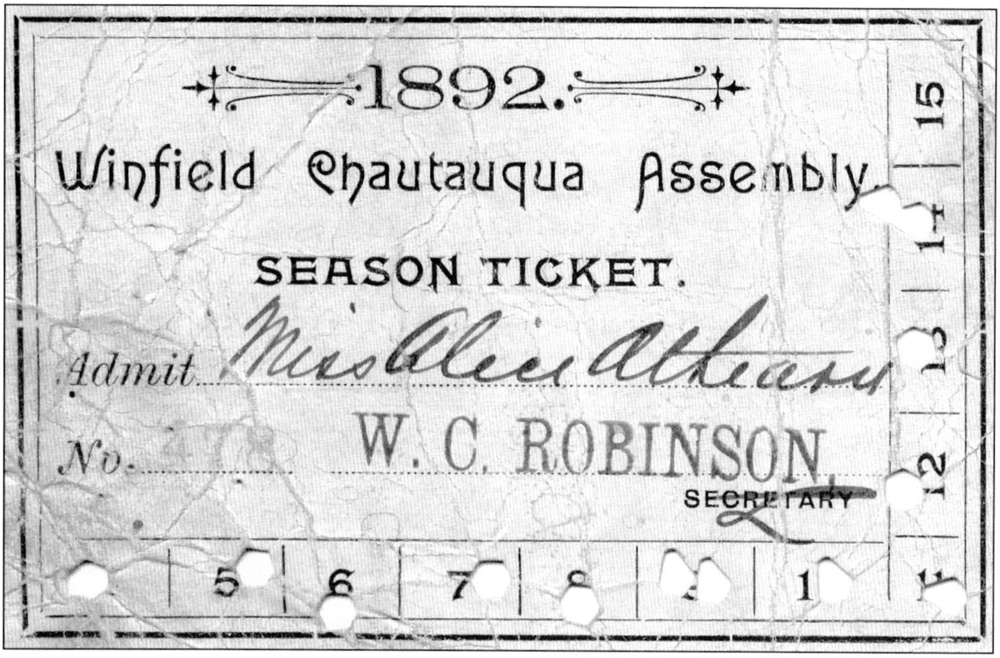


A season ticket to the Winfield Chautauqua Assembly cost about $2 for 10 days of educational and religious lectures, musical and dramatic presentations, art classes, and recreational opportunities planned by the association's local board of directors. Attendees were encouraged to camp to receive the full benefit of the Chautauqua experience, and even local people rented the more than 200 tents provided each year.

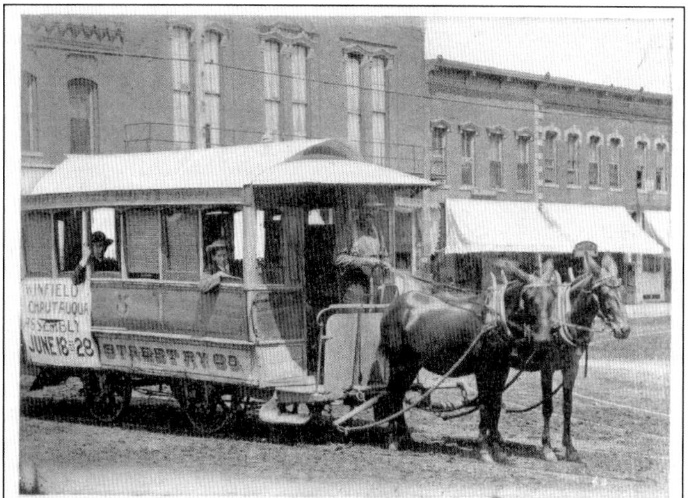


The Union Street Railway mule-car service, chartered in 1886, dedicated some cars for shuttle service during the Chautauqua and advertised that it met all trains. The stables for the mules were located west of Island Park, and the track ran from Island Park down Main Street to the Santa Fe Depot on Fourteenth Avenue, providing easy access for Chautauqua visitors not only to the park but also downtown Winfield.

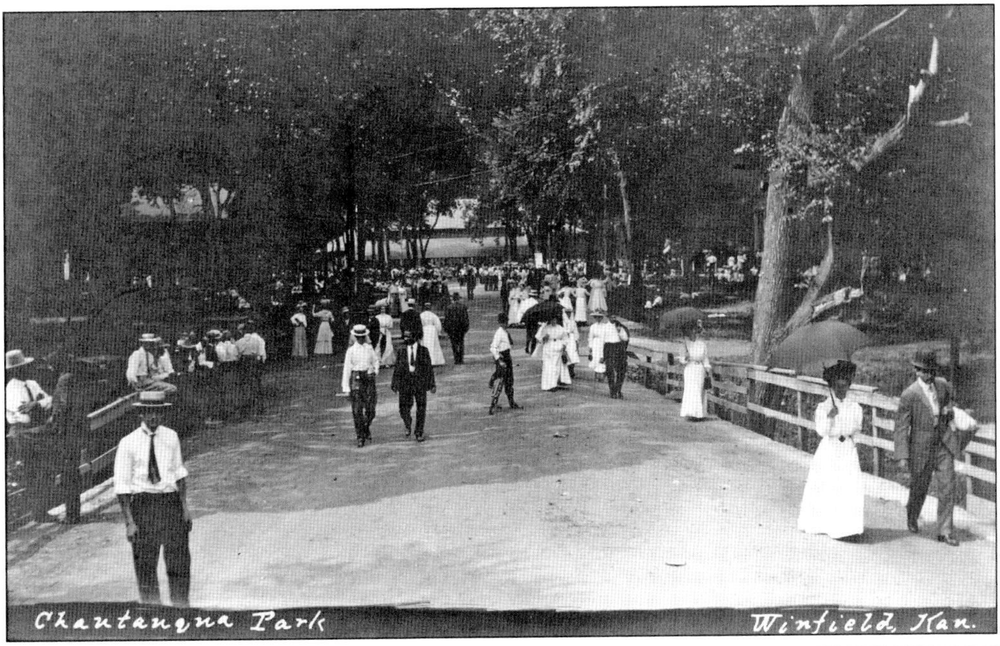


Once the Chautauqua took the park as its permanent home, its board of directors encouraged city ownership. An 1891 bond election accomplished this and provided the official name Island Park, but it remained Chautauqua Park for many years in the minds of the public. The park's entrance featured a grand archway and ticket booth at its outer edge and provided a promenade for Chautauqua attendees as shown in this card.

Chautauqua Assembly
JULY 11 TO 21
ISLAND PARK, WINFIELD, KANSAS

Program of C. L. S. C. Round Table
4:00 p. m. each day
Henrietta V. Race, A. M., Director

July 12—Monolog, "A Certain Rich Man," F. L. Gilson of Southwestern College.
July 13—Reading, Sarah M. Willmer, Chicago.
July 15—Recognition Day. Processional. Passing of Golden Gate and Arches. Address, H. J. Waters, Pres. Kansas Agricultural College. Presenting of diplomas to class of 1912.

Kansas History Series, Mrs. Margaret Hill-McCarter

July 16—"Nature's Masonry."
July 17—"The Footprints of Spain and France."
July 18—"Historic Highways."
July 19—"The Shadow of Old Glory."
Jule 20—"The White Man's Burden."

*"To Thine Own Self Be True"*
Motto, Class 1912

HULVEY PRINTING CO.

This program from the 1912 Chautauqua demonstrates the assembly's major focus: the Chautauqua Literary and Scientific Circle (CLSC). This four-year home-study program culminated in an annual recognition ceremony, complete with diplomas, held at the assembly for those people completing the cycle. Winfield became known as the "Chautauqua Capital of Southern Kansas" due to its large number of CLSC graduates, which, by 1912, was reported to be about 400.

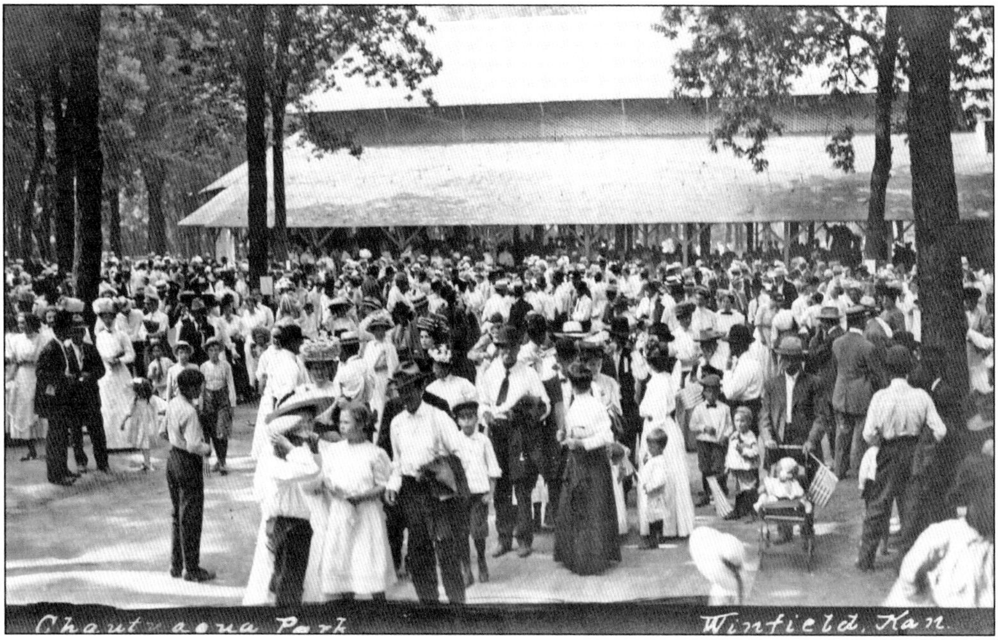

The tabernacle served as the central meeting place and was first lit by electric lights in 1888. A 1903 remodeling project enlarged it to seat 3,000 with room for 500 on stage. Money for improvements to the park was set aside from each season's returns by the Chautauqua Association Board of Directors.

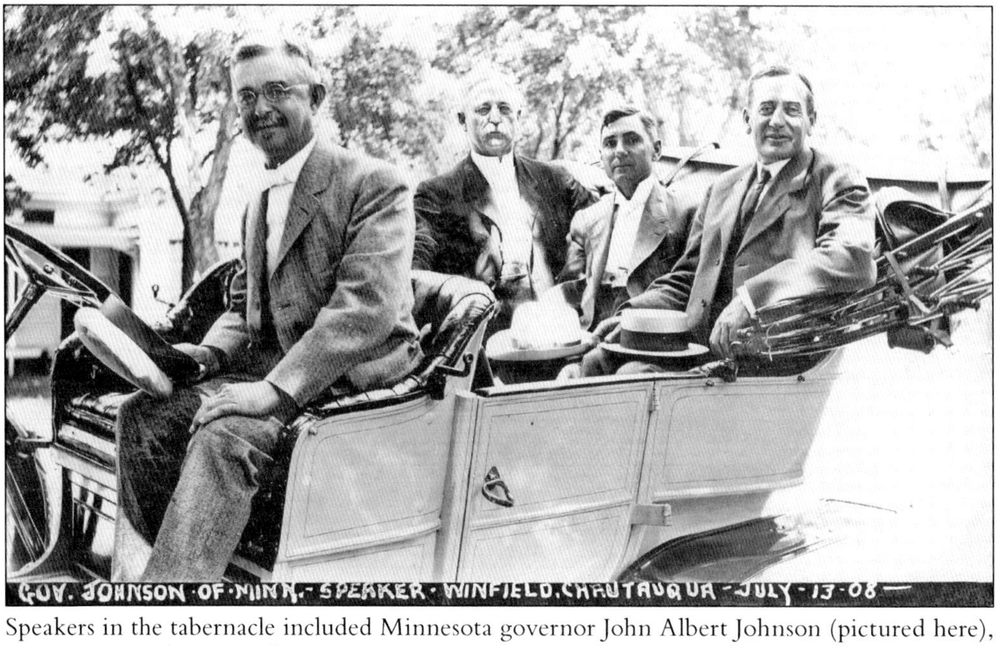

Speakers in the tabernacle included Minnesota governor John Albert Johnson (pictured here), US senators Robert LaFollette and Joseph Bristow, author and newspaper editor William Allen White, and Kansas governor Henry J. Allen. The most popular guest was no doubt William Jennings Bryan, who appeared in 1895, 1898, 1905, and 1912. Many writers, clergymen, musicians, scientists, artists, and judges of note also participated in the Winfield Chautauqua Assembly over the years.

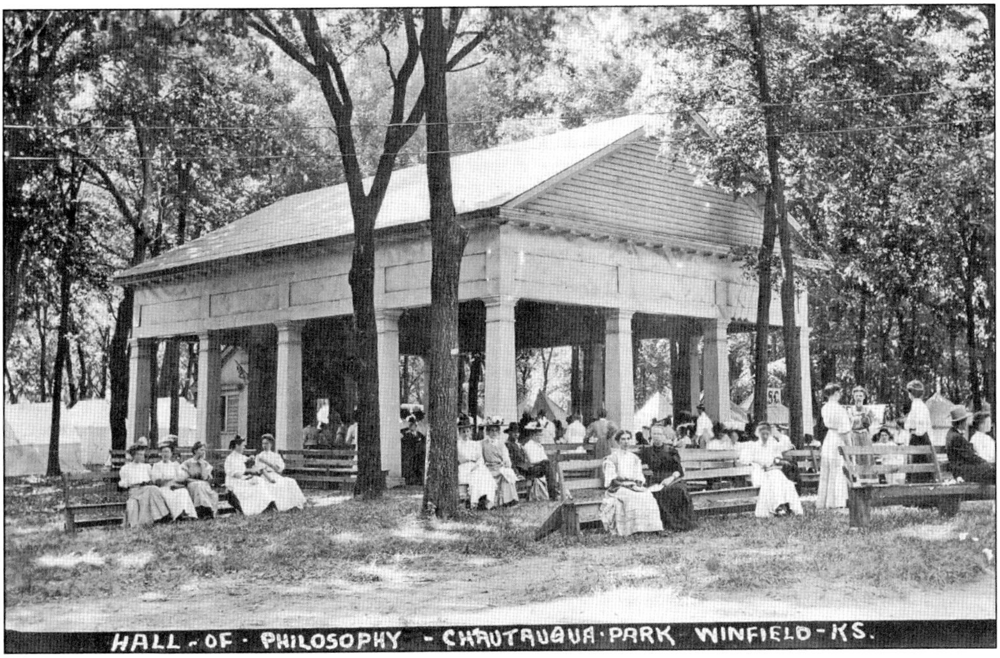


The Hall of Philosophy echoed the Greek-influenced design of the Hall in the Grove at Lake Chautauqua, a reminder of the link between the Winfield assembly and the national movement from which it grew. It served as a meeting place for roundtable discussions for the CLSC participants and for classes. Note the tents behind this structure on the west side of the park.

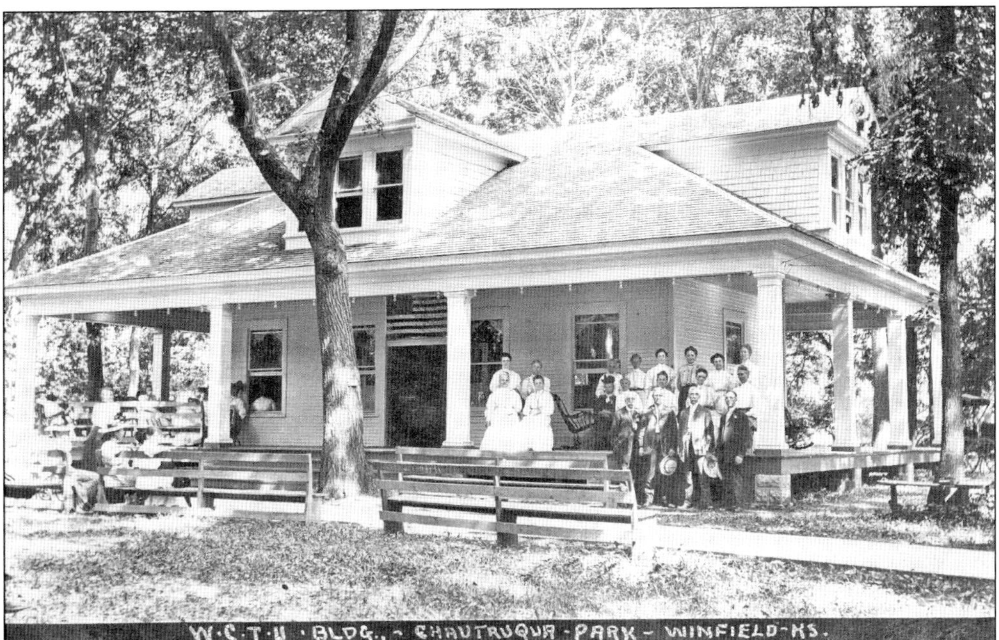


In 1909, state and local chapters of the Women's Christian Temperance Union financed the building of this bungalow on the east side of the Chautauqua grounds north of the Lecture Hall as an annual meeting place. This organization promoted limitations on the consumption of alcohol and women's suffrage. Its most famous Kansas member was Carrie Nation.

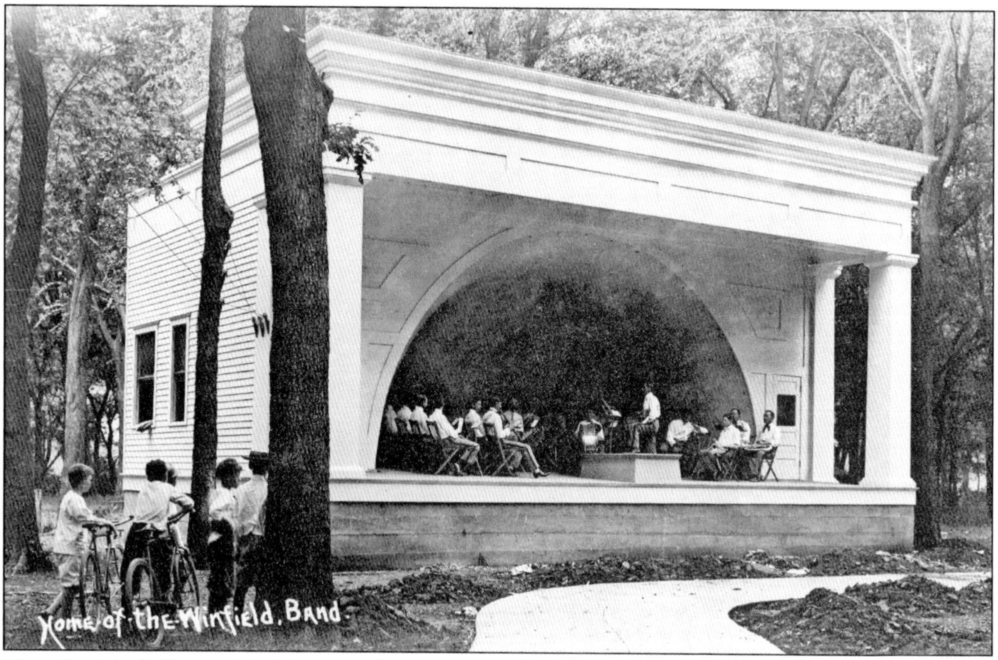

The final building added during the Chautauqua years was the band shell, constructed in 1910 north of the Hall of Philosophy with funding raised by local merchants and income from concerts. On July 14, 1910, the Winfield City Band played to a crowd of over 1,000. In 1916, the shell was moved to the corner of Ninth Avenue and Loomis Street, facing the courthouse, and torn down in 1927.

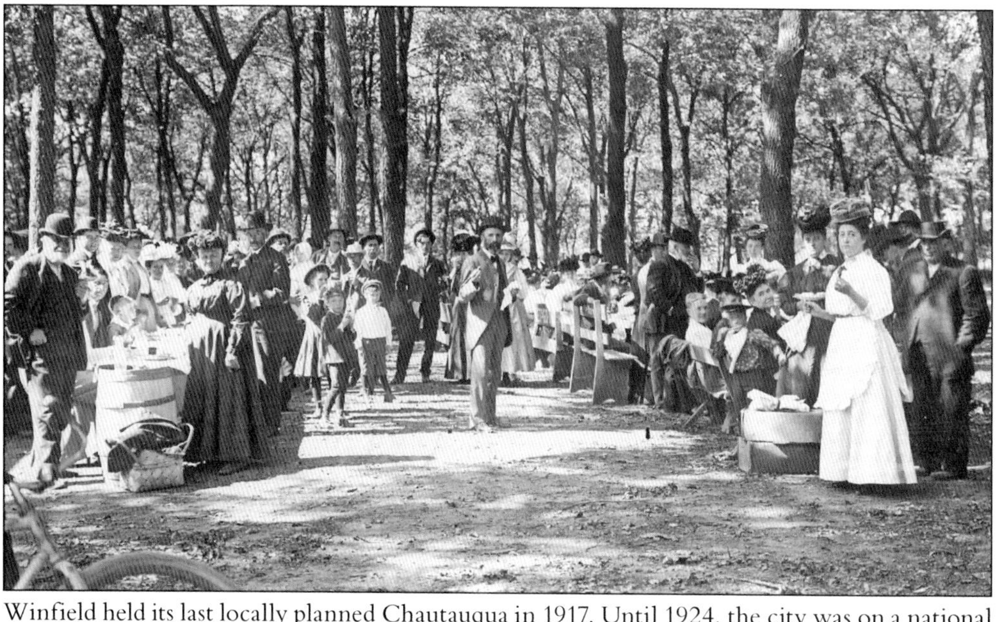
Winfield held its last locally planned Chautauqua in 1917. Until 1924, the city was on a national Chautauqua circuit. By 1967, the Hall of Philosophy became the final building to be demolished, but the Chautauqua spirit did not die. In 1984, and again in 2004, the Great Plains Chautauqua Association chose Winfield as one the host cities for five nights of evening programming. Winfield encourages art and education to this day.

# *Eight*

# Where Winfield Lived

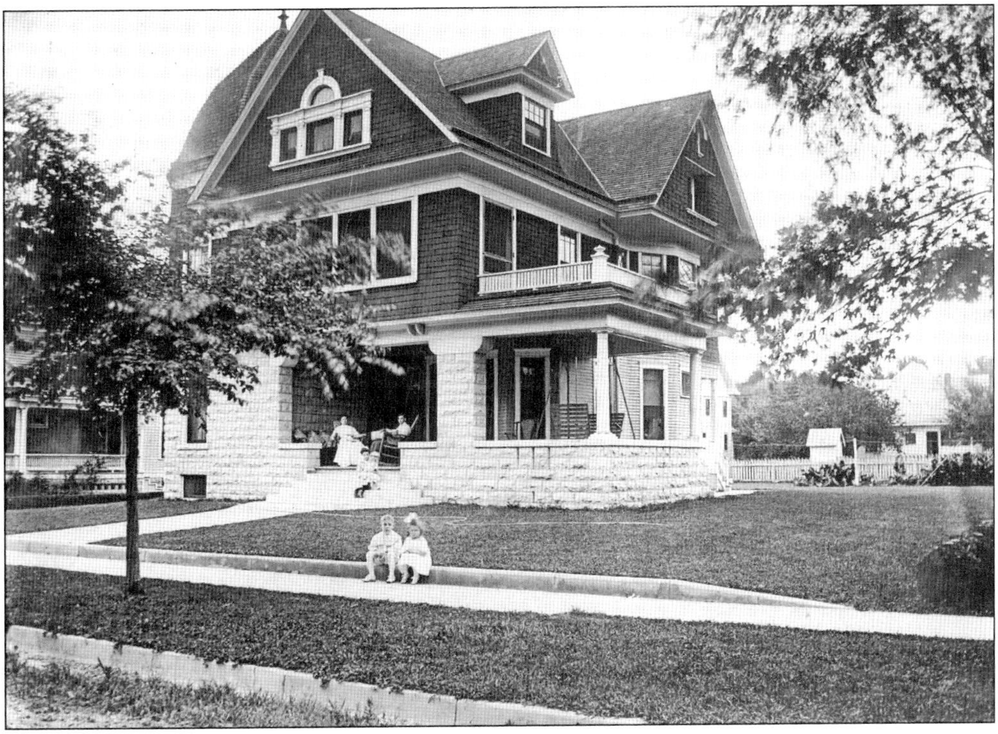

The March 23, 1882, *Winfield Courier* stated, "One of Winfield's crowning glories is her beautiful residences and snug, comfortable homes. Nothing is more indicative of permanency and prosperity than these and nothing shows more strongly the character of her people." An example of such a home was built by local mill owner Charles Wallace at 1010 East Ninth Avenue.

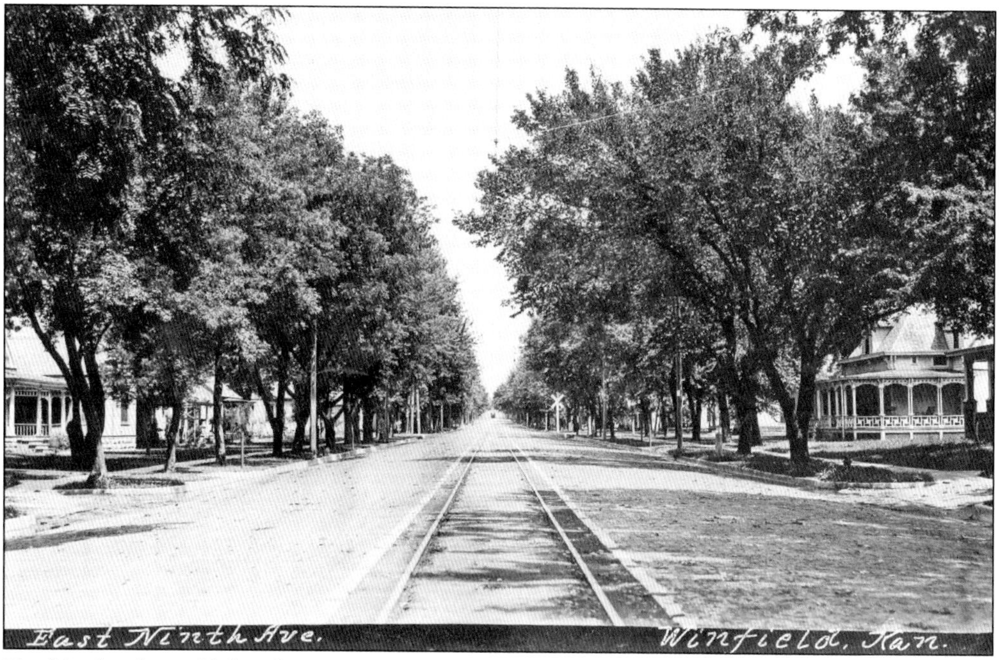


To this day, beautiful and spacious homes line Winfield's East Ninth Avenue that was and continues to be one of the town's main thoroughfares. The trees on East Ninth Avenue were planted by E.C. Manning. Its broad expanse was divided by tracks for the trolley and later the interurban. This view shows the street prior to 1914 before brick paving.

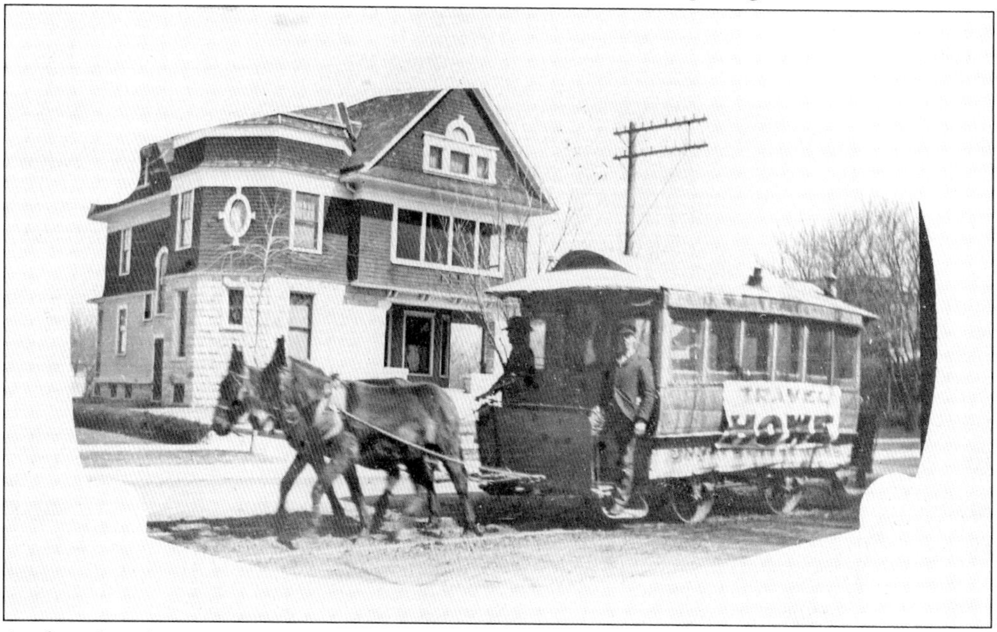

As the advertisement states, a mule-drawn trolley could indeed provide a ride home if the rider lived along its route. Here, a trolley passes the home of Charles Wallace on its way back from College Hill. Wallace ran a local mill, served on the city council, and had two terms as Winfield's mayor. He moved to California in 1932 and returned to Kansas a few years before his death in 1956.

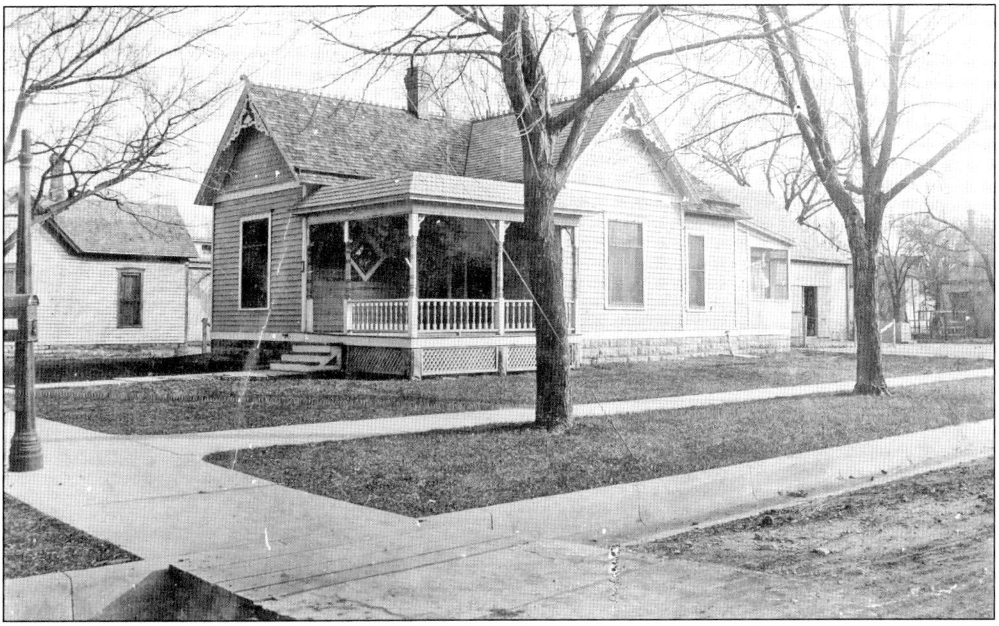

This neat frame house at 221 West Ninth Avenue was owned by Henry Jarvis until 1925. In 1930, Jarvis purchased an auto-parts store on Main Street, which grew into the successful Jarvis Auto Supply Company with branches in several area cities.

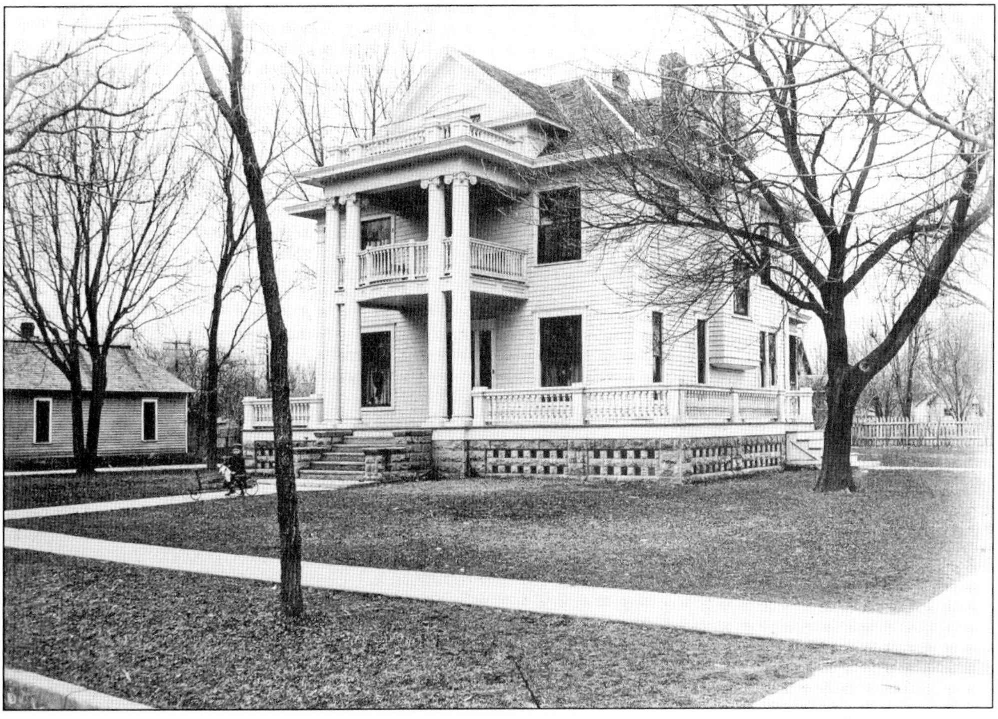

In the early 1900s, E.W. Bollinger built this imposing home at 918 East Ninth Avenue. He worked as a cashier at the First National Bank and later moved to California. The home changed hands in 1939, when George Jarvis purchased it. It remains recognizable today, a glimpse into Winfield's past.

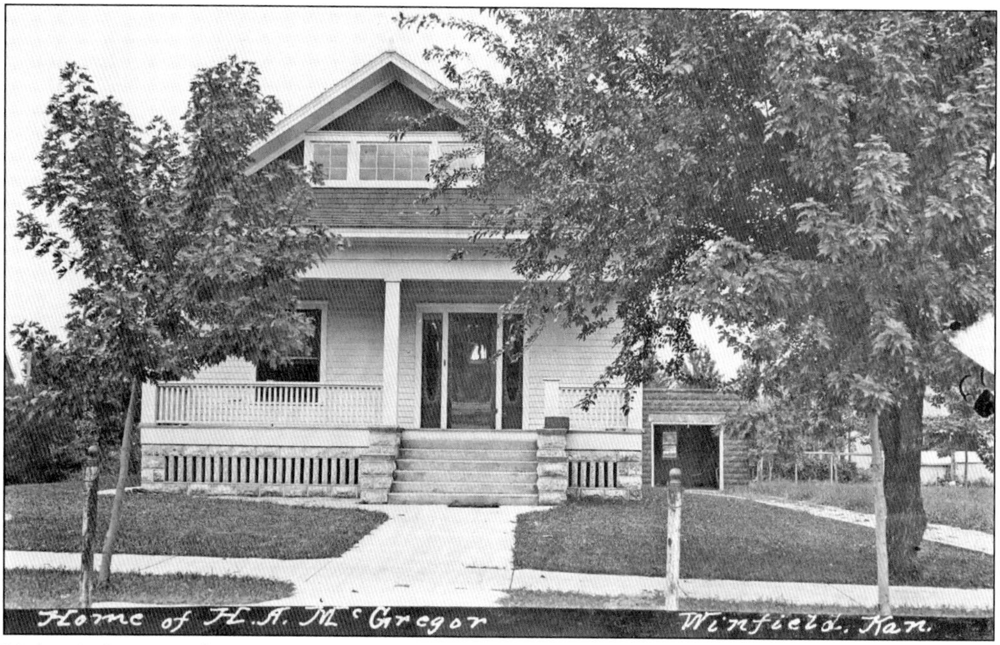


H.A. McGregor, who owned McGregor Hardware at 117 East Ninth Avenue, moved in 1924 to the corner of Ninth Avenue and Millington Street, formerly occupied by Stuber Brothers auto dealership. He also served as a director for Caman's Band and as Winfield's mayor from 1913 to 1917. His home, at 1411 East Ninth Avenue, retains its charm in the 21st century.

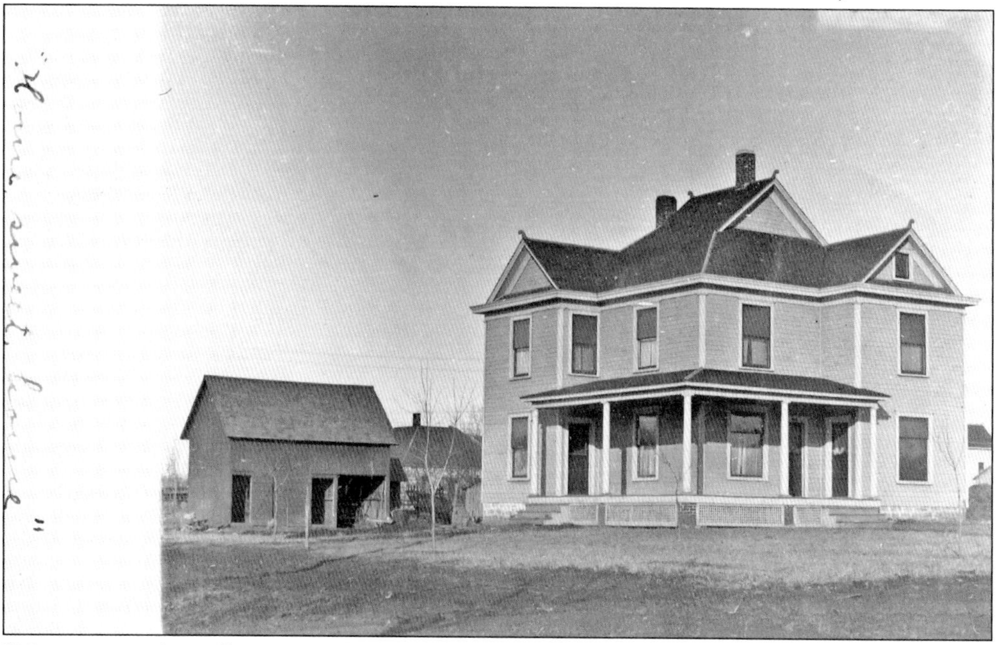


"Home, sweet home" expressed the sentiment of the owner on the back of the image of this home built in 1906 at the corner of Sixth Avenue and Gary Street. It also states, "Built 1906. Moved July 16, 1906," which likely refers to the date the family took up residence, but the moving of buildings did occur. In the 1880s, Robert Hudson ran a moving business using a steam-powered engine.

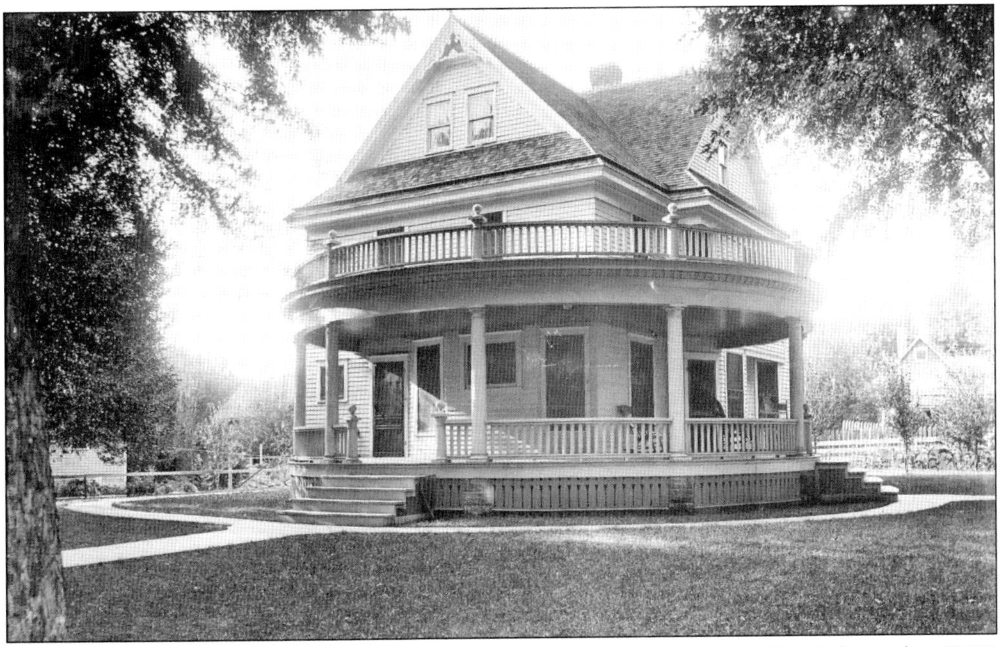

Often called "the round house," this home at 1120 East Seventh Avenue first belonged to C.W. Bailey, Winfield's register of deeds in 1903. The Winfield *Free Press* of May 29, 1905, records the home being struck by lightning. In later years, it was home to the Calvert and Albertson families, and it still stands today with its inviting porch at the intersection of Seventh Avenue and Cherry Street.

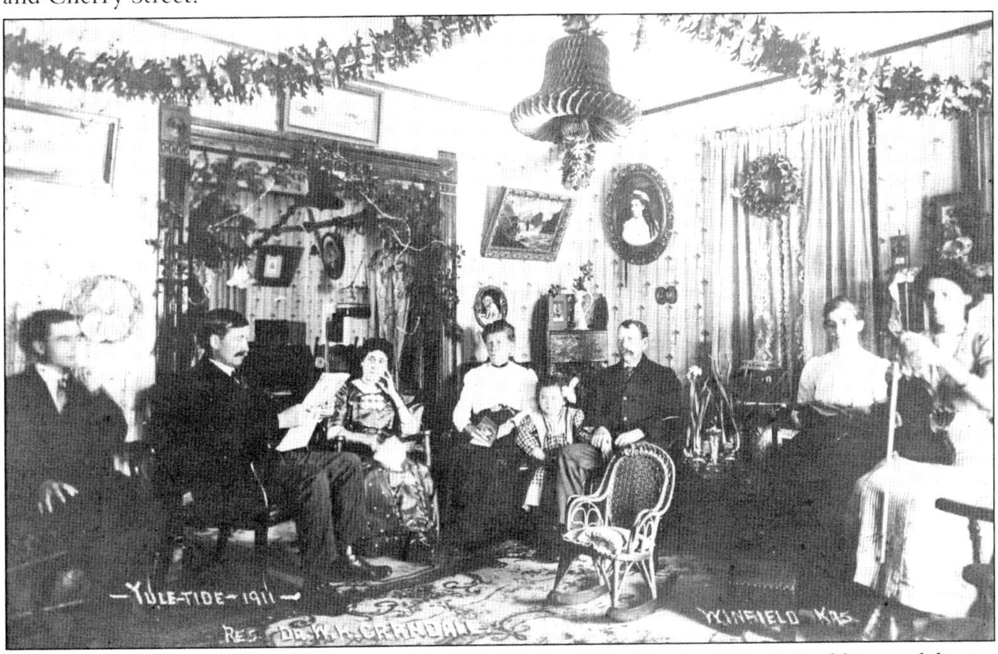


W.H. Crandall, a Winfield dentist with offices in the First National Bank building, celebrates Yuletide 1911 with his family in their home at 1222 East Eleventh Avenue. Crandall's daughter Mary, no doubt holding the violin, was an accomplished musician. The home hosted many club meetings and parties.

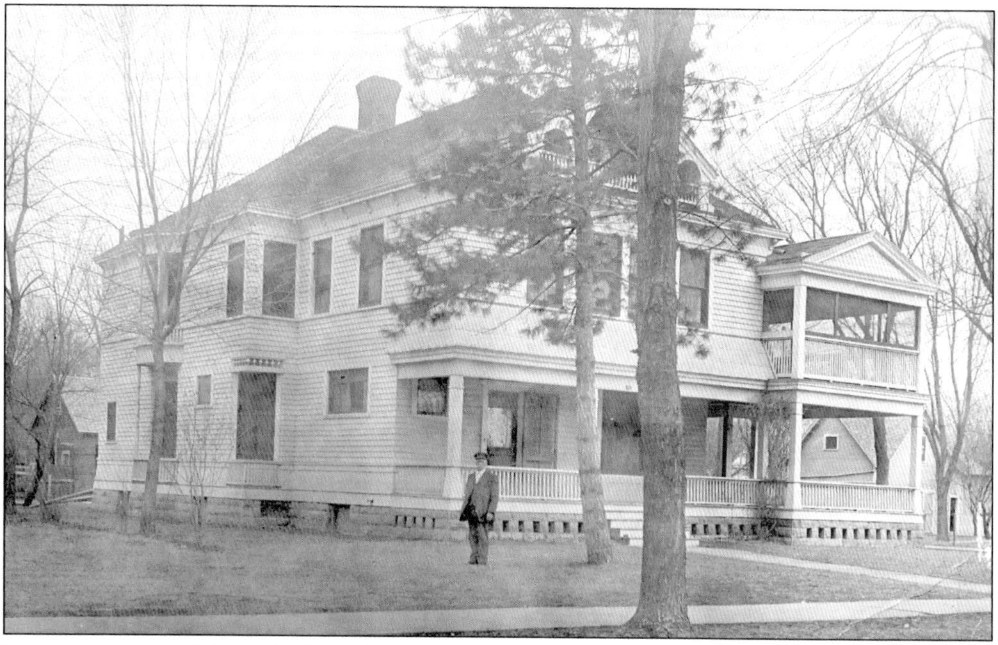

This card, sent in 1912 by the home's owner, features E. Klauser's fine home at 420 East Eleventh Avenue. Klauser, a builder by trade, came to Winfield in 1885 with his wife. In 1903, he opened a shop at 320 East Ninth Avenue. Upon his death in this home in December 1916, Klauser was remembered as a prominent Winfield citizen.

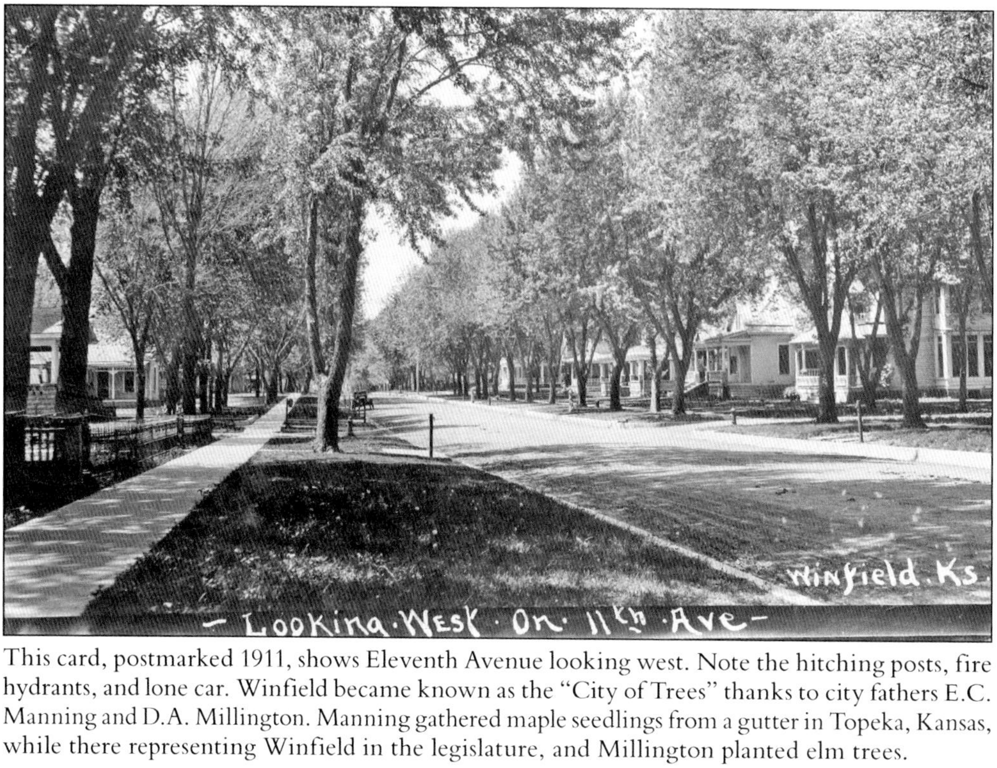


This card, postmarked 1911, shows Eleventh Avenue looking west. Note the hitching posts, fire hydrants, and lone car. Winfield became known as the "City of Trees" thanks to city fathers E.C. Manning and D.A. Millington. Manning gathered maple seedlings from a gutter in Topeka, Kansas, while there representing Winfield in the legislature, and Millington planted elm trees.

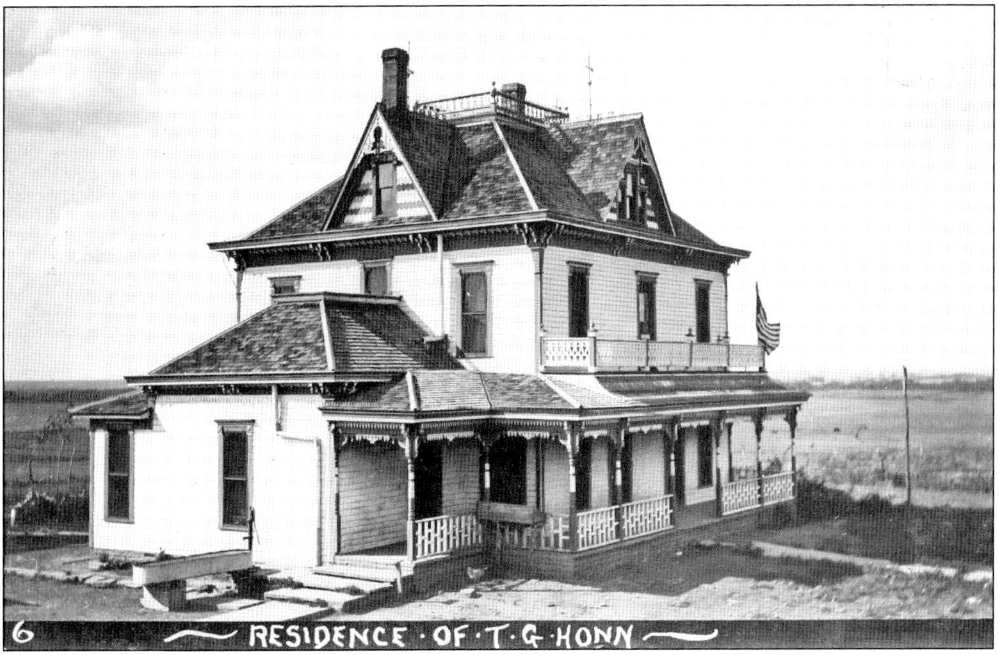


This grand residence, built by T.G. Honn, was located at 317 West Eighth Avenue between Mansfield and Menor Streets, one of the first constructed in the area. Streets running parallel to Main Street were named after early settlers such as Mansfield, Menor, Stewart, and Lowry on the west and Millington, Fuller, Loomis, Gary, Bliss, Hackney, Torrance, Maris, and Platter east of Main Street.

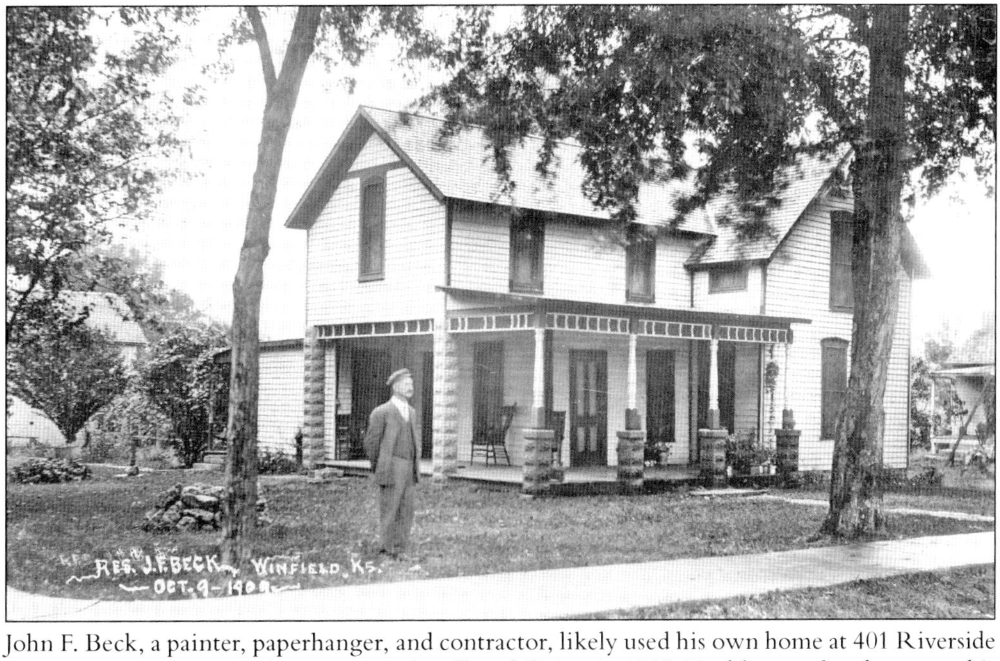


John F. Beck, a painter, paperhanger, and contractor, likely used his own home at 401 Riverside (now Fourteenth Avenue) as an example of his abilities. In 1909, Beck's own daughter sent this card to a friend in Wellington, Kansas, writing, "Being as you won't come over and see me, I'll send you a picture of my boarding house. Ha, ha!"

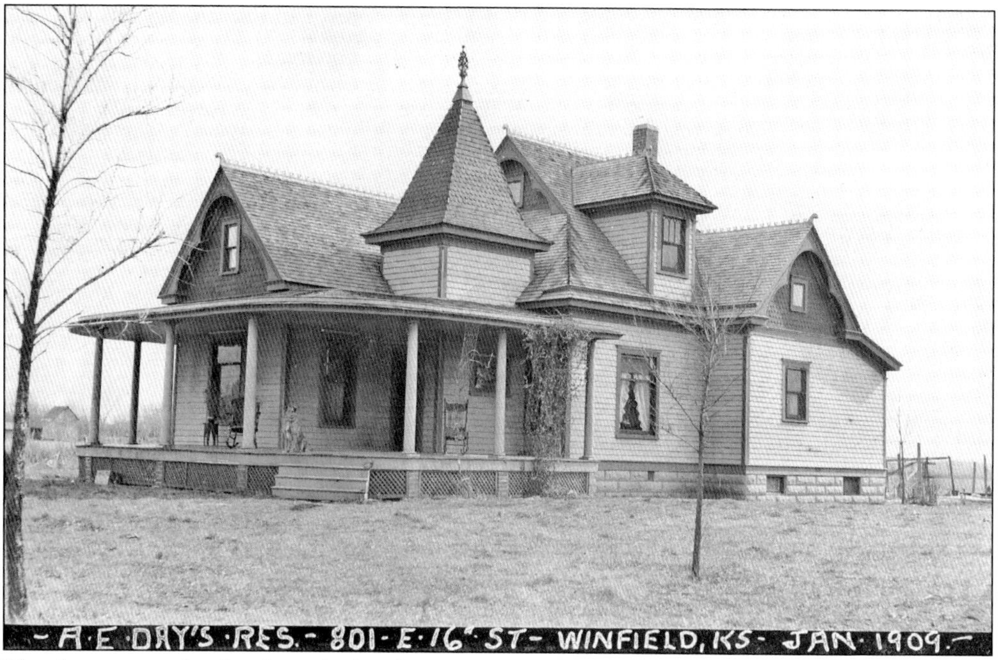


The dog appeared to be the only family member at home when the photographer came calling at A.E. Day's residence at 801 East Sixteenth Avenue in 1909. Sixteenth Avenue is another street with an earlier name in Winfield's history. It was originally named Walnut Street, with Maple and Park Avenues on either side of it. Eighteenth Avenue was once called Osage Street.

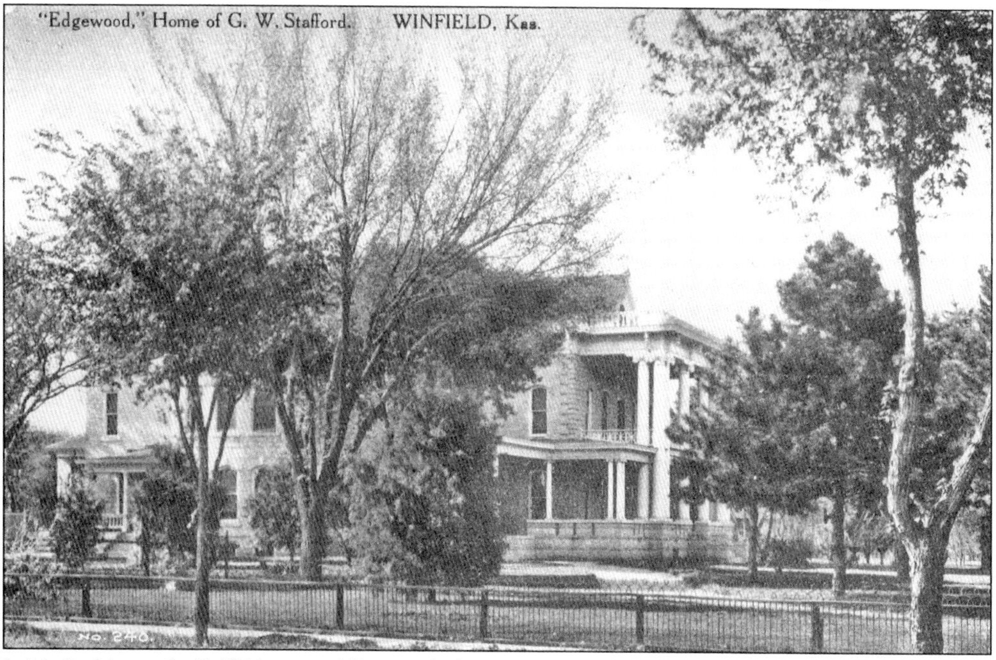


L.M. Robinson built "Edgewood," a stately home at 1209 Menor Street. It later became the first sanitarium in Winfield that, by the time of this postcard, belonged to Grant Stafford, a senior partner with P.H. Albright in abstracting and real estate. The home burned in 1940. Walnut Towers senior apartments now occupy the lot.

# *Nine*

# Winfield's Social and Medical Services

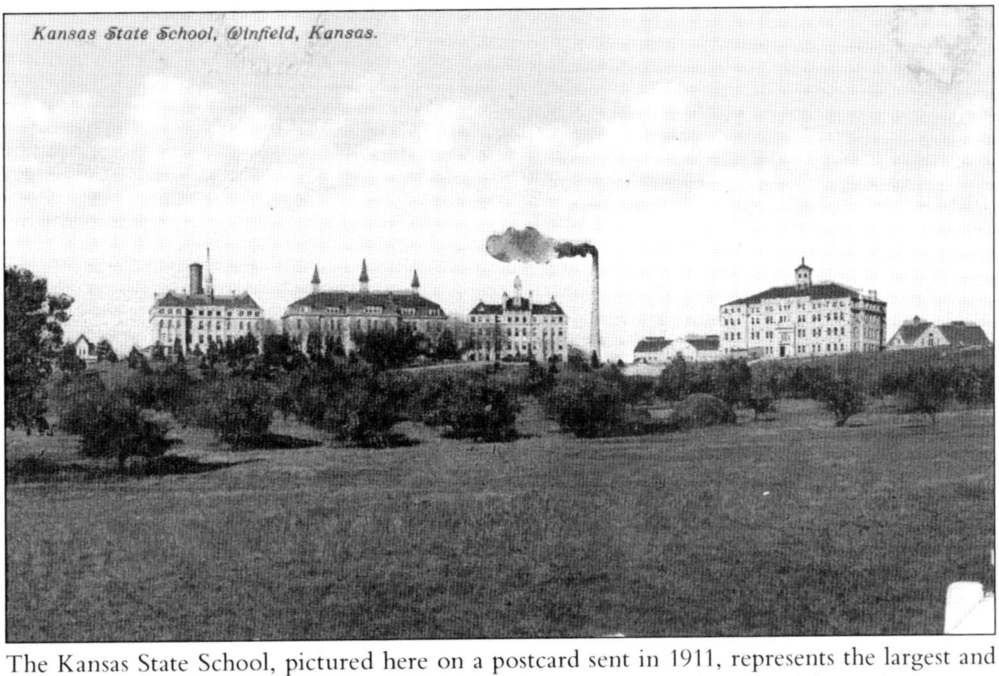


The Kansas State School, pictured here on a postcard sent in 1911, represents the largest and most far reaching of Winfield's social and medical services. Opened in 1887, it housed a program addressing the needs of the mentally handicapped begun in 1881 at the University of Kansas. In its 116 years on a hill north of Winfield, the school's name and mission changed to reflect the current treatment of its population.

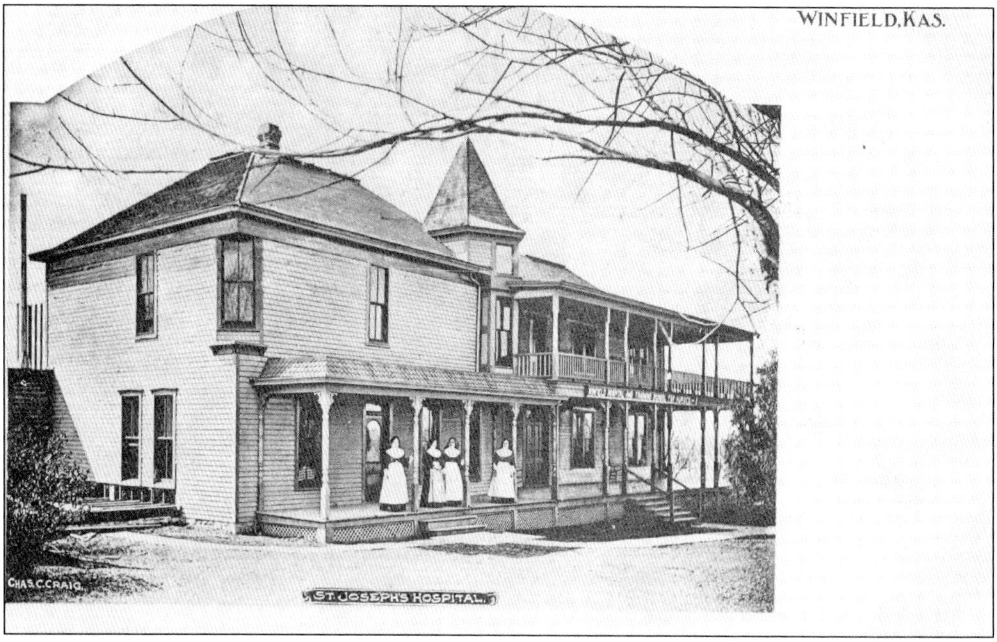


Hospital service came to Winfield in 1899. A group of local citizens, including J.P. Baden, F.K. Robinson, and W.H. Somermeier, formed the Winfield Hospital Association to establish a hospital and nurses' training school at the northeast corner of Ninth Avenue and College Street. It included 10 rooms, a surgery, and a reception chapel. In 1903, due to financial difficulties, the group gave the hospital to the Sisters of St. Joseph.

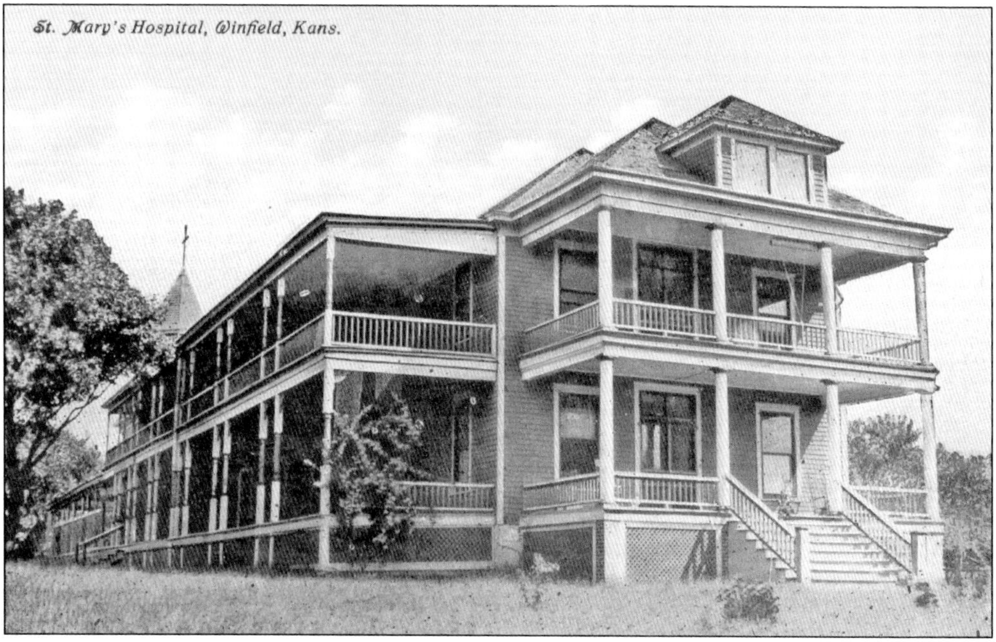


The Sisters of St. Joseph made additions to the hospital, renamed it St. Mary's, and closed the nursing school for a time, reopening it in 1913. A heating plant and laundry were later added. This postcard view shows the other side of the enlarged wood-frame hospital with porches on both floors and the turret retained from the original building.

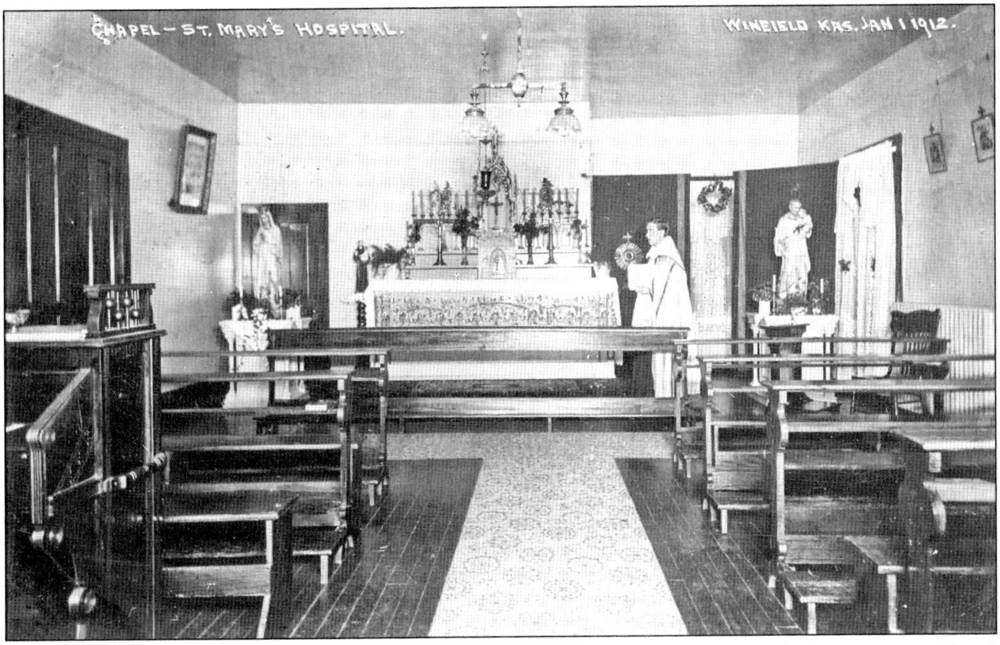


Befitting its Catholic sponsorship, St. Mary's Hospital included a chapel with the services of local priests. Despite its excellent location and additions, the hospital began to show limitations by the time the nursing school reopened. The Sisters and the City of Winfield began a fundraising campaign to build a larger, safer all-brick hospital.

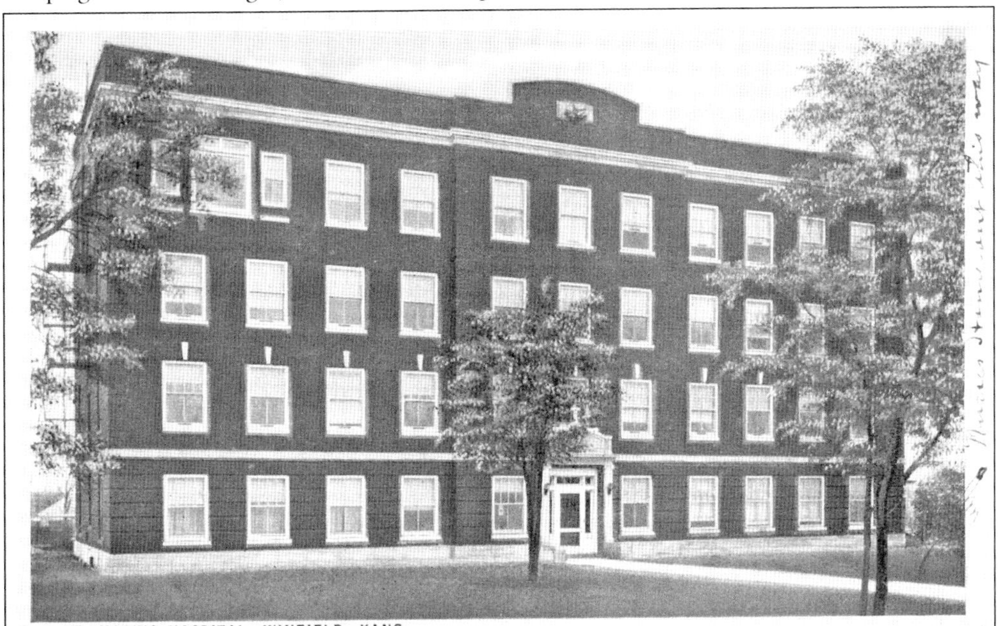


A new St. Mary's Hospital, located at the corner of Ninth Avenue and Mound Street, opened in 1918. The sender of this card noted on its right side, "Nurses' home out this way." With three operating rooms, an x-ray department, 50 beds, and kitchen, it served until 1961 when it became the Good Samaritan nursing home. The early 1970s saw it razed to make way for the Village East apartment complex.

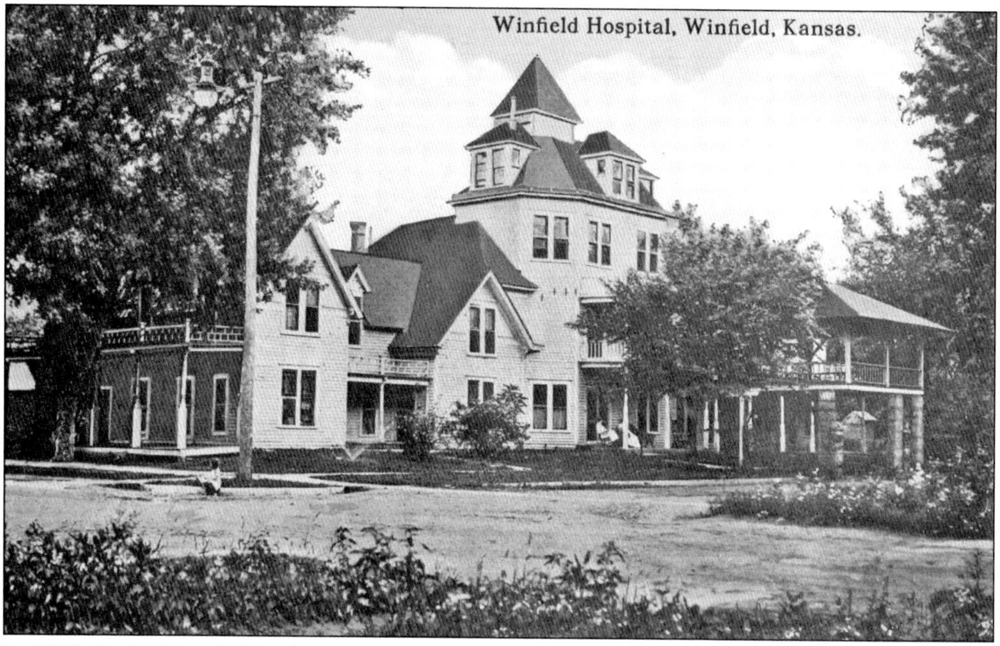


In 1899, Dr. F. Hoyt Pilcher began a private hospital at the corner of Tenth Avenue and Manning Street, dedicated to the care of surgical patients. Patients coming from around Kansas and beyond led to the doubling of the hospital's size within a year. Upon Dr. Pilcher's death in 1908, Doctors Edward O. and Flavius R. Smith took ownership and changed the name to Winfield Hospital.

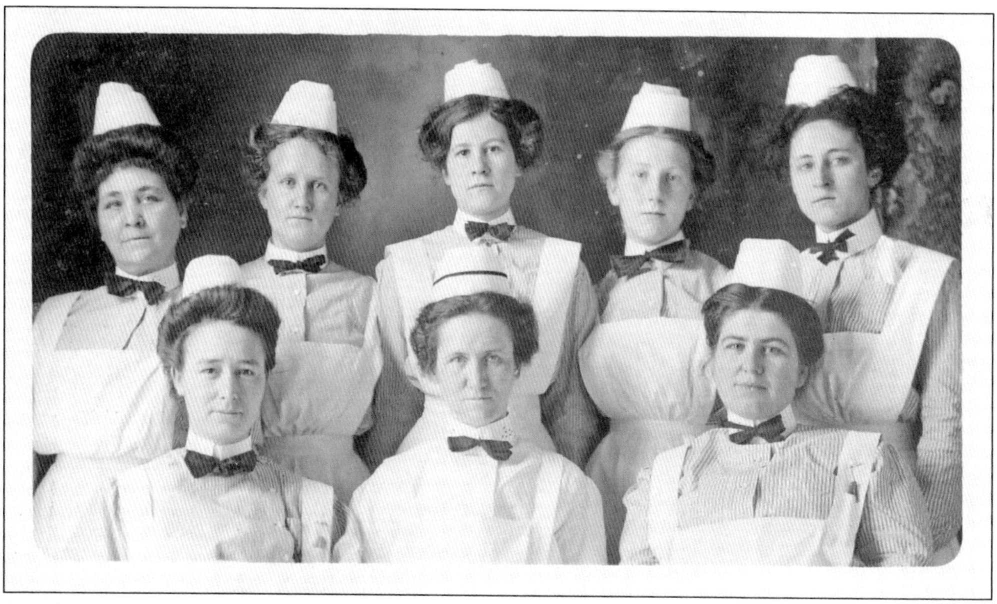

Winfield Hospital also offered training to nurses. The back of this postcard states that this photograph is of the first graduating class. Winfield Hospital lasted until the death of Dr. E.O. Smith in 1926 and Dr. F.R. Smith in 1927. At that time, the newer part of the structure became an apartment building with the original wing demolished.

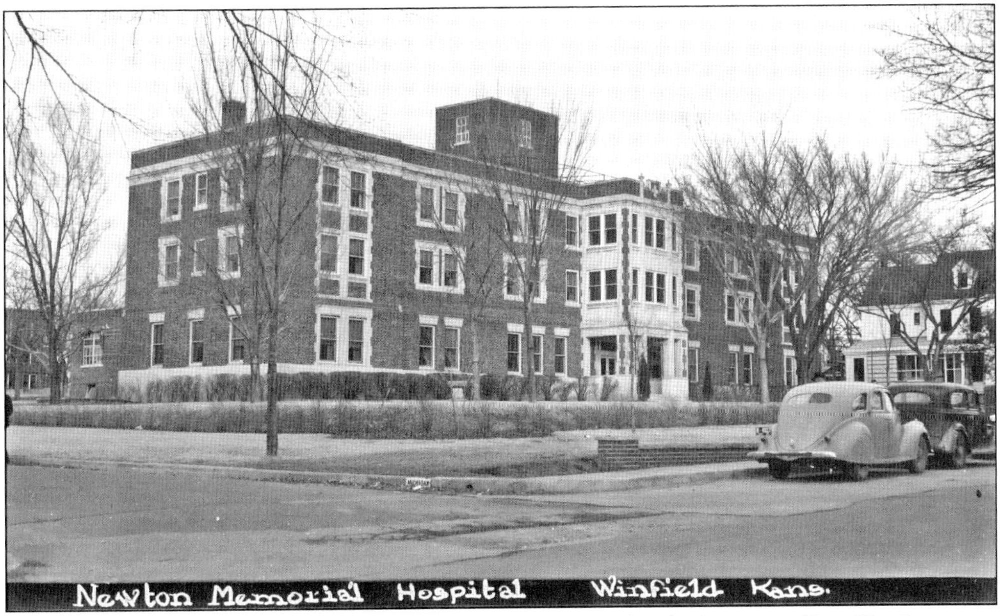


Winfield received its current hospital on East Fifth Avenue by the bequest of local businessman and landowner William Newton upon his death in 1922. When it opened in 1927, the fully equipped hospital displayed 52 patient beds to crowds who gathered for a guided tour. It received the coveted approval of the American College of Physicians within only seven months of its opening.

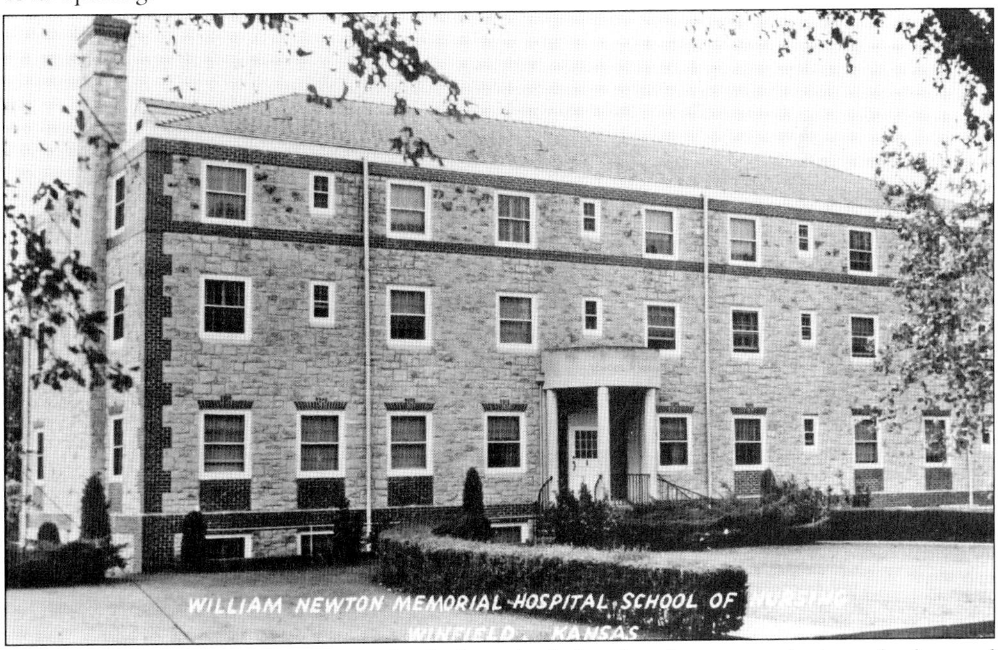


William Newton Memorial Hospital relied on the help of student nurses in its early days and established a three-year nurses' training program in 1928. Nurse trainees lived in local homes, including one east of the hospital. In 1947, Virginia Hall, named for Newton's wife, went up at Lynn and Massachusetts Streets. It provided a home for 60 students as well as lecture halls and laboratories until its 1969 closing.

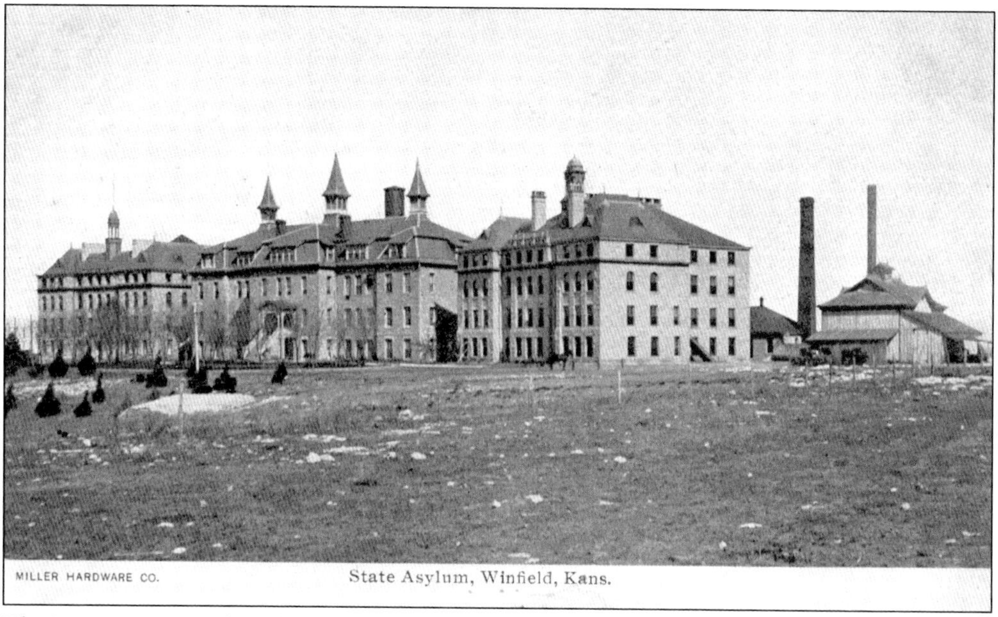


The Kansas State Asylum for Idiotic and Imbecile Youth, begun in Lawrence, Kansas, in 1881, moved to Winfield in 1887, and 100 children were brought to a four-story building constructed on 40 acres of land north of Winfield. By 1900, residents numbered 209 and the campus grew to 250 acres to include a dormitory for girls, two barns, a laundry, bakery, hospital, pump house, and two wells.

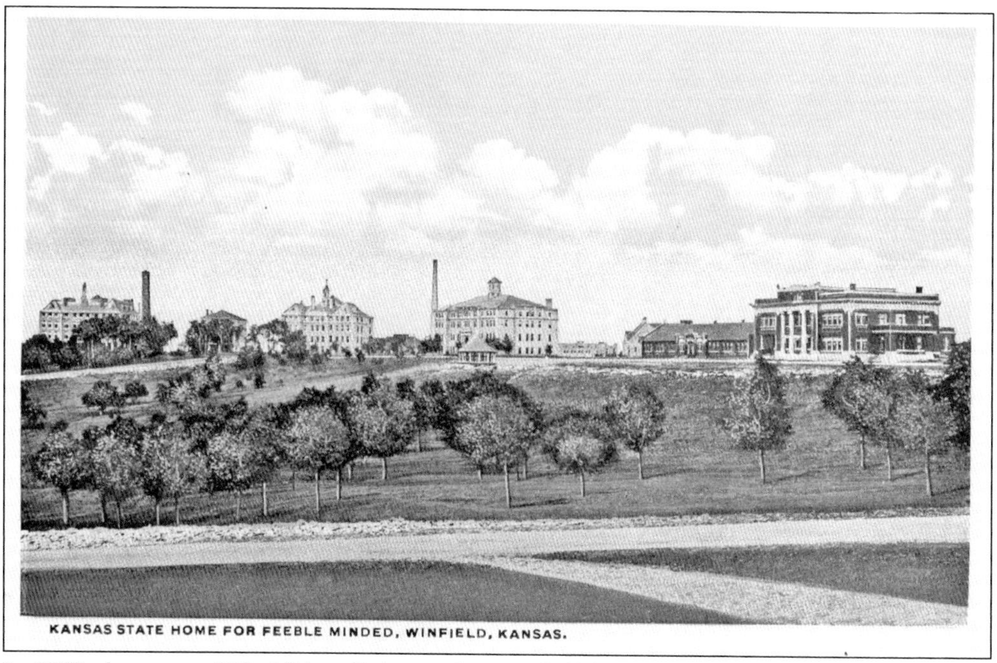


In 1908, there were 379 children living at the Winfield home. This postcard reflects the 1909 name change. That same year also marked the removal of the age limit of 15. With the original building destroyed by fire in 1911, a brick administration building and hospital were added in 1914. The residency rate grew to 645 in 1917.

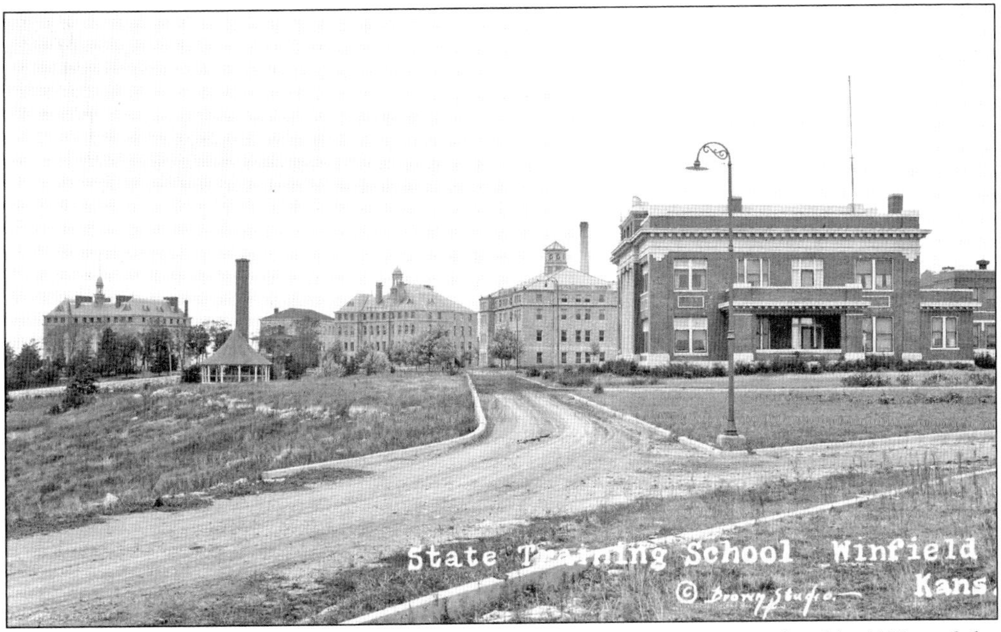


A special commission recommended the name change to State Training School in 1919, and the school's population reached its peak of 1,245 in 1942. In 1957, with the downsizing of facilities for the mentally disabled, another name change occurred. The Winfield State Hospital and Training Center, once Cowley County's largest employer, closed in 1998. Its grounds and buildings now form the Winfield Correctional Facility.

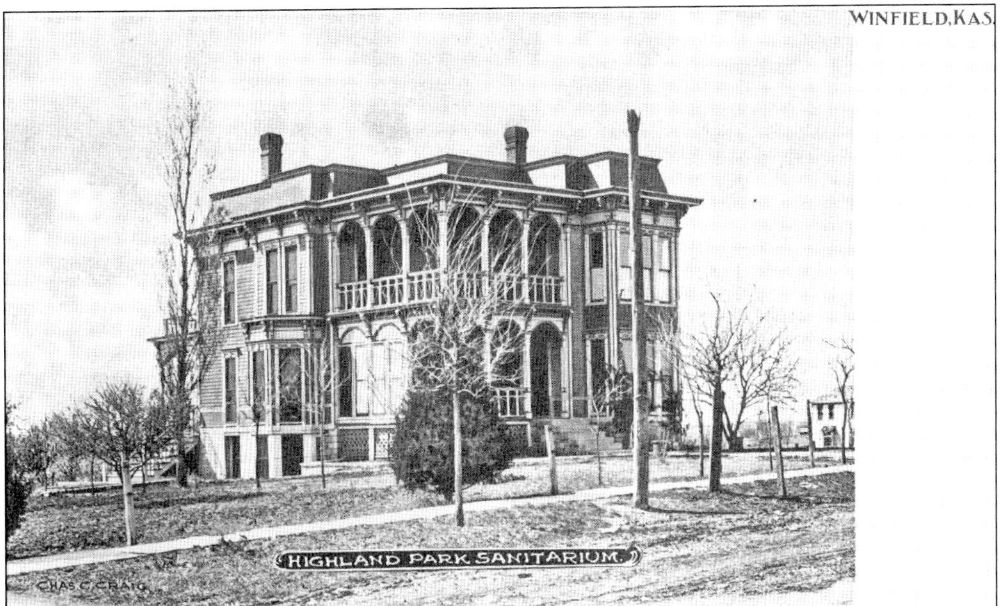


The Highland Park Sanitarium, located at 411 Park Street, placed an advertisement in the 1905 Southwestern College *Moundbuilder* extolling its location as being "away from the noise and dust of the city and . . . always cool and salubrious in summer." The facility accepted "all classes of cases except contagious diseases," and its operating room was free to physicians and surgeons.

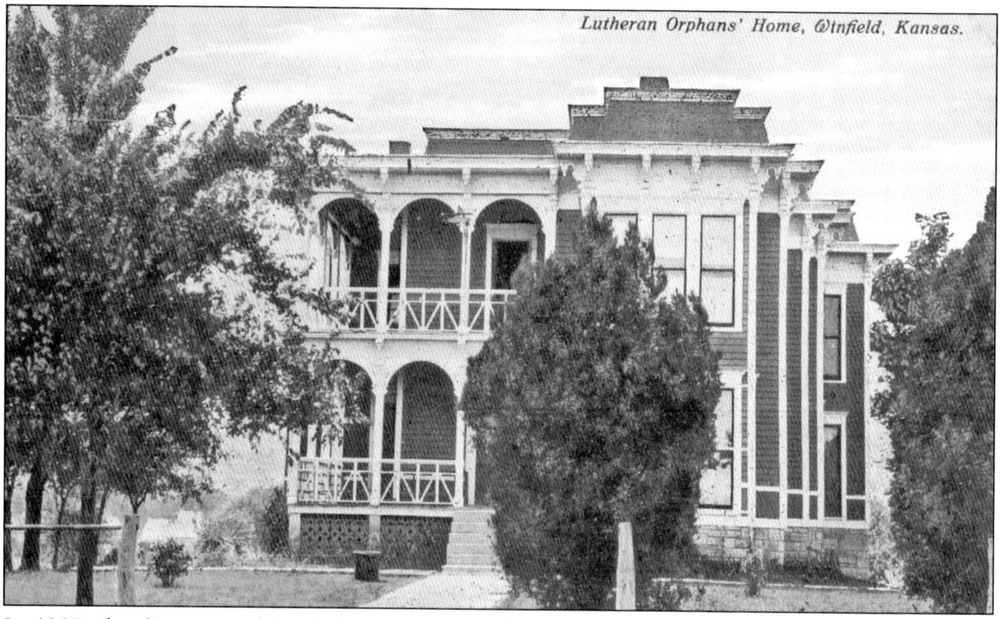


In 1907, the directors of the Lutheran Children's Friend Society in Topeka, Kansas, accepted the offer by Adelaide Elizabeth Baden of a building to house their Lutheran Children's Home. That building was the former Highland Park Sanitarium, and it housed about 25 children at a time. The society's goal was to find permanent homes for the children, and children's religious affiliation did not bar their admittance to the home.

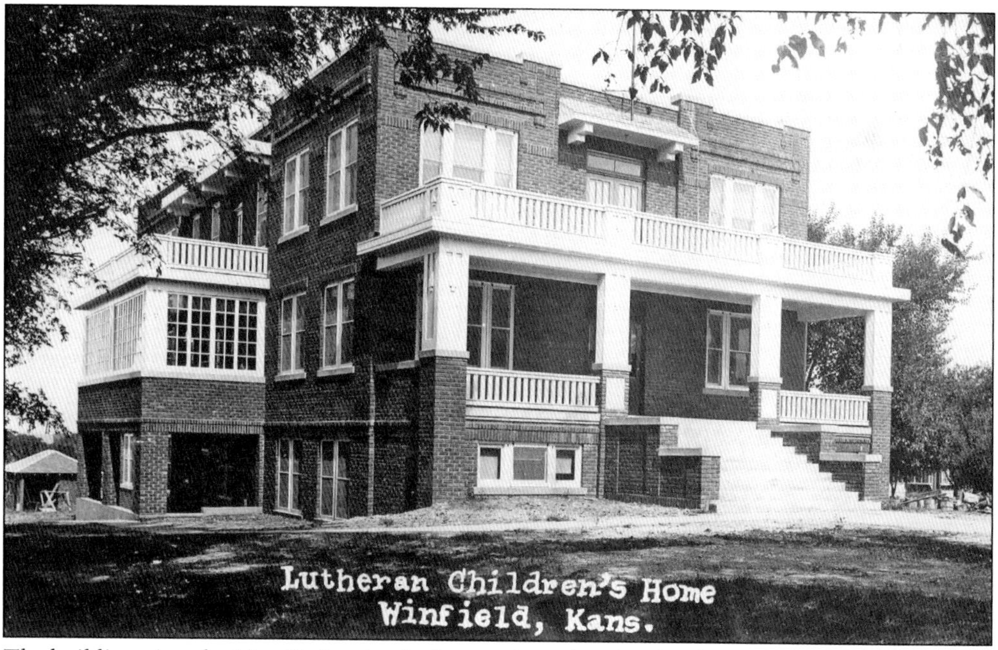


The building given by Mrs. Baden that had seemed spacious in 1907 began to show its limitations by 1921. In that year, a large, new brick home was dedicated at 411 Park Street, and the old home was moved to 421 Michigan Street, where fire later destroyed it. When the children's home closed in 1960, the building served several uses until being demolished in 1981 to provide land for Newton Memorial Hospital expansion.

*Ten*

# ALONG THE WALNUT

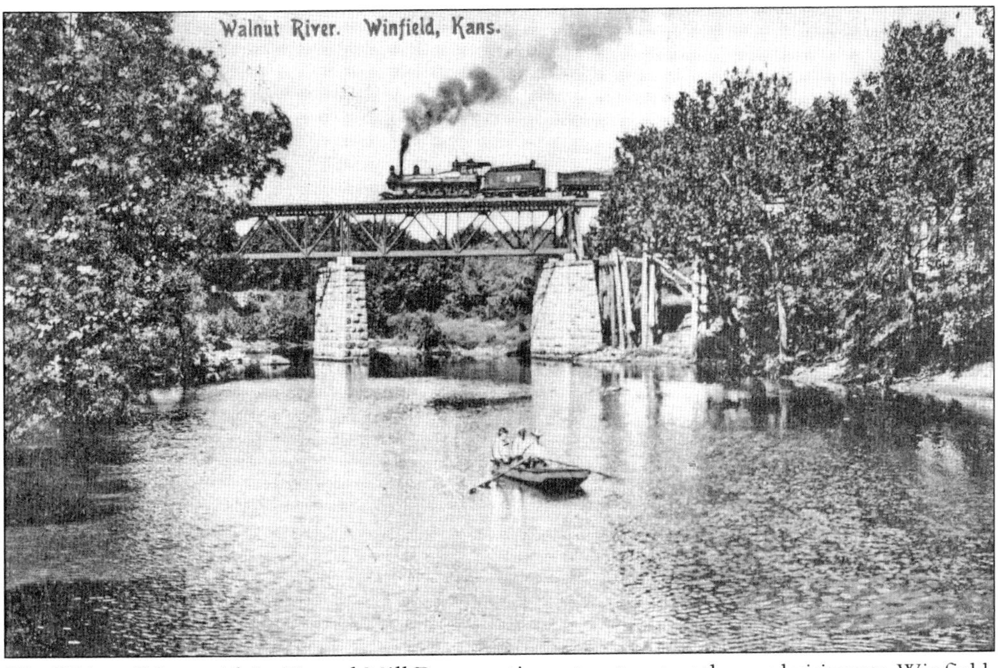


The Walnut River with its Tunnel Mill Dam continues to attract settlers and visitors to Winfield. Its waters provide recreation, as shown in this photograph of the Frisco Railroad Bridge. But, in years past, the Walnut River, which brought power and scenic beauty to the area, also brought peril that took many forms.

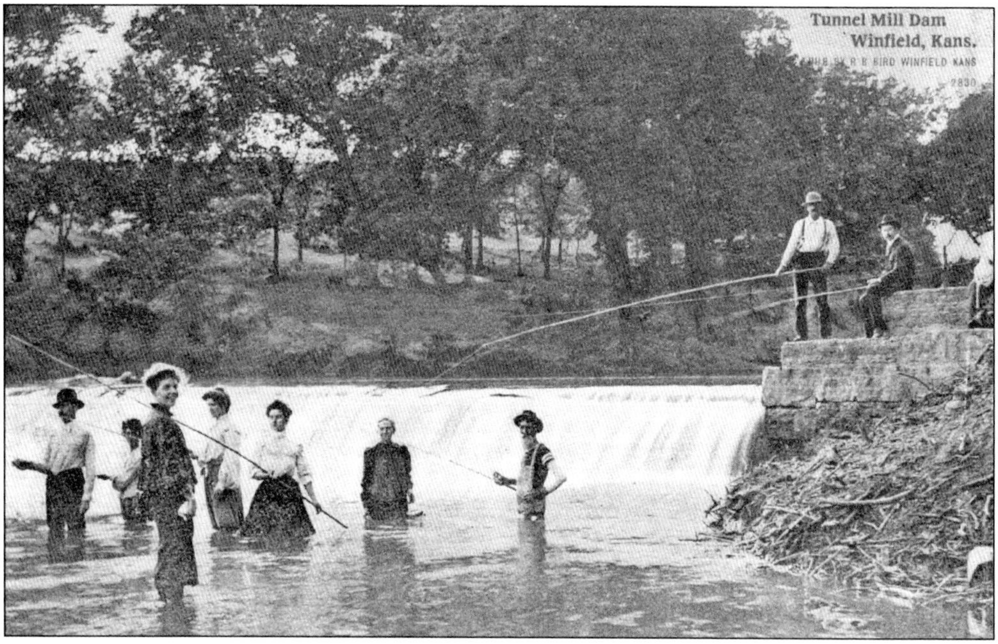


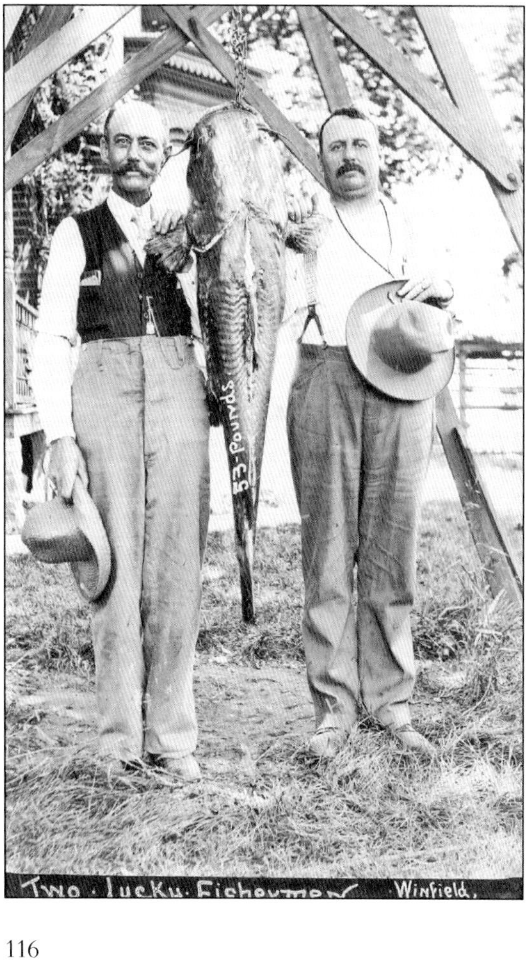


Tunnel Mill Dam received its name from the Tunnel Mill, built in 1872 downriver from the dam. Even before a 1923 flood washed it away, the area brought anglers, picnickers, and campers. West of the dam site was the Kickapoo Corral, used by Indians to hold livestock before Winfield's settlement. Remains of it, including an 18-foot-tall limestone kiln, may be seen today.

The Walnut River retains its reputation as a haven for catfish even today. The sender of this card noted, "We caught several small catfish . . . but the one on the front was the father of them all." Another claim to fame of the Tunnel Mill Dam was its deadly whirlpool south of the dam, created from a hole deep in the river's limestone bed, providing a prime but dangerous spot to fish.

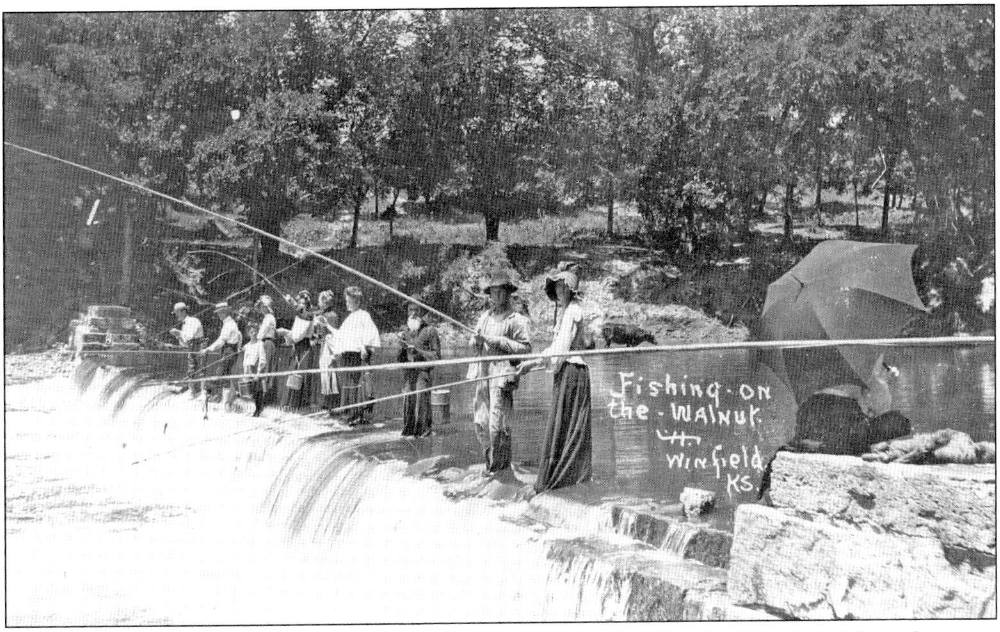


Despite the danger, even children fish with impunity on the dam in this view. More than one person met their death on the Walnut River. The *Winfield Free Press* mourned on July 17, 1908, "The Walnut River swallowed up yet another young life yesterday afternoon," reporting the drowning of a 21-year-old man near the Baden Mill while swimming with a friend who was unable to save him.

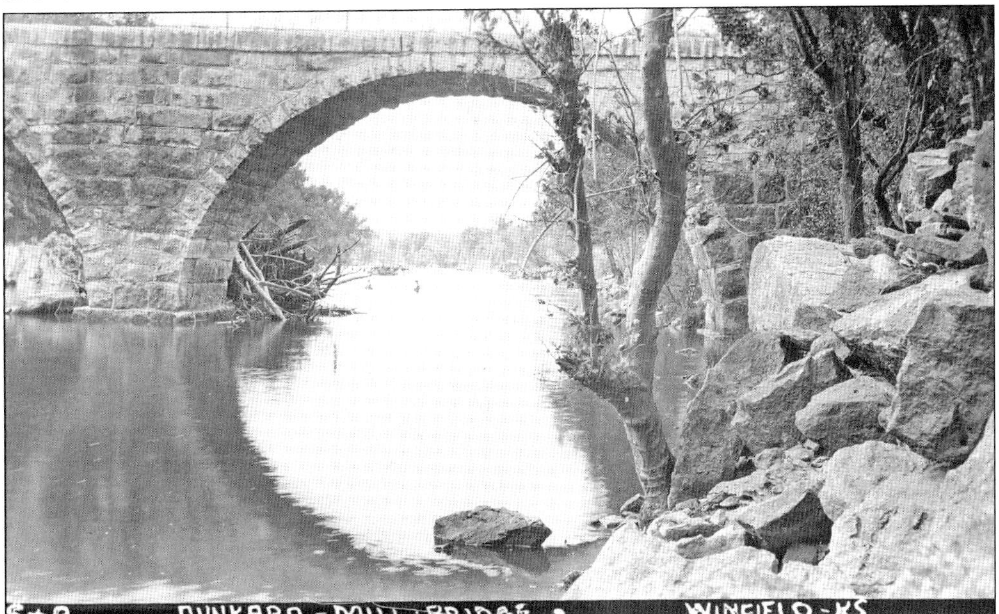


Cowley County features many limestone bridges, including this one south of Winfield. Limestone from the Walnut River and the nearby hillside contributed to the construction of Dunkard Bridge in 1903. The bridge stood until a 1944 flood washed it away, but it was rebuilt in 1945. Dunkard Mill, established by a man of the Dunkard faith, stood south of the bridge but ceased operation by the turn of the century.

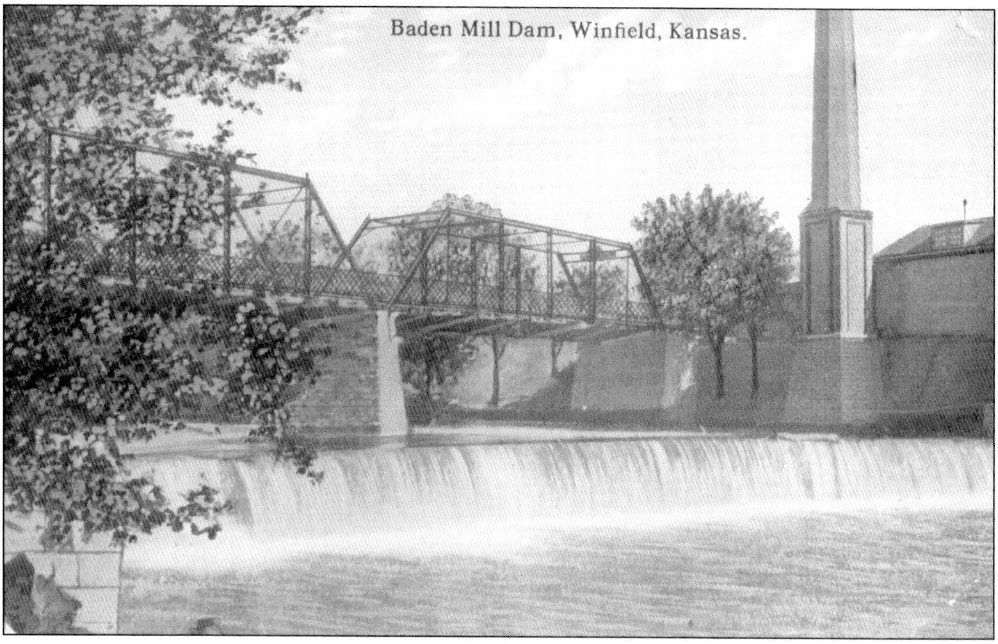


This 1915 postcard shows the Baden Mill and dam to good advantage. The mill's first owner, C.A. Bliss, dammed the river to provide power for the flour mill. In 1885, an 18-foot-wide iron bridge was built across the Walnut River, which bordered the mill. Because of its location, the mill suffered repeated flood damage. After the 1923 flood, electricity replaced the power of the Walnut River.

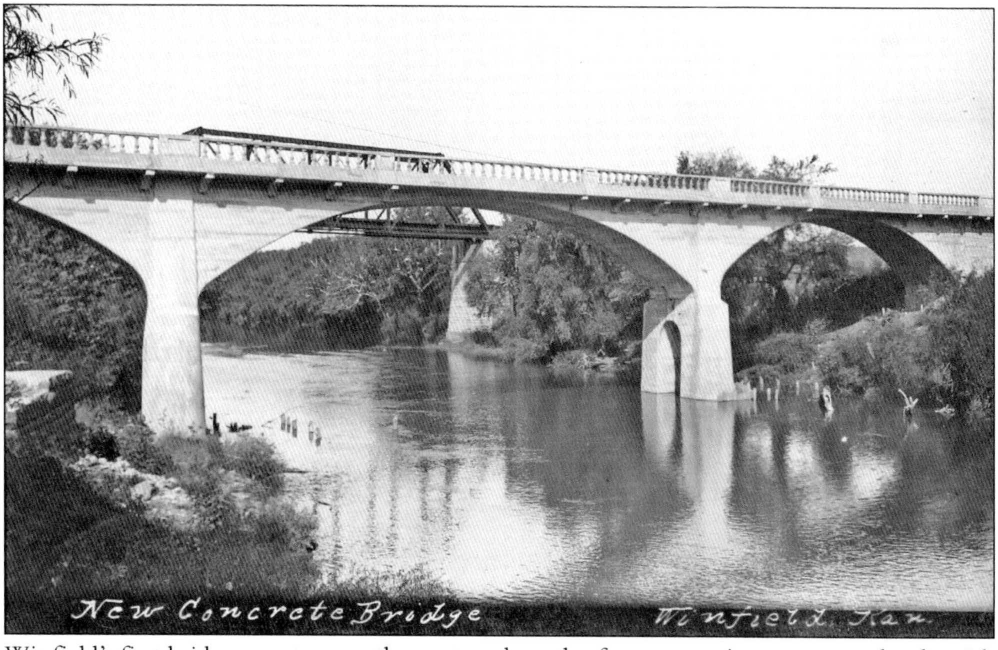


Winfield's first bridges went up south, west, and north of town, starting a constant battle with the elements. Over the years, wood gave way to iron, but limestone abutments were no match for Winfield's frequent floods. This concrete bridge on South Main Street, east of the railroad bridge, brought its city into the modern age and was cause for celebration.

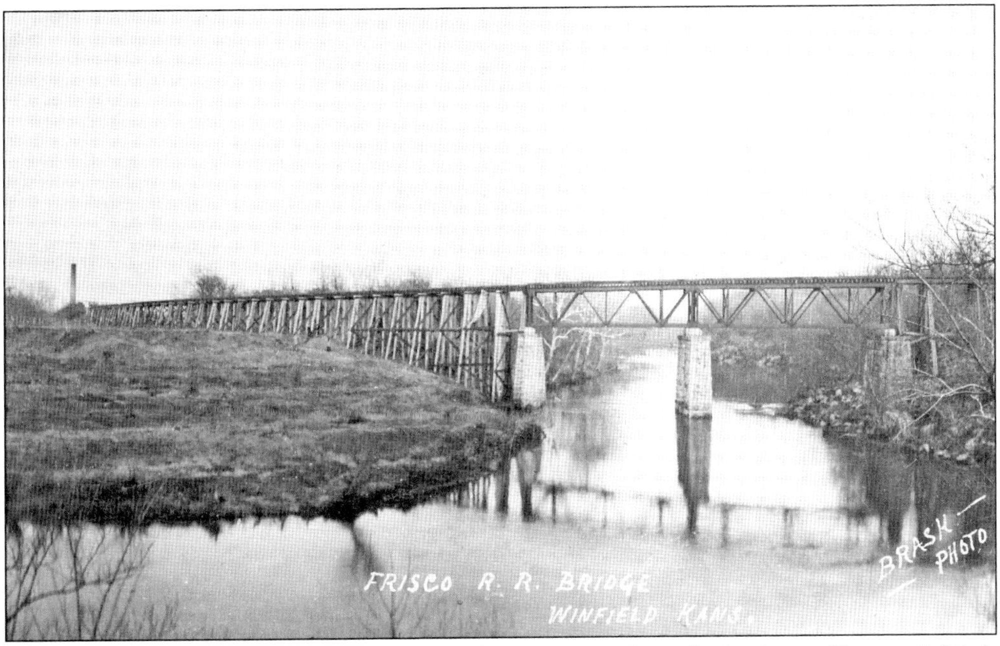


The Frisco Railroad Bridge spanned the Walnut River and caught its share of logs and debris when it flooded, prompting the stationing of men with sticks to direct the flotsam between its limestone abutments during floods. Eventually lost to one, its limestone supports remain visible to this day south of the West Fourteenth Avenue Bridge, built in 1928.

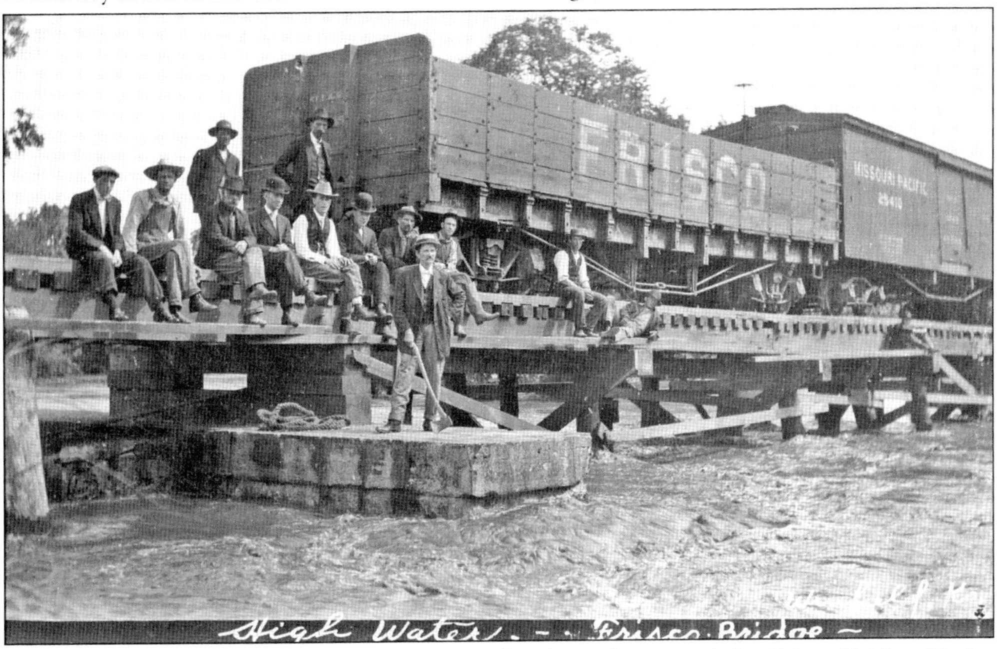


A 1904 flood, said to be Winfield's worst at the time, threatened the Frisco Bridge. Trains abandoned service until the water receded. During Winfield floods, railroad trestles provided a means of navigation by foot when railroad service was cancelled and streets were impassable. During the 1904 flood, some people left their homes and went to the top floor of the city building, where rescuers showed up in boats.

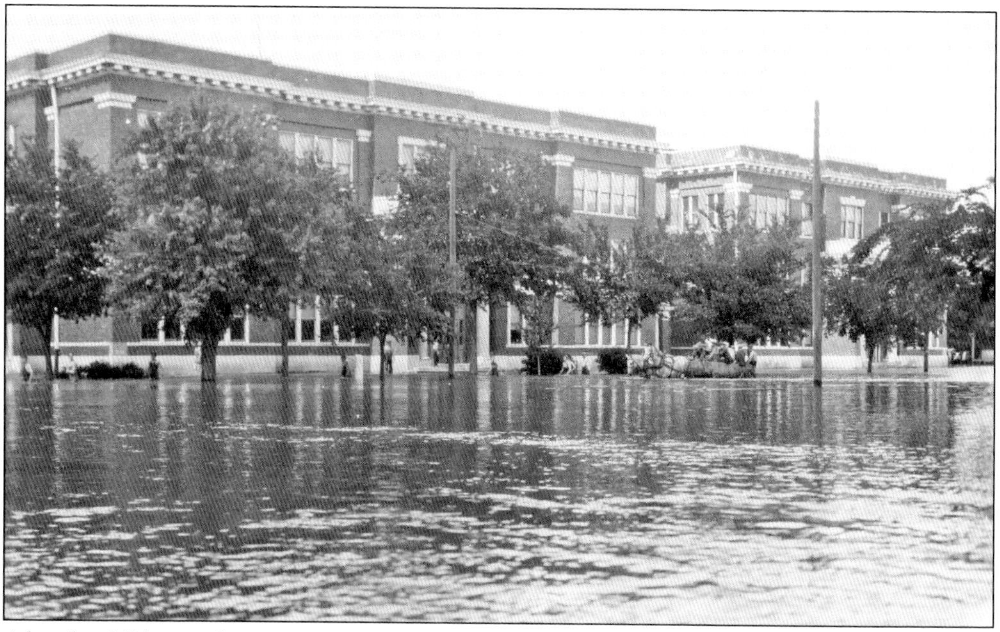

A barely visible two-horse wagon navigates East Ninth Avenue after a flood in November 1928 made travel by automobile impossible. Floodwaters lapping the bottom entrance step of Winfield Junior-Senior High School did not keep people away from it or from wading around in the waist-deep water in the schoolyard. This flood claimed one life before its waters receded.

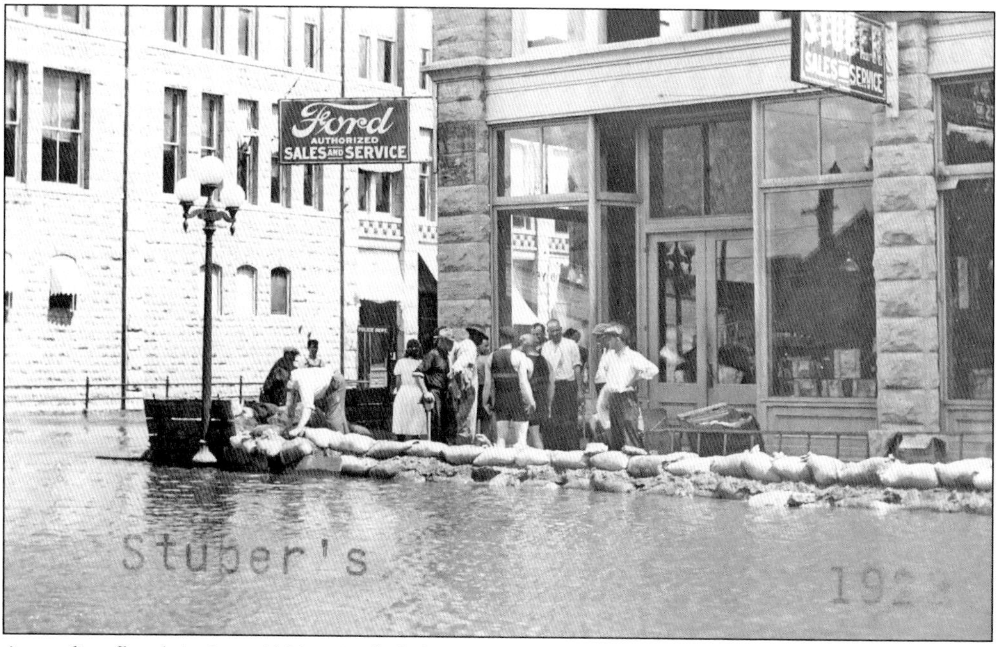


An earlier flood, in June 1923, crippled the city and cost a Southwestern College student his life when floodwaters swept him away. The water covered an area of over three miles, damaging crops and homes alike. Businesses such as Stuber's Ford dealership at East Ninth Avenue and Millington Street sandbagged in hopes of keeping the water at bay. Note the two volunteers who came prepared in swimsuits.

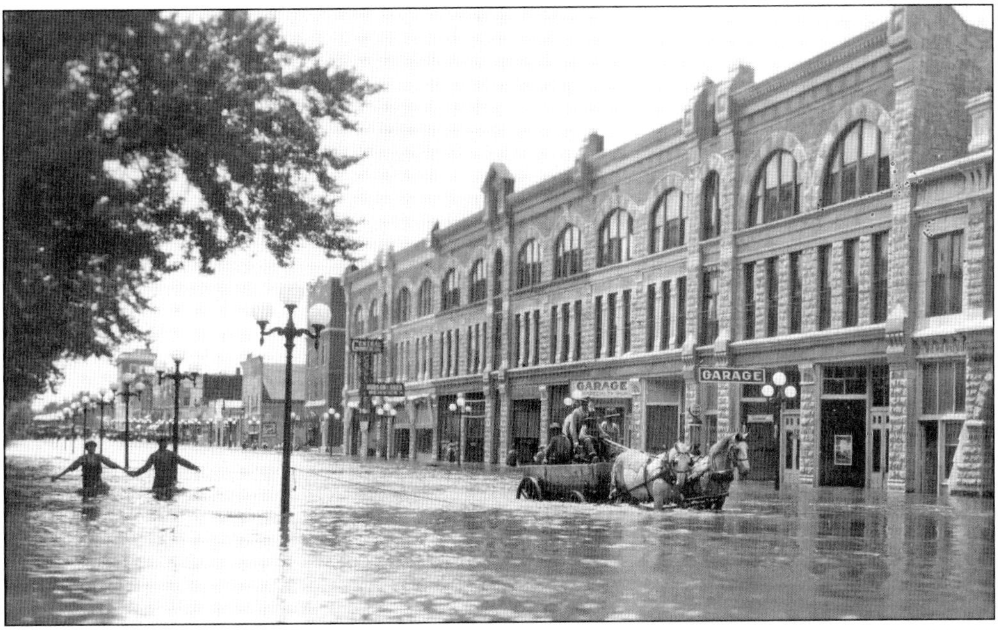


This postcard provides a different view of East Ninth Avenue and the wagon at the height of the November 1928 flood. The Caton Block, which at that time housed the Central Commercial College and several garages, is in the foreground, while the Lagonda Hotel can be seen across the street and the State Bank towers in the distance. Two people take their chances walking in front of the courthouse.

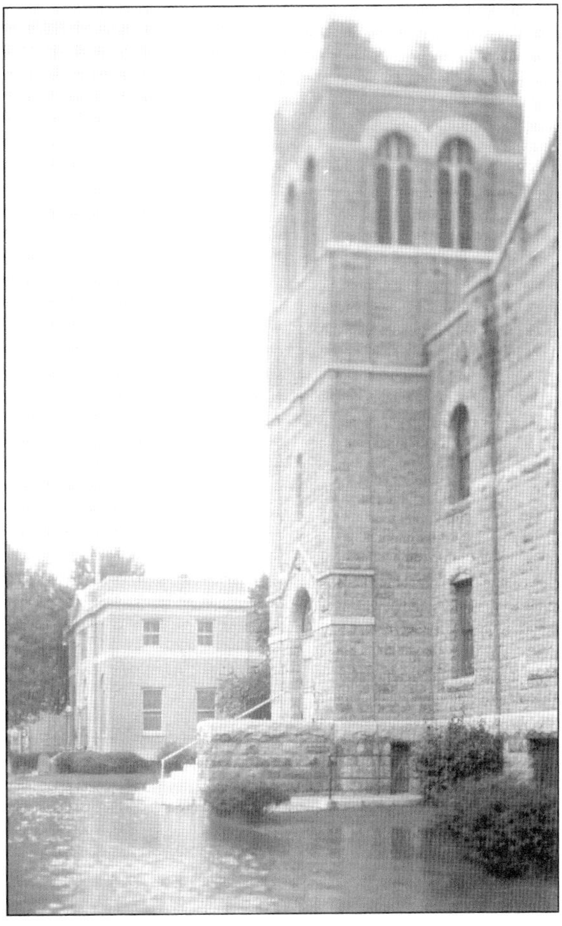

A block off of Ninth Avenue, south of the *Courier* office and the new city building (not around for the 1923 flood), floodwaters surround the post office and the First Methodist Church on Millington Street during the 1928 flood. The public library across the street suffered the loss of its periodicals collection when its basement flooded. While local volunteers got to work, the National Guard came to offer assistance.

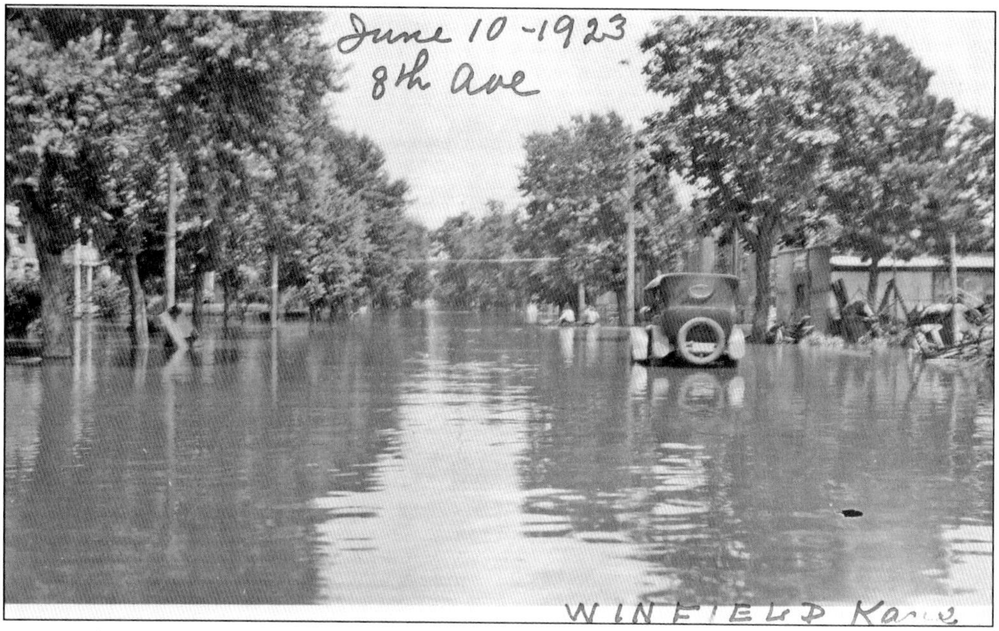


During the June 1923 flood, water rose to a height of over 36 feet. Electrical and water services were out, and the Chautauqua assembly had to be cancelled. Dikes were constructed in 1924 and 1936, but the continued flooding into the 1970s led to the creation of the Winfield Lake and Timber Creek Watershed District, which has a system of dams to retard floods.

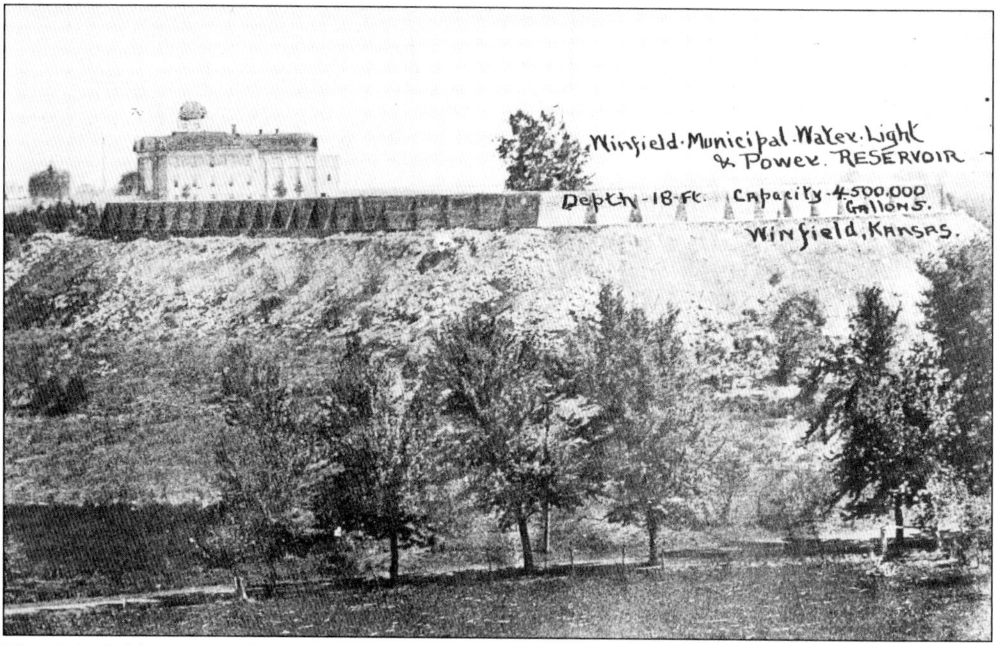


The Winfield Municipal Water, Light, and Power Reservoir brought pride to its city. Originally built in 1883 to hold water supplied from the Walnut River, the reservoir's walls were raised in 1913 for it to begin receiving water from wells west of Winfield. This postcard provides a view of its location east of College Street between Sixth and Seventh Avenues. Southwestern College is visible north of the reservoir, possibly superimposed.

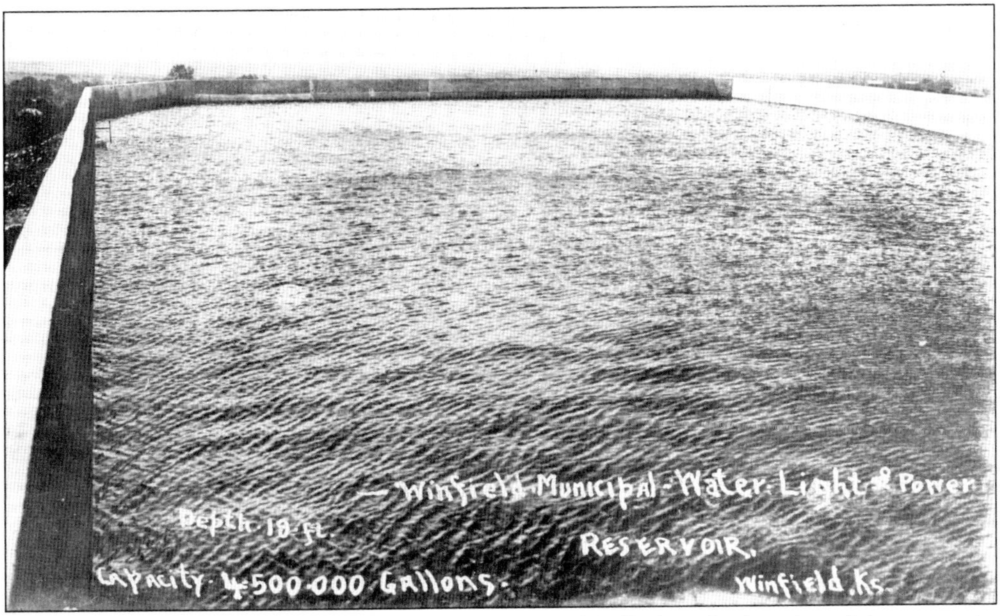


This view based on a photograph taken on June 2, 1916, displays the interior of the reservoir. While the water received from the wells did not require filtration, other problems developed that led to periodic draining and refilling of the reservoir. The June 8, 1914, the *Winfield Free Press* reported the reservoir drained for the second time in two weeks due to "the great number of tadpoles that are hatching out."

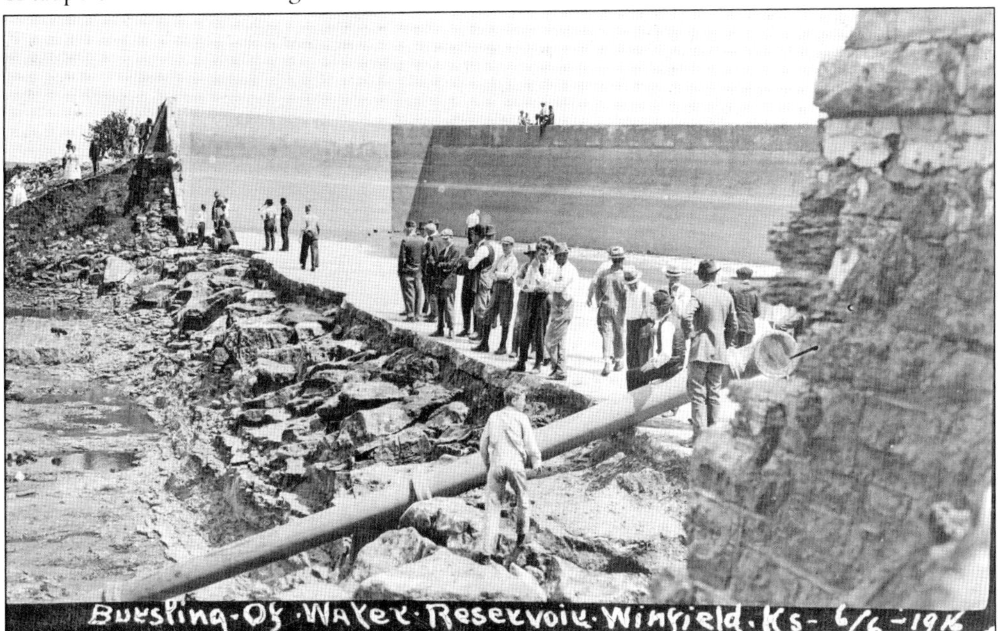


Water superintendent Jack Welfelt began keeping an eye on leaks in the reservoir in June 1916. On June 6, 1916, following heavy rainfall, the leaking increased. Local officials closed surrounding streets and warned neighbors. Shortly after Welfelt ordered draining to begin, the earthen wall supporting the west side of the reservoir slid down. Just before 10:00 a.m., a 200-foot section of the exposed concrete wall of the reservoir burst.

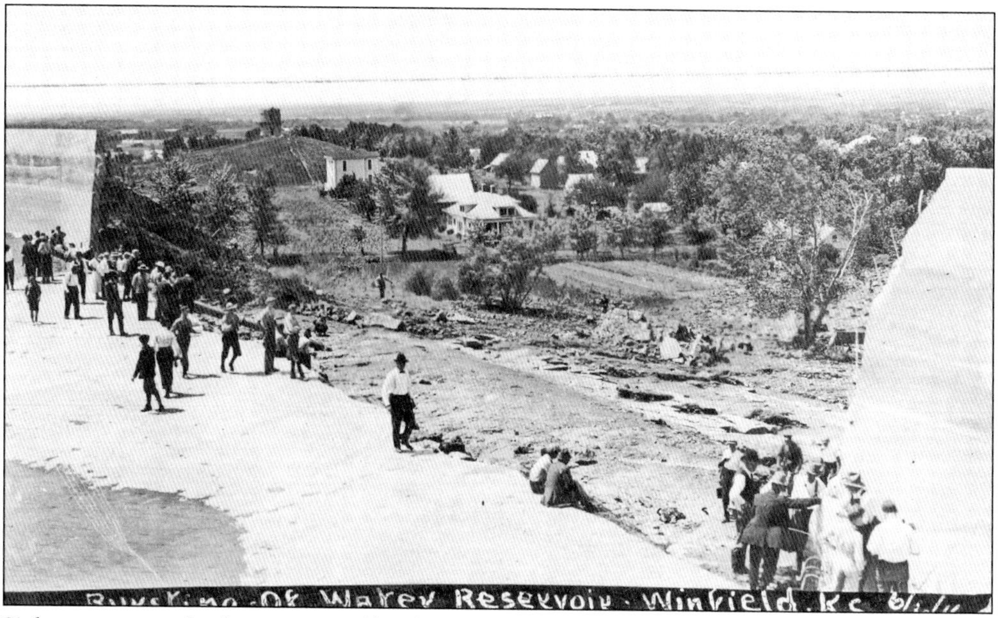


Sightseers survey the damage caused by three million gallons of water bursting from the reservoir. Broken trees and cement weighing 100 tons littered the street below and the lawn of St. John's College across the street. Homes on Seventh Avenue suffered flood damage. The event caused no injuries or deaths, and a St. John's student standing across the street and north even caught the moment of the break with his camera.

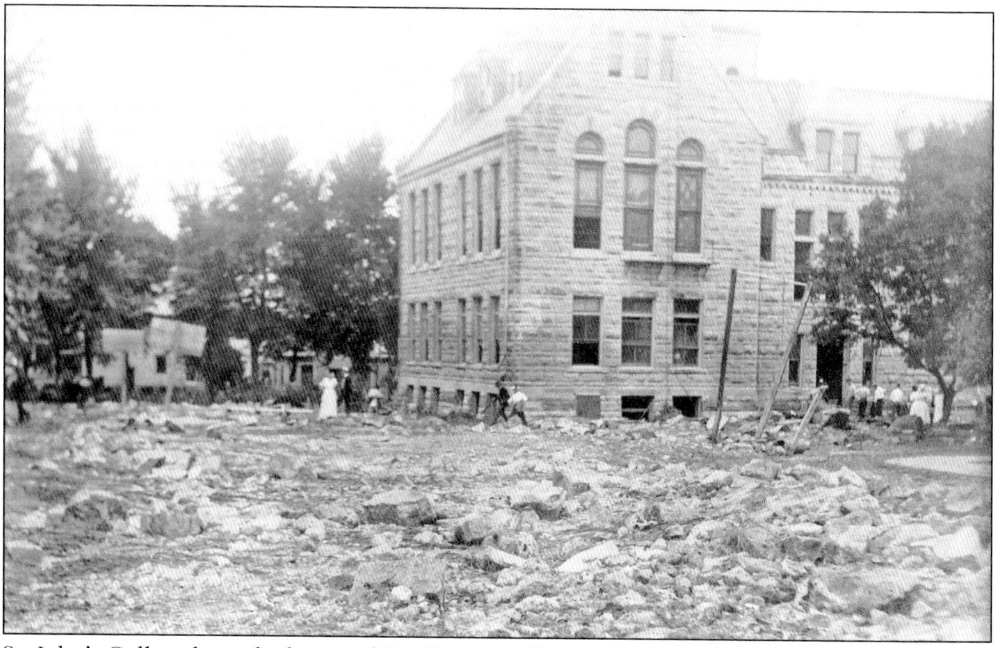

St. John's College bore the brunt of the disaster. All of its basements were flooded, and Baden Hall, pictured here, lost windows on the first floor. The college steward's vehicle was swept from a garage at the rear of the hall. The Commercial Club, with rooms downtown, took over feeding the 100 students, and the school's commencement exercises were moved a day ahead of schedule to allow students to go home.

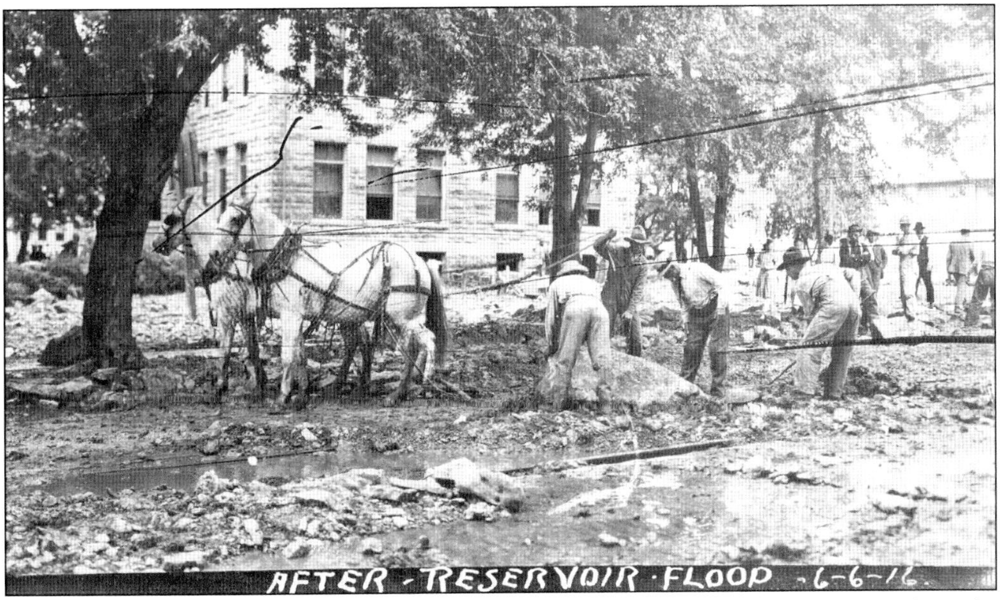


Clean up by horse and manpower began right away, as did the payment to St. John's students for their losses, many of whom had trunks stored in Baden Hall's basement. The college received a mutually agreed–upon payment for their losses in March 1917, and the reservoir went back into use in May 1918. Until then, the public enjoyed reservoir parties on the site with skating, dancing, campfire suppers, and picnics.

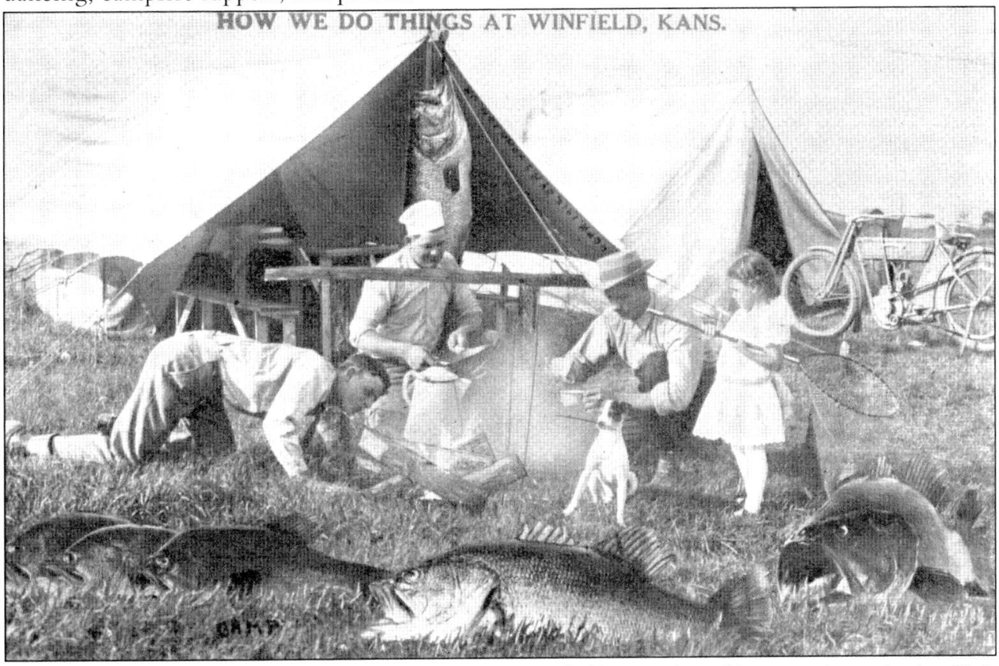


This humorous card, sent in 1917, held true as Winfield grew in a big way through the 20th century. Gott Manufacturing started in 1916 and grew into Rubbermaid in 1986, and the Binney and Smith Crayola plant came to town in 1952. Today, acoustic music fans all over the world know Winfield, as the Walnut Valley Festival has been held each September along the Walnut River since 1971.

# Bibliography

Baker, Rae Lynne and John Baker. "And the Band Plays On: The Winfield Municipal Band, 1895–2006." Paper presented at the annual Celebrate Winfield History conference, Winfield, KS, 2007.

Barnard, Adelaide Baden. "John Peter and Adelaide Elizabeth Baden, Philanthropists." Paper presented at the annual Celebrate Winfield History conference, Winfield, KS, 2001.

Behrhorst, Wallace. "The Land and Buildings of St. John's College, 1893–1936." Paper presented at the annual Celebrate Winfield History conference, Winfield, KS, 2005.

Brewer, Gary. "Memorial Park: Winfield's Own Battleground." Paper presented at the annual Celebrate Winfield History conference, Winfield, KS, 2010.

Cales, Joan. "Winfield Public Library, 1913–2013: A Century of Service." Paper presented at the annual Celebrate Winfield History conference, Winfield, KS, 2013.

Cowley County Heritage Book Committee. *The History of Cowley County Heritage.* Winfield, KS: Cowley County Heritage Committee, 1990.

Flottman, Rex and Gary Hanna. *Winfield Then and Now.* Marceline, MO: Heritage House Publishing, 1993.

"History of Winfield." Compiled by the fourth-hour Winfield High School senior history class under instructor Maude Andrus, Winfield, KS, Spring 1924. On file at the Cowley County Historical Museum.

Seaton, David. "Winfield State Hospital." Paper presented at the annual Celebrate Winfield History conference, Winfield, KS, 2005.

Taylor, Sharon. "Winfield Newton Memorial Hospital: The Early Years, 1927–1937." Paper presented at the annual Celebrate Winfield History conference, Winfield, KS, 2008.

Ulbrich, Gloria. "Island Park: A Gathering Place." Paper presented at the annual Celebrate Winfield History conference, Winfield, KS, 2013.

Wilcox, Sally. *Winfield and Walnut Valley.* Arkansas City, KS: Gilliland's Publishing, 1975.

*Winfield Daily Courier.* Souvenir edition, March 14, 1901. Reprinted by the Cowley County Historical Society, 1973.

# Index

NR indicates buildings placed in the National Register of Historic Places and their date of inclusion.